1939 = Into The Dark

PAULA PHELAN

ZAPmedia • New York

ZAPmedia
New York, NY
info@zapmedia.com

ZAPmedia is a registered trademark of ZAPmedia, LLC.

Cover designs by Sandy Frye
Cover photography © ZAPimages

Manufactured in the United States

Publisher's Cataloging-In-Publication Data

Phelan, Paula A.
    1939 : into the dark / Paula Phelan.

    p. ; cm.

    ISBN-13: 978-0-9778192-1-8
    ISBN-10: 0-9778192-1-3

1. Nineteen thirty-nine, A.D.--Fiction. 2. New York (N.Y.)--History--1939-1945--Fiction. 3. New York. World's Fair, 1939-1940--Fiction. 4. Artists--New York (State)--New York--History--1938-1945--Fiction. 5. World War, 1939-1945--Fiction. 6. Historical fiction. I. Title. II. Title: Nineteen thirty-nine

PS3616.H45 N567 2008
813/.6

Dedicated to the Memory and Work of Varian Fry

LIST OF CHARACTERS

Jason Rothman ~ ascending playwright and idealist

Miriam Rothman ~ aspiring poet with parents in Germany

Bill Curran ~ talented dancer and thug

Sarah Karofsky ~ successful harpist

Karl Klyne ~ classical pianist turned labor organizer

Kim McIntyre ~ undiscovered painter and museum curator

Alex Bridges ~ talented architect and gigolo

Ernestine Robertson ~ ballerina with the Metropolitan
Opera Ballet and ballroom dancer

Bud Rawley ~ patron of the arts and arms merchant

Alan Stipple ~ cultural commentator and critic of the arts

Nancy Ames ~ war correspondent for the Negro Associated Press

JANUARY

The Bronx

Bill Curran stepped into the cramped elevator on the sixth floor of the Remington typewriter factory in the Bronx and turned to face the closing doors. Behind him stood two men with briefcases. While Bill towered a good seven inches above them, both men were compact with barreled chests, making up in girth what Bill had in height.

All three wore new gabardine suits, silk ties and camel hair overcoats. Bill noted the squat men did not wear their finery with the same panache as he. They looked like off duty cops, hired to transport the factory's payroll to the bank.

The small elevator left precious little space between the three men. The dingy building was old and the elevator slow. As the lift made its way to the street, Bill spoke over his shoulder to the men behind him.

"So, you boys taking in the fight tonight?"

The men turned to one another confused, like someone had forgotten to invite them to a party. The man to the left shrugged. The other spoke up.

"What fight, mister?"

Bill spun around and kneed the silent man in the balls, who sank to the floor, grabbing his partner's coat for help. As his companion looked down in surprise, Bill's left hook caught his chin slamming his head back against the wall of the elevator, knocking him out cold.

The door opened. Bill reached down calmly and collected both mens' briefcases. The silent man began to yell for help. Bill kicked him in the face, then once again in the stomach for good measure.

As he stepped casually out of the elevator Bill pushed the button for the seventh floor, sending the groaning man and his associate upward. Out on the street the wind spit snowflakes into Bill's face. He buttoned his overcoat against the winter storm and pulled his hat down to shield his eyes. He walked to the corner and hailed a cab. A dusting of snow covered the sidewalk. Feeling exhilarated, Bill performed a brief soft-shoe routine before getting into the taxi.

"Hey, buddy, you're good," said the driver.

"You ain't seen nothin' yet," said Bill. "Take me to Times Square."

The Exitus

Bud Rawley was known for his parties. He gave screamers that lasted for days. Up in his penthouse overlooking Manhattan, one had the sense that New York was a city of limitless potential. Everything appeared clean, fresh and full of possibility. His guests always left feeling certain they could scale the tallest mountains. After all, Buddy had. What's more, he made them feel good about themselves and the world. No one wanted to miss a Bud Rawley party.

Buddy had titled tonight's party 'The Exitus' and only artists were invited. No one remembered Buddy naming a party before nor could they recall such a select guest list. The invitations were unambiguous. Each guest was required to bring a sample of his or her work. How famous you were proved immaterial; you simply had to have something that supported your claim.

Young artists were thrilled at the possibility of being discovered. Established artists felt the 'prove it' premise was beneath them, however, they didn't mind showing off something the critics might have panned. Especially since Buddy had made the provision that all critics would be turned away at the door, even Walter Winchell, Louella Parsons and Alan Stipple.

Actors brought playbills, ads, or publicity photos of their recent work. Musicians toted their instruments and sheet music. Dancers had their shoes and posters.

Buddy had turned his China room into a four-sided, multi-shelved art display case. Five butlers carefully received the works from guests, filled in small parchment cards with the artist's name and a description of the piece and then placed the offering directly into the awaiting cases.

When asked why he'd restricted the attendees to artists, Rawley claimed, "I'm looking to create a moment when we can come together as comrades-in-arms, not as competitors, as a united creative force." He said he couldn't explain it any better. The entire town was abuzz with the notion.

The critics were outraged. Walter Winchell sniped, suggesting it was a communist gathering and plainly stated that the police should bust it up. An unlikely event since Buddy and Mayor LaGuardia were friends and the mayor knew Buddy wasn't a Red. What's more Buddy had invited the mayor's daughter, an up-and-coming muralist, to join the festivities. LaGuardia, being nobody's fool, knew this event would go down in history and that he would earn a special place in his daughter's heart should she attend. If guests were arrested while she was there... well, it would never happen. Instead, LaGuardia doubled the police force outside the building at Central Park West. He helped make sure only bona fide artists made it through the door and gave approval for the removal of interlopers, no matter what their social status or political connections.

No one ever talked about where Buddy's money came from, yet everyone knew he had plenty of it. There was speculation that he had gotten out of the stock market before the crash. Others thought he had been a bootlegger during prohibition. There were rumors he owned large tracts of land in New York City, had ties to the railroads or even organized crime. In truth, no one knew. If asked, he would laugh and say, "Born lucky." Then he would get you talking about yourself, a topic no one could resist.

The playwrights were the first to arrive, each dutifully bringing a marked up script or playbill with their name highlighted with arrows or underlined in blue ink. Clifford Odets offered up his original script of Lefty, dog-eared and heavily noted. Lillian Hellman garnered her current playbill from The Little Foxes. Dashiell Hammett, at her side, came with a third edition of The Thin Man.

As Jason Rothman, a tall handsome man in his early forties entered Buddy's apartment he suddenly realized a good number of spouses would be excluded from the festivities. Frequently the partner of a famous artist didn't entertain the muse. He was thankful Miriam, his young German wife, had her poetry chapbook in hand.

Upon further reflection, Jason realized there actually were a great many artistic partnerships: Fitzgerald and Zelda, Stieglitz and O'Keeffe, Frida and Diego, a stream of actors who seemed to exclusively marry other actors, and hapless singers who married a member of their band. The new talk about town this month was the union of W.H. Auden and Christopher Isherwood, poets and bon vivants.

Jason wondered if William Powell would be there with Carol Lombard. She and Powell had been close friends since Harlow's untimely death and the 'accidental' shooting of Russ Columbo. Jason wanted to talk to Lombard about his play.

"So what should we make of this, that the playwrights are the first on the scene?" Odets said, eyeing the crowd.

"Either we're considerate guests," replied Lillian Hellman, "or we're planning to devour all the best food before the drunks get here. They wouldn't know the difference anyway."

"Here, here," replied several members of the tight knit group, raising their champagne flutes in a toast.

"Or perhaps it's that you all have nowhere else to go and forgot that sex is a superior way to start the evening." Dorothy Parker emerged from the shadows, greeting those in her path with a kiss, men and women alike.

"You know, Dorothy, you may have something there," said Noel Coward. "We writers are so filled with dialogue and the conversations of others, that it never occurs to us to go to bed with anybody else. Why would we, when we have ourselves so close at hand."

"Noel, you dear." Dorothy kissed him. "How in the world could you be here? Aren't two or three of your hits running in the West End?"

"Only one, my pet, and it's doing just fine without me. I decided to come over here and catch 'The Exitus'. Buddy was good enough to send me a cable. Besides, I figured with the end of the Federal Theater Project, I might find myself an American starlet or two." He took a Martini off a passing tray and then pulled Dorothy close to him.

"What's more, my love, someone needs to keep you cut down to size at this party and I don't see any great American wits ready to joust with you in all the best places." He bumped against her and the crowd laughed. Dorothy grinned. Noel was right. There wasn't anyone in the great Metropolis that could match wits with her as well as he.

"Noel dear, I read Design for Living." She paused theatrically. "Loved it – but it'll never play in the States you know. Much too risqué. All that sexual ambiguity exposed."

"I know, my dear, luckily the Brits adore it and who knows? Maybe in fifty years you Yanks will loosen up your puritanical corsets."

As they spoke, the musicians began to arrive. They were setting up in separate thematic rooms. There were classical artists, stride piano masters like Fats Waller, and out on the terrace Artie Shaw's big band. Buddy had thought of everything, including portable heaters for the terrace.

Sarah Karofsky was hired to play with the famous musicians. When she arrived at nine-thirty p.m., dressed in a shimmering gown of bronze that highlighted her coppery red hair, the party was already in full swing. Sarah pulled out her contract to see if she'd gotten the time wrong. No, she was to start at ten p.m. It was going to be a long night, but she was used to that.

Mr. Rawley approached her as she maneuvered her harp dolly into a back bedroom devoid of anything but a few chairs. He was a man in his mid-forties, and his confidence in himself and his place in the world made him attractive. Sarah noted that she always felt a kinship with red-haired people.

"Miss Karofsky. Do you have everything you need?"

"Why, of course, Mr. Rawley."

"I'm flattered you remember me," said Buddy.

"No sir, I'm the one who's flattered. Thank you for thinking of me for your party this evening."

"Nonsense, Miss Karofsky. I'm a devotee of your Sunday Palm Court recitals. I haven't missed one in the last two months."

Sarah blushed. They weren't recitals, playing at the Palm Court represented nothing more than a paycheck. And no, she hadn't noticed him, but then she didn't usually notice middle-aged men. On closer inspection, Buddy was good looking in a burly sort of way.

"I'm not surprised. You haven't seen me. I usually sit behind one of the fuller palms so that you don't think the worse of me."

"In that case, you must be familiar with my repertoire. What would you like me to play this evening? Your coordinator mentioned other musicians might be joining me."

"Ah yes, but mainly I want you to enjoy yourself."

"Your coordinator expressed that as well Mr. Rawley."

"Do call me Buddy. And yes, enjoyment is key. Please join me for a moment." He held out his arm to her and since the harp was still covered, she felt comfortable leaving it. She followed him into the main living room, which was the size of a small ballroom. "Miss Karofsky, I...."

She interrupted him. "Sarah."

"Sarah, I have distinct types of music being played in each room. For instance, I've invited Aaron Copland to join us this evening and thought he might want you to accompany him. I've already told him that the finest harpist in all of New York would be here."

"You're too kind, Mr. Rawley. I mean Buddy. I'm just a strummer for hire."

He considered her words for a moment, started to speak, censored his retort and then said, "If my idea ends up being a crazy one, I hope you'll stay for the party."

"I'd be honored."

He smiled and escorted her back to her harp. Outside the room where Sarah was to play, she noticed a sign that read, 'Classical'.

"You've thought of everything."

"It's a special night." He studied her as a lover might, which startled and excited her.

He was the first to break the spell. "Please excuse me while I greet my other guests."

"Of course," replied Sarah.

He bowed, kissed her hand and left Sarah beside her harp.

A Conversation Between Artists

From the foyer a woman's voice called out, "Stieglitz, you old so-and-so."

"Dorothea, I hear you've been scaling the Chrysler building. Big footing King Kong are you?"

"You're just jealous because my photos are in focus." Dorothea Lange, in her mid-thirties, offered a vivid contrast of youth against Stieglitz's sixty years. "Is O'Keeffe still with you, or has she finally wised up?"

"Don't give me that. I know you like that little man without any clothes."

"You mean Gandhi? As a matter of fact, I am kind of partial to him. I was there last week. He's a pretty smart guy."

"Ah, you're a believer then."

"In a word, yes. Here is this little fellow, armed only with his brain, a law degree and a loincloth, standing up against the most powerful nation in the world. I kept asking myself if he was insane or a genius."

"Of course it does help that the British have other things on their minds at present," said Steigletz.

"No doubt, but I don't think India will be under British rule by the time this war is over," replied Lange.

"So you think it'll come to that?" asked Georgia O'Keeffe as she joined them, with three fresh drinks in her hand.

7

"I do. The climate everywhere outside of the U.S. suggests there's no other choice. Although Americans are not yet emotionally committed to the war, the industrial machinery is gearing up right under our noses and no one is saying a word."

"But what about the Neutrality Act of '35?" asked Arthur Dove standing at O'Keeffe's elbow. "Doesn't that prevent the U.S. from selling arms to the Europeans?"

"Technically, yes, but manufacturers have found ways around it, loopholes in the language. Actually, if we go to war it will probably hurt the arms dealers because they'll only be able to sell to the allies. Right now they're selling to the Germans, Russians, Italians and Japanese equally."

"I'm merely an artist," began Dove.

"And an obtuse, abstract one at that," quipped Stieglitz.

"Admittedly, however selling to the aggressors and the allies, doesn't that sort of defeat the purpose of the Neutrality Act?"

"Dear boy. Where there's a lawyer there's a way," said Dorothy Parker as she joined the clique. "Come on, did you all really think we wouldn't go to war? It's just too luscious to avoid," she licked her lips. "War solves so many ailments – the economy, us free thinkers. And as a bonus, it gives the U.S. the chance to claim our birthright as a world power." She paused. "Wake up and smell the gun powder."

Parker left the group to join the heavy drinking writers in the corner. The authors were deep in conversation.

"It's true, Dash. Europe's gone mad. Jews walk around like stunned sheep, wearing armbands and identification markers. I don't think even Wells or Lovecraft could have come up with something this diabolical." F. Scott Fitzgerald was in the first flush of a half dozen drinks. He had been away for years, having left the U.S. when he was the golden boy. He and Zelda had moved to Europe after the crash, saying they couldn't bear to witness their bejeweled city reduced to ashes. Now Zelda's mental health had deteriorated and Fitzgerald needed money. His hands punctuated the air with dramatic emphasis. His drink sloshed onto the plush rug.

"Listen to me. The Jews can't work. They can't beg on the street or buy food in any of the stores. They are dying in these fenced off ghettos surrounded by barbed wire. And it isn't just the Jews. It's gypsies, homosexuals, as well as, anyone with a physical or emotional infirmity. Hitler expects America to buy back the people slated to die. Will we do it? How do people here feel about it? Why isn't anyone else shouting besides me?"

"Sounds like you all are talkin' about the South," drawled William Faulkner. "I never thought about Jews like the colored, but I suppose if you've got to have someone to blame, a Jew will do." The group gaped at him as though he had sprouted horns.

"What?" he continued. "Come on now, you know that all men are not created equal. We all need someone to dump on occasionally. Luckily, we in the South always have the niggers."

Dashiell Hammett responded by pouring his drink on Faulkner's foot. "You're talking sludge, Faulk. Excuse me, I need a fresh drink."

"What did I say? What did I say?" asked a confused Faulkner.

Lillian came up beside him, having seen the anger in Dash's face. She knew Faulkner needed to keep his mouth shut or a communist left hook might knock him out. "Faulk, I suggest you go listen to some music. There's a delightful red-headed girl playing harp in the other room. Either go listen to her or say your prayers before Dash gets back."

Still muddled, Faulkner shuffled away.

"That's just what I'm talking about," said Fitzgerald, "I need to get drunk."

"I'm right behind you Fitz," said Hellman.

Somewhere around midnight Buddy called everyone into the little display room. Only a few dozen people fit in the space, but Buddy's words carried out into the hall.

"Friends, I've called you here tonight because you represent an era. The best and the brightest the last decade had to offer. You each overcame hardship and challenge. At the same time, you enjoyed a cocoon of aesthetic encouragement unparalleled in modern times." There were murmurs in the crowd. "As many of you know I have ties to the federal government. I spend a good deal of time in Washington and am privy to things that I wish to share with you tonight.

9

January

I entitled this evening 'The Exitus' to celebrate the end of the decade, not because the forties will begin next year, but because by then, many of you will no longer be here. In New York City that is." He heard people turning to one another, puzzled and asking, "What did he say?"

"Hear me out. You all know the war is coming." He heard several no's and ignored them.

"Another World War is approaching. Roosevelt has been a good president and he has provided artists with a nurturing atmosphere enabling each of you to create masterpieces for posterity. We're the beneficiaries of his policy, a policy that is about to end. I have it on good authority that the WPA will cease as of July."

A gasp went up in the crowd.

"Many of you already know that the Federal Theater and Federal Writers Project will end at the same time. What you may not know is that the Un-American Activities Committee has identified Jews and communists in the arts as undesirables. Those of you with left-leanings must assume you will no longer be able to work in your chosen profession after the war begins. Those of Jewish heritage will experience severe persecution – it has started in Germany, and the waves of hate will wash up on our shores as well.

"You must prepare yourselves for it and determine now what you can do to help your relatives and friends in Europe, because no one else will help them. I repeat. No one will help them. We will go to war, but it will not be to help the Jews or the repressed. We will fight in order to maintain the status quo and keep Britain and France in power. The brief time we have had with FDR and his creative encouragement will be gone with the wind."

A few in the crowd chuckled with the reference to the much-hyped movie.

"The artists who grace this house tonight shall never come together again. This era will be the last great artistic movement for perhaps another millennium. I want you to enjoy yourselves tonight, because friends, when this sparkling moment in history is over, some of you will be gone, others forgotten and some destroyed."

The guests sober enough to listen were befuddled. Yet no one doubted Bud Rawley's sincerity.

"I'm honored to have known you all." He began to leave the room, then stopped and turned.

"For those who would not find it a hardship, I would like to keep the art you brought tonight. I promise never to sell the pieces and that they'll remain in my collection for as long as I live. Upon my demise they'll be offered to a museum of repute. Tonight's a night for history and I would like to share it with future generations."

The room erupted in a buzz that sounded like the hum of electric motors. No one knew what to make of it. Everyone was aware Buddy had friends in high places, but what could it mean? How could all they had created and been through in the last ten years disappear? This was America, the land of the free. How could it happen here?

There were some who knew, F. Scott Fitzgerald, Noel Coward and Dorothea Lange, who had crossed the Atlantic, and people like W.H. Auden and Christopher Isherwood who had gone to China. They had each seen the face of war and knew in their hearts that Buddy's statements rang true. Everything was about to change and not for the better. What was to come would make the depression seem, if not like a picnic, then a foggy day at the beach.

Buddy walked to the back of the apartment, where Sarah Karofsky had set up her harp.

Sarah did not question Buddy. She sensed that what he had said had come at a high price. While she didn't know who held the debt, she knew he felt very alone. She also registered that he had come to her for solace.

"Buddy would you like me to play something for you?"

"Please. The Blue Danube."

An Evening of Mirth

One week later, Miriam Rothman exited a cab and handed the driver a generous tip with a smile. She slipped out of her coat, removed a scarf from her white gold hair and entered the vestibule of the Music Box Theater. There she found her agitated husband pacing the lobby, lost in his own private world of pitchfork-bearing demons. His handsome face was drawn into a scowl, his shoulders hunched.

"Hello darling," she said.

Jason turned on her savagely. "You're late. The third act is almost over. I hate your superstition of not being here for opening night. I need you here." He grew silent and thrust his hands deep into his pockets, unable to meet her gaze. He focused instead on the clever marquee posters for An Evening of Mirth.

"Shush now." Miriam said, kissing his cheek. "I've seen the play a hundred times. It's going over fine." Coaxing a hand from his pocket, she eased open his clenched fist and placed her hand in his.

"Really, darling, it'll be fine. Everyone will love your play. It's brilliant. The actors are superb, the sets are stunning, and the production is simply marvelous. Please don't worry, dearest. This play will be your glory."

Jason relaxed slightly, his jaw no longer clenched. "Or I'll be crucified," he said under his breath.

She ignored his comment. "Besides," she said, "the wife of a famous playwright should dress the part, don't you think?" She backed away and gave a brief twirl, displaying her full-length satin gown. The dress seemed to be poured over her, caressing every perfect curve of her body. Its color was the blue of the evening sky long after sunset – a blue so deep her skin seemed like an unblemished sheet of paper. Her eyes were the shade of winter violets.

"Miriam, you're dazzling."

Jason realized suddenly that it had been a long time since he had truly seen Miriam. The play had consumed all of his attention. But here before him was his wife, a ravishing beauty dressed in the height of fashion. He wished he could provide her with such fine couture every day, however, they couldn't survive on his income as a playwright. They depended upon Miriam's part time position at Bergdorf Goodman to make ends meet. Miriam had no doubt "borrowed" the dress from the formal gown department where she worked.

Jason wished their parents could be here tonight to enjoy this success. But Miriam's parents, who had helped them out so much finan-

12

cially, were trapped in Germany, unable to leave despite Jason and Miriam's best efforts. And his own parents, who supplied him with endless encouragement, had both died during the 1918 influenza.

"I'm glad you approve," Miriam smiled and slipped on her fur coat.

He looked at her, aghast. "Miriam, where did you get that?" He pointed at the coat as if one of the little minks had raised its head and hissed at him.

"Not to worry, handsome husband, it's borrowed from Mrs. Cohen. She's certain this play will mark your success and thinks your wife should appear ready for your public's adoration. Besides, you're taking me out dancing afterwards."

Jason took her hand and kissed it. "Alright, Miriam, I will take you dancing as long as the play isn't a dismal failure and I don't decide to jump off the Empire State Building."

Their conversation was interrupted by a thunderous wave of applause that filled the lobby. Miriam and Jason parted as the doors swung open and critics with notepads and pencils raced out, along with enthusiastic theatergoers. Alan Stipple, the critic for the New York Sun, approached them.

"Congratulations, Rothman. It looks like you have a hit on your hands. It's about time you stopped feeding us all that 'making the world a better place' crap. Drawing room comedies, that's what people want. Make 'em laugh." Nodding to Miriam, Alan put on his hat and walked into the night jotting down notes.

Jolted by a slap on the back, Jason turned to see the familiar face and red hair of Bud Rawley. Bud Rawley, the affable man who always had faith in Jason and proved it time and again by producing Jason's political plays for the past two decades.

"Well done, Rothman. I'd say An Evening of Mirth is going to prove a very good investment indeed." Bud offered Jason a cigar. Jason shook his head no.

"Thank you, Buddy." Jason looked over at Miriam. "We appreciate your believing in the play. If it hadn't been for you…"

"Nonsense. You, sir, you are destined for greatness. I knew it the first time we met. Come along. I've invited the cast and crew to celebrate at the Stork Club."

Miriam gave Jason an I 'told you so' smile. He squeezed her hand. As they left he chose not to mention seeing J. Edgar Hoover standing in the shadows outside the theater. Instead he happily followed Buddy uptown.

One Woman Show

In a small third floor gallery on Fifty-Seventh Street, Kim McIntyre in her early thirties stood beside a plate of crackers and cheese. She held a glass of red wine. A man in overalls entered the exhibition room and noted it was empty except for the artist.

"How did it go?" asked Karl Klyne.

"The good news is the liquor held out." Kim raised a half-full bottle of wine in salute.

"Nothing sold?"

"You don't see any red sold tags do you?" She set down the bottle and lit up a cigarette. "Sorry, Karl. I don't mean to take it out on you. It's just, well, my WPA contract ran out last week, and I'm going to need a job. I was hoping for a sale or two tonight."

"None of the critics stopped by?"

"Nope," Kim responded.

"Their loss. Your work looks great." Karl stood back to admire her vibrant abstracts. "Hey, how about we get out of here and I take you to dinner?"

"I've got a hankering for pie," said Kim.

"You're on. I'll take you to my favorite automat and tell you tales of the coal miners' strike in West Virginia. You'll be pleased to know I was only arrested once this time."

The Stork Club

The party at the Stork Club was the stuff movies are made of – a room full of the famous and would-be famous – men in evening attire and women wearing chic gowns. The revelry went on until morning.

When Miriam and Jason finally made it home, Jason appeared worried.

"What is it, dear?" Miriam asked tenderly.

"I'm not sure I can do it again. Expectations are low for your first Broadway play, but they'll demand so much more from the next one. Audiences are like hungry animals; they're only briefly satisfied."

Miriam followed him to the bedroom and sat on the end of the bed as he paced, his thoughts spilling into the room.

"Worse yet, I feel like Prometheus chained to the stone, with the eagle coming to feed on my liver every day. Don't get me wrong, Miriam. I must write. I'm a part of the theater. We share a symbiotic relationship. But the ravenous audiences.... "

Miriam recognized his almost incoherent ramblings for what they were – an anxiety attack. She knew from experience it was best just to let Jason tire himself out. She patted the space on the bed beside her. He sat and she pulled his hand into hers and began stroking it.

"I don't know what to do next," he said, calming slightly. "Truth is, I've already finished the outline for the next play. I'm glad I didn't wait to start it, because that was the first question everyone asked tonight. When should they expect the next play from Jason Rothman?"

He turned to Miriam, his expression changing to one of chagrin. "I'm sorry, darling. Here I am ranting and raving like a lunatic, and here you are, so beautiful and patient with me. What have I done to deserve you? Did you enjoy yourself this evening?"

"I did. I can see you're not ready to sleep. Let's play some cribbage like in the old days. I'll make you eggs and we'll watch the sun come up."

He stood and drew her to him. Jason kissed her gently. Any other wife might have thought this a prelude to sex, but in Jason's case, excitement lived in his head, not his loins. She led him to the small table where they ate their morning meal and went to the credenza for the cards and cribbage board. Then she turned on the radio before proceeding to the kitchen.

The voice of a woman with perfect diction filled the room:

January

> The editors of the Associated Negro Press have asked me, Nancy Ames, to pick up where I left off after the Great War as a correspondent-at-large. For those of you familiar with my dispatches twenty years ago, I assure you that I will once again report what I see.
>
> There will be no sugar coating. I will cover not only the who, what, and where, but also the why. My dispatches will not be for the faint of heart. I will travel from country to country providing eyewitness accounts of what is really happening 'over there.' If war is to come to America again and men of color are called up, you will know the truth. I will not serve up any of the usual simplistic patriotic propaganda.
>
> Since I arrived in Berlin I have witnessed atrocities and injustices that are reminiscent of the slavery era in the U.S. Shortly after this dispatch I will leave Germany for Austria because it is no longer safe for anyone not of the Aryan race. As of January first this year, Jews in Germany and its occupied states are no longer allowed to...

Miriam returned to see Jason absorbed in the report. Now was not the time for such thoughts. Miriam turned the dial to a station playing music, a Duke Ellington tune.

"The eggs will be ready in a moment," she said over her shoulder. She didn't want to cast a shadow on Jason's success with bad news. She had already chosen not to mention that her position at Bergdorf Goodman's appeared to be in jeopardy. While Christmas and New Year's sales were excellent in the formal gown department, they didn't warrant keeping on as many girls as they had hired for the holiday season. And now that the returns had been made, pink slips would be issued this Friday. Miriam assumed she'd receive one.

She had taken the job anticipating that their WPA checks might one day disappear. She and Jason had survived for the last three years on the dole, he in the Federal Theater Project and she with the Federal Writers Project. Together they scraped by, aided by the occasional check from her family in Germany. All the support had paid off, and now her husband was a star – albeit an anxious one. As for her own career as a poet, she had her doubts, but she'd worry about that later. She placed a plate of eggs beside Jason. She picked up the cards, shuffled and dealt.

"Fifteen for two," she said, placing her seven of clubs against his eight of spades.

"Twenty five." He responded with the queen of hearts. Jason began to relax as their game continued.

Miriam sighed, grateful for these simple moments. "Thirty-one for two," she said as she laid down the six of hearts. Beyond the window the lavender light of morning illuminated their future.

In Karl's Room

The room was small. Claustrophobically small. It held a bed, a sink, and atop a small dresser the pride of the room – a Zenith cube radio whose dial glowed in the dark and from which the voice of a woman spoke with conviction and without apology. Karl and Kim, immersed in each other, heard little of what was being reported:

> *Jews in Germany and its occupied states are no longer allowed to*
> *- Attend movies, concerts or cultural performances*
> *- Drive automobiles*
> *- Enter or reside in the city of Berlin*
> *- Practice as a pharmacist, veterinarian or dentist*
> *- Own a business*
> *- Work, except directly for a German without pay*
> *- Appear in public without written approval....*

Karl reached over and switched off the radio. Instead of silence filling the room, the sounds of the apartment building and neighborhood crowded in - children screaming, parents yelling, sirens, and traffic. Karl turned on the light and put his arm under Kim's head. Clad in bed sheets they looked toward the water stained ceiling.

"What do you miss most?" Karl asked, as he rolled onto his side, propping his head up. He wanted to see Kim's face as she replied. Her expression always revealed every emotion before she uttered a sound.

She stretched her lithe body like a cat and closed her eyes, retrieving the memory.

January

They had been dating for a couple of months. Karl had gone to the opening of her show in the Village. He liked her paintings and her. Kim was easier to be with than his political friends. She certainly carried as much angst, but of a different kind. He gazed now at her soft face framed in black curls.

"Describe to me where you are," he said gently.

"I'm twenty-one. It's the fall of 1926, and I live here in New York. Optimism is in the air. My friends and I believe that only good things will happen to us. Everyone is making money. The sky is the limit, and we all imagine ourselves as famous artists. I even receive two commissions from important collectors."

"From whom?" he asked, pulling her from the daydream.

Kim opened her eyes and raised herself up on her elbow. "Did you know the Bacons – Fredrick and Karen?" Karl shook his head no. She dropped back down onto her back. "They were big collectors in the twenties. I think they lost everything in the crash and moved to the Midwest."

She paused for effect. "But the other one, you'll know. Mr. Nelson Rockefeller. It was the highlight of my career and quite the coup. I was in a show with half a dozen artists uptown, and who should walk in opening night, but Mr. Rockefeller – complete with white tie and tails. Even more handsome than his photograph in the papers."

"What did he see first? You or your painting?" Karl teased. Kim blushed and pursed her lips. Karl leaned over and kissed them.

"You may be a few years older, Kim McIntyre, however, you're still beautiful. You must have cut quite a figure back then. How could Rockefeller resist?"

"Oh you," she said, pushing on his shoulder. "He saw my painting first, and sure, he flirted with me a little, but he bought it."

"What was the picture of?" Karl hadn't seen Kim paint for months. He assumed she couldn't afford the supplies. He believed her to be a gifted painter. He had seen people admiring her work at galleries. If the Depression hadn't descended, who knows how far she might have gone?

"A lovely little cityscape, very impressionistic, you know." She snorted at that – it was an inside joke of theirs for anything blurry or with distorted proportions. "The city at night, with a sprinkling of stars in an indigo sky.

"Unfortunately, Georgia O'Keeffe was showing as well," Kim frowned in annoyance. "She, of course, stole all the accolades. If it hadn't been for Stieglitz, no one would have paid any attention to her stupid flowers. I bet a rich sugar daddy would have done wonders for my career as well. And it wouldn't hurt if he were a famous photographer. I wish she'd just stay out in New Mexico. The weather must be better there in the winter. Then again, if I lived in a penthouse on Forty-Ninth and Lex, I might not complain much either."

"And lose all the ambience of an East Village flat?" He gestured to his room, barely large enough to hold two people.

"You silly boy." They wrestled playfully for a moment. "Fact is, she doesn't have you, and for that she'll always be jealous." Kim squeezed him between her long legs and stroked his chest. If nothing else, the hours with nowhere to go and nothing to do left plenty of time for exploration.

The Devil and the Cafe

"What a fool." Bill Curran crumpled his newspaper into a ball and threw it to the floor in disgust.

"Is there anything wrong, sir?" asked the pretty waitress, coffeepot in hand. Her face lined with concern.

"The man's an idiot. That King of England, Edward, or I should say the Duke now."

The waitress held up the coffeepot and Bill nodded.

"What do you mean, sir?" she asked, as she poured.

"He's the King of England, the most powerful country in the world and what does he do? He quits it all for a woman. A woman. No skirt is worth that even if she is an American." He glanced up. The waitress's face radiated innocence, which usually brought out his wolverine instincts, but not today. Right now he desired an equal, someone who understood the world and how it worked, the way he did.

"I think it's romantic," she said. He chortled in disgust.

"Excuse me, friend," said the nondescript man sitting at the next table. "Did I overhear you say that love is for saps, especially when the whole world's up for grabs?"

The man's bluntness made Bill smile. It sounded like something he'd say. Bill responded, "That's right, mister. Italy, Germany, Spain, Japan – everyone is on the move, and what does Edward do? He settles in Sussex with a pair of legs."

"I'm with you, brother. A damn waste. If it were me, I'd expand my empire, not let it be gobbled up by these greedy would-be kings. Why don't you join me for a cup of coffee?"

"I'd be glad to." Bill changed chairs in one fluid movement. Despite being six-foot-three he moved with exquisite grace. The stranger noticed – Bill saw him notice and wondered if the guy was a homosexual. That kind rarely strayed above Canal Street, but here at Rosie's on Twenty-Third, a queer may have been separated from the herd. 'If he's one of them. I'll kick his teeth in', thought Bill.

The man continued, "So I guess that means you didn't go off to fight for the Loyalists in Spain?" He took off his hat in deference to Bill exposing a baldhead. "Name is Fred, Fred Cochran."

"You kidding? I'm not stupid enough to fight someone else's battle when there's plenty to capitalize on here. The way I see it, the only reason to go to war is for the spoils. The saps in this country have been rolling around in this Depression for so long, it's like they've lost their marbles."

"You can say that again," said Cochran. "Bunch of fools. Only the Vanderbilts, Astors, and the other hoity toities got it right. They let us poor jerks lay in the filth while they clean up with real estate and industry. When this thing is over they'll be even richer than they were, and the rest of us…"

"We'll be left with the scraps," said Bill finishing Cochran's sentence.

Cochran nodded. Bill guessed the man to be upwards of fifty, a tough nut with a proposition.

"Hey, Cochran, I don't have all day to talk politics. I don't care what Hitler, the emperor of Japan, or Mussolini does. What I care about are my own fortunes. What's on your mind?"

Fred gave an appreciative laugh.

"I like you, mister, and you're right, I've got an angle. Who doesn't these days?" He pulled out a pack of store-bought cigarettes and offered one to Bill. Bill had been rolling his own lately and appreciated a proper smoke. He lit up and nodded for Fred to continue.

"Here's how it is. Certain Jewish and Italian families in the city handle the prostitution and drug trafficking. The Fifth Avenue boys own the banks and manufacturing. So what does that leave us?"

"The slag heap," answered Bill.

"That's right, and we deserve better. I do a little work now and then for a group that supports foreign interests in this country."

"So what do you want?" asked Bill, unimpressed.

"Let me lay it out. I need some favors done from time to time, and I can make it very worth your while."

"Define 'very'."

"We're talking fifty to a hundred bucks a job." Fred leaned back in his chair.

"Am I killing someone for all that scratch?" asked Bill.

"Nah, only if they get in the way, but nothing like an assassination or anything." Fred took a sip of his coffee. "We pay more for that," he winked.

Bill considered Fred's offer as he finished his coffee. Then he stood up, placed his hat on his head, and while pulling on his coat, he reached out his hand to Fred. "Yeah, I'm your man. Bill Curran. I'm at the Roosevelt. Call me when you need me." And he left.

Fred smiled as he watched Bill cross the street toward the Flatiron Building. Murder Inc. and Meyer Lansky would be pleased with this new recruit.

FEBRUARY

Art Enthusiasts

The gallery was only a few blocks from the Plaza and a friend had told Sarah that Kim McIntyre's show was well worth seeing. When she climbed the three flights of stairs and entered the dimly lit gallery she saw two men standing apart looking at the canvases. One a tall handsome brooding fellow who appeared to be a cross between Cary Grant and Gary Cooper who Sarah wouldn't mind meeting. The other she recognized immediately as Alan Stipple the critic, whom Sarah read faithfully and knew casually. She crossed the room to start a conversation.

"Hello, Mr. Stipple. You're a fan of Miss…," she glanced at the flyer she'd picked up at the door, "McIntyre?"

"I am. Unfortunately, she doesn't have a chance. She might as well give up. There's no room in the art community for women these days. No matter how good."

"That's a discouraging statement."

"Except for you, Miss Karofsky. Do you ever get a rest between

Out of the Dark

by Alan Stipple

THEATER:

Rocket to the Moon

Clifford Odets has another hit on his hands. The dialogue is confusing, the characters unlovable and yet somehow, everyone in the audience sympathizes. The white lies and grand lies are the very ones we cherish. Taken all together, everything in this play works. You'll leave the theater with lines of colloquy dancing in your head.

MOVIES:

★★★★☆ Gunga Din

Despite William Faulkner's name not appearing in the credits it doesn't take a genius to realize his fingerprints are all over the script. Cary Grant is, of course, as handsome as ever.

★★★☆☆ You Can't Cheat an Honest Man

If you are looking for some sidesplitting fun, *You Can't Cheat an Honest Man* is just the ticket. If you don't belly laugh at least once during this movie, I'll eat my hat. Perhaps W.C. Fields' best movie ever, his one-liners are nonstop and are answered by none other than Charlie McCarthy, who gets his in the end.

★★★☆☆ The Little Princess - Once again

Shirley Temple saves the day. This movie is sort of Cinderella in reverse. Prince to pauper. But all's well that ends well. We hope the same holds true for Miss Temple's career since the little princess is showing signs of growing up.

record contracts, opera performances, and concerts? You, my dear, are the city's de facto queen of the harp."

Sarah curtsied at his praise.

"I do sometimes feel as though I am sprinting for some undefined finish line." Sarah spoke to Alan, but her eyes strayed to the handsome man in the camel hair coat. Regaining her poise she asked, "Alan what movie should I take in this week? What are you recommending?"

Stipple, showed his pleasure at the question and focused all his attention on Sarah. "Well, I wouldn't miss John Ford's film Stagecoach. It's not your typical shoot 'em up western but rather a soul-searching expose into one of the toughest hombres of the Wild West – Johnny Ringo. Played by my favorite swaggering bad man Marion Michael Morrison – who just changed his name to John Wayne.

But if your tastes swish the other way, there is Only Angels Have Wings, which explains why all of Hollywood says Rita Hayworth, has IT. She steals every scene she's in from Cary Grant and Jean Arthur. The story isn't hot, but Rita is!"

Alan watched as Sarah's eyes once again traveled to the other art lover in the room.

"I've got to go my dear. A critic's job is never done. Besides," he leaned over and whispered in a conspirator's voice, "I'd say you have your work cut out for you." He tilted his head towards the other man. "Happy browsing. Ta Ta." He blew her a kiss from the doorway.

Attempting not to be obvious, Sarah worked her way around the room slowly, taking time to study each painting until she reached the only other patron in the gallery. As they stared at the same canvas he spoke to her without turning, "Do you know whose work this is? I'm captivated by the imagery. The use of color and light is so beautiful. The artist obviously understands the emotion behind architecture and buildings." Taking his eyes from the painting he glanced at Sarah.

"Please excuse me, I'm Alex Bridges."

"Sarah Karofsky. The artist is Kim McIntyre. She's actually a muralist. She did that big mural in the lobby of the Thirty-Third Street Post Office." Sarah was pleased she had read Kim's bio.

Alex's eyes returned to the painting.

"I'm an architect. This artist and I share the love of light on buildings."

Awkwardly Sarah searched for something to say. She wanted Alex to look at her the way he was admiring the painting.

"I understand that this is Miss McIntyre's first one-woman show," said Sarah.

"She's a real talent I'd love to own this piece. Then I'd feel like I had made it." A look of shame passed over his face and Sarah's heart went out to him.

"I confess, I'm between jobs at present," he said. "Yet I'm certain something will come through soon and this would be a great reward."

"Yes, it is a beautiful. Wait a minute. Didn't you say you're an architect and your last name is Bridges? Come on, now, you're pulling my leg."

"No, it's true. I couldn't tell you if my last name influenced my choice of profession or it was mere coincidence. It does sometimes help people remember me when I go on job interviews. Sometimes they call me Mr. Building and I never correct them."

Sarah smiled with relief that he had abandoned his discouragement and returned to the present.

"Are you an artist, Miss Karofsky?"

"Of a sort. I play the harp."

"Let me guess. You're a regular at the Metropolitan Opera House and sit in at Carnegie Hall."

"Mr. Bridges, you're good. Yes to both. Should I be frightened? Are you a psychic?"

"Lucky guess. I'm afraid I've never had the good fortune to hear you play. Would you like to go for a coffee and you can tell me about the musician's life?"

"I'd love to, but I have to go to work now. I play at the Plaza's Palm Court during high tea on Mondays and Tuesdays. Maybe some other time?"

"How about this Wednesday? Here, please write down your number and I'll call you. I have a few interviews coming up this week. Perhaps I could take you out to celebrate if I land a position."

"That would be lovely." Worried that he might not call unless he found a job, she added, "Let's get together no matter what."

"It's been a pleasure to meet you, Miss Karofsky. I hope to see you soon."

Sarah was certain waiting for his call would be the longest two days of her life.

Calling Home

After leaving the gallery Alex stood on the corner of Sixth Avenue and Fifty-Seventh Street collecting his thoughts before entering a neighborhood bar to call home. He had moved from Colorado because there was no work. His family was starving, and he didn't want to be one more mouth to feed. What's more, he and his father had never gotten along and the grinding poverty had made his father meaner. Without provocation his dad would lash out with verbal insults, or worse, reach for the closest object at hand, a cup, spoon, belt, or even a burning log from the stove. Alex could bear the scars, yet feared that his presence made the house a powder keg in which the rest of the family had to live. He couldn't stand to see the anguish on the face of his younger sister, Ruth.

Ruth was his better half, full of spunk and optimism. She had married poorly, and her husband had left her and their son after the banks collapsed. Ruth returned home to keep the men of the Bridges family afloat, where her father and their two other brothers blamed the world for their troubles. Alex swore he would never be one of them.

He walked into the small dark bar and placed two liberty dollars on the counter.

"I'd like to get some change for the phone."

"You callin' long distance?" asked the bartender.

"Colorado."

The man gave out a short whistle. "All the way out to Colorado?"

"Yep. Thank you," said Alex, as he took the change and headed back to the privacy of the phone booth.

"Hello, operator? Connect me to Ruth Bridges in Fort Collins, Colorado."

"Right away sir. You're in luck; the lines are open." After a few clicks the operator continued. "Hello, this is a call for Ruth Bridges."

"Yes, operator, I'm Ruth. I'll take the call."

"Here's your party, sir. Please deposit one dollar-fifty. Would you like me to stay on the line?"

"No, operator. Thank you." Alex heard the satisfying sound of the change falling into the phone box. "Sis, is that you?"

"Alex!" She paused. "What's wrong?"

"Nothing, I just missed you Ruth, all of you. How is everyone?"

"Just fine. Your nephew Rusty has a cold. Besides that everyone's well. How's it going? Have you found a job yet? How are you affording to pay for this call?"

"I've been getting some fix-it work, handyman jobs here and there." Alex hesitated. "Ruth, it's not what I thought it would be. I thought there'd be plenty of jobs in New York, instead there are plenty of people standing in lines wanting a job."

"That's still better than back here. There aren't even any lines in Fort Collins. Everyone's sitting at home hoping something will happen."

"Yeah, I know." Alex had sworn he'd be cheerful during this call. "Hey, Ruth, I went down to Frank Lloyd Wright's studios the other day. Remember I told you about him? The guy's a genius. Crazy, yet brilliant."

"Great, does he have any work for you?"

"Nah. Maybe I'll move to California. There seems to be employment out there and maybe I could connect with that architect Julia Morgan. She's getting more commissions than any man or woman alive."

"But Alex, you want to build skyscrapers."

"That's right."

"They don't build skyscrapers in California, remember?"

"Yeah, I know, earthquakes. It's just – I'm at my wit's end, Ruth. I need to find something soon. I'm losing faith."

"Don't be silly. You're the best architect in all of Colorado, and you have the awards to prove it. Have you been to the World's Fair yet? Don't they need help?"

"I was too late. All the commissions had already been awarded."

"Do you have a piece of paper, Alex?"

"Huh? Yeah."

"And a pencil and an eraser?"

"What are you getting at?"

"I want you to sit down and draw something. Nothing is going to impress a prospective employer more than seeing your drawings. Get out there and show them the skyscraper of the future. You can do it, Alex. We're rooting for you."

"Thanks, Sis. You're quite the fan." He wished he could hug her, yet at the same time he wouldn't want her to see the disappointment in his eyes.

"And Alex, when you do get something, and I know you will," her voice dropped to a whisper, "if you could see your way clear to send a little something along, it'd help a lot, now with the mine closed and with winter and all."

"I know, Ruth. I know. I'll get something to you as soon as I can. Big hugs."

"Love you."

The operator's voice broke in as though she'd never left. "Sir that'll be an additional thirty-five cents."

Alex dropped the change into the phone and stepped out into the bar. The bartender frowned. "If I were you, son, I'd save my money, not be spending it on long distance calls. Money doesn't grow on trees, you know."

"No, no it doesn't." Alex pocketed his fifteen-cent life's savings and raised his collar to the wind.

He didn't notice the man sitting alone at the table by the door.

WAR CORRESPONDENT

Nancy Ames - Madrid

Thirty-two weeks ago the sovereign nation of Spain democratically elected a new president. The rest of world refused to support the citizens' decision and instead backed the fascist dictator, Francisco Franco Bahamonde. Russia, France, Germany and Italy joined Franco in his crusade by testing their newest weapons against Spain's citizens. With the end of the Spanish Civil War the U.S. and its allies have lifted the embargo against Spain.

But Franco is making no secret of the fact that he is determined to kill every person who supported the loyalist party against him. Policemen, teachers and postmen are being rounded up and murdered. Franco is killing hundreds of individuals daily – now that the war is over.

At present, fifty thousand Spanish refugees, mostly leftist intellectual writers and artists, along with their families, have attempted to flee the Levante area. 15,000 were trapped at the port causing waves of suicides. People chose to kill themselves, rather than be captured by Franco's soldiers. When the soldiers arrived they fired on the crowd. In the end, only a few hundred people remained alive. They were rounded up and taken to labor camps. This correspondent doubts that they'll survive the year.

Karl and Hemingway

Karl Klyne sat in the small dark bar, his head in his hands, feeling done in. The joint was a mere hole in the wall, just big enough for a handful of stools at the bar, four small tables against the wall and a phone booth in the back. Karl sat at a table near the door unwilling to engage in conversation.

A rousing tale of Dick Tracy blared from the radio. Two men sat at the bar with glasses of weak beer in front of them. One had a whisky chaser. All three patrons were silent, lost in their own regrets.

Karl had been fighting for the rights of workers. He had assisted on seminal labor reform legislation. The Bill of Rights and the Constitution were the documents upon which he based his arguments and drew his strength. He advocated democracy in all of its manifestations. He'd been jubilant when the Spanish people elected their first self-ruled democratic government in 1936. There'd been parties and bonfires in the streets of New York, celebrating the birth of another democratic nation.

Yet even before the last ember had cooled, reports arrived that the new Spanish government was resistant to American and European business interests. As the days and weeks progressed, it became obvious that the U.S. would support a fascist military dictatorship over the Loyalists. America was advocating tyranny over democracy. It seemed inconceivable.

The only organization willing to help Spain confront the barbarity was the International Brigade, a collection of recruits from around the world. The Brigade's charter was deemed communist because much of the funding and leadership came from Russia. In the name of freedom and democracy, Karl was content to be called a communist. He foresaw that communism would be the next major party in the United States destined to speak for the working people.

He picked up his beer and drained the glass.

"Could I buy you another?" A big man wearing a hunting jacket loomed beside the table. "You look like you could use a few."

Karl couldn't argue with that. "Sure."

"Forgive me for asking friend, but are you drowning your disappointment over Barcelona?" The big man paused, "If so, I'd like to join you since that's what brought me into this hot spot." Karl sensed he knew this man.

He stood up and held out his hand. "As a matter of fact, comrade, that's exactly why I'm here. Karl Klyne, with the Abraham Lincoln Brigade."

"Ernest Hemingway, but everyone calls me Pa."

"I thought you looked familiar. Did you lose any friends?" said Karl as he sat back down offering the other seat to Hemingway. "I mean, that you know of yet?"

"I don't know. I've been home for two years. Most of the people I fought with were in Madrid or in the south, but I imagine…" Hemingway eyes drifted. If there had been a window he'd have stared out of it, but the only view available was the stamped green tin wall of the bar. He shrugged. "Seems hard to believe doesn't it? I mean being American and all."

"That's what I keep thinking. Somehow the logic evades me. Why should we take the side of a self-proclaimed fascist? Franco has systematically killed over a million of his people and we continue to send him arms and support." Karl stopped and shook his head. "And they call me a traitor for not supporting him."

"Yeah, I know. They tried to stick that label on me, but I prefer 'adventurer'. If I didn't write though… Barkeep, how about another round? Ah, to hell with it, just bring over a bottle of your best whiskey." He turned back to Karl. "I wouldn't expect much from the whiskey or our country, I guess." Hemingway took the bottle from the bartender and poured a shot for Karl.

"Here, have a shot. It'll help take the edge off." They both downed the liquor in a single gulp. "I can only say," continued Hemingway, "that I'm not going back over there to fight. I don't care what patriotic drivel they use to defend another war."

Both men fell silent for a resonant moment letting the significance of a world gone mad wash over them.

"Hey, we know the score," said Hemingway. "And there's nothing we can do about it right now. Let's you and I go have some fun. I know of this art opening in Harlem. There should be some knockout dames there and I could use a few laughs."

Karl hesitated.

"Oh, come on comrade, the war isn't going to go away today or tomorrow. You'll work out the problems of the world later this week. For now, let's tie one on."

Karl couldn't resist the big man's magnetism.

"You bet, comrade."

Hemingway threw a handful of dollars on the table and put his arm firmly around Karl's shoulders, ushering him out into the harsh afternoon sunlight of Third Avenue.

Sarah Karofsky – The Palm Court

Sarah filled the room with her music. On the harp she spoke a language without guile. The patrons of the Plaza Hotel's Palm Court were, for once, quiet and listening, transported with her to a magical land of billowy clouds and serenity. Her fingers flew over the strings, offering a view into Ravel's complex world. Playing the harp was the only true thing she knew.

But moments of musical bliss like this were infrequent. These days Sarah played by rote, rarely applying herself. Yet sometimes the harp forced its will upon her and she became inspired. During these rare and precious episodes Sarah recalled why she played the harp, and why she had come to New York.

As she reached the composition's crescendo, someone coughed; a waiter dropped a dish, and the spell was broken. The lunch traffic began once again, the loud voices were drowning each other out, reducing her virtuosity to unacknowledged background music.

Mostly, Sarah didn't care. She had given up on her musical aspirations, maybe because it was too easy. She had more engagements than she could possibly play, while her colleagues struggled to get by.

The rest of the afternoon at the tearoom was filled with the usual requests for Strauss, a favorite among the regulars because it was the composer's seventy-fifth birthday and he was being featured in a retrospective at Carnegie Hall. She wondered for a moment if Strauss felt that he too had sold out, dispensing waltzes to audiences who couldn't get enough while all he actually wanted to write was opera. Engrossed in her thoughts, she left the stage without applause, only to be startled by a man blocking her path to the exit. Bud Rawley's flaming red hair made him unmistakable.

"Miss Karofsky." He bowed slightly as she imagined they did in Europe. "I just wanted to tell you how much I enjoy your playing. You are a true talent."

Sarah blushed, "No, I'm just part of the atmosphere." She waved her hand to take in the potted palms and gilded columns of the room. "But thank you for the compliment. Sometimes I wonder if anyone is listening."

"Be assured, Miss Karofsky, as one of your ardent fans, I listen intently to every note. Thank you for your beautiful music." With that he took her hand, kissed it formally and bowed again. "If you have some time this evening would you consider taking dinner with me?"

Sarah had not seen Buddy since the party. She had forgotten what a robust man he was. All she remembered about him was their age difference. But now she saw something more. A man enamored with her, who thought her perfect. Seeing her reflection in the eyes of one so smitten was impossible to resist.

"Why yes Mr. Rawley. I'd love to take dinner with you. Let me put away my things and I will join you presently."

Bud lit up at her acceptance. He unconsciously puffed up his chest based on sheer pleasure of her acquiescence. "Wonderful Miss Karfosky. How absolutely wonderful."

He reached out and kissed her hand again. As Sarah turned toward the manager's office, she realized Harry Liam the piano player had witnessed the interaction. He winked at her and nodded approvingly as she approached.

Kim McIntyre – Waiting in Line

Kim found herself standing on Fifty-Seventh Street, in a line of three thousand people. The wind whipping down the street made it difficult to ignore the cold. While long lines were common, this one was unique because at its end stood a pot of gold – three hundred jobs. At the height of the Depression, hungry people had waited in queues almost as long for just two jobs. Now, in 1939, one-in-ten odds were considered a sure thing. What's more, each position held prestige because the openings were for the New York World's Fair. The event had been so heavily promoted that nearly everyone had something, a calendar, salt and pepper shakers, key rings, etc. branded with the Trylon, the tall triangular-shaped monolith that resembled a three-sided Washington monument and the Perisphere, a globe so large that it could hold an eleven-story building inside.

Kim, like many, had adjusted to hard times by cutting down to one meal a day. Her features stood out in sharp relief and she wrapped her coat tightly around her slim frame. Prosperity wasn't waiting around any of the corners in her neighborhood. She reflected, not for the first time, that life might not get any better than this – ever.

Ten minutes later the line had progressed only five feet. Based on a quick calculation she reasoned she'd be inside the building by the afternoon of the following day. Kim hoped for a curator position. She spoke fluent French, the language of the world, and her ability to identify the masters as well as the avant-garde artists was without peer.

"From my lips to God's ear, let me be a curator for the Impressionists." She must have spoken aloud, because the little man in front of her spun around and said in a thick German accent, "Me too."

Startled Kim asked, "You too, what?" She hadn't wanted to start a conversation because it represented something of a commitment, considering the length of the line.

"The Impressionists – they're my favorites. My lifelong passion."

Kim assumed he must be a Jew. The city was overflowing with European Jews escaping the Nazi regime. She knew very little about what was happening in Europe. Her own misery great enough that she didn't feel able to share anyone else's.

WAR CORRESPONDENT
Nancy Ames - Vienna

As preparations for the next World War move forward, oil once again plays a major role in the decisions of the allies and aggressors. Britain has assured Arab leaders that the Jewish refugees will not settle in Palestine in exchange for assurances that oil will continue to flow to British shores. Following suit France has made similar arrangements regarding its Jewish population with Algiers.

Jews are disappearing from sight throughout Eastern Europe. Additional concentration camps and ghettos are being erected in every major city including Warsaw, Milan, Venice, Krakow, Munich and Berlin. Open discussions suggest moving the Jews from the country into the cities in order to be 'better managed'. Meanwhile Jews are required to turn over all property, precious stones, gold and silver to German authorities.

In the U.S., senators Wagner and Rogers sponsored a bill to allow America to admit 20,000 Jewish refugee children. The proposal died in committee.

During this past week the Yugoslavian premier has been removed from office and Germany has annexed Lithuania.

This reporter wonders when the U.S. will emerge from its apathetic slumber.

"The Impressionists!" the man repeated with rapture. "They are so full of light and beauty, when today such things are especially important. Hans Zimmer at your service, madam." He made a formal bow.

"Mr. Zimmer." She nodded. "Miss McIntyre."

"It's a pleasure to meet you, Miss McIntyre. Who's your favorite Impressionist, and why?"

"I adore Monet's scenes of French flags, and the lily ponds at Giverny. I find them soothing."

"Ah, a good choice," said Hans in solemn reflection. "My favorite…"

Kim interrupted. "Oh, Monet is not my favorite. I respect Cézanne, during his more angular period, and Bonnard, for the liveliness with which he paints."

"Such happy colors," Hans broke in.

"Exactly," responded Kim. "Which brings me to my favorite, Edouard Vuillard. His paintings of interiors move me. They represent everyday life, without the exactitude of Sargent. Vuillard provides enough detail for the viewer to know what is portrayed, yet leaves much to the imagination."

"Agreed," said Hans. "I know Mr. Vuillard's work. He makes everyday life appear exquisite. My favorite is the German, Max Slevogt. His work borders on realism, but he adds that magical vibrancy seen in all the great Impressionists work. As for the modernists, I am partial to Kandinsky. He's a musician of color. His spheres and lines seem to float in space, like a Miro mobile."

He studied her for a minute. "So you're applying for the curator position?" Kim knew that most people aspired to something so glamorous, of course they would be happy with any job including sweeping the streets in the, 'The World of Tomorrow'.

"That's my heart's desire, Mr. Zimmer."

"I suspect we will be in this line for most of tomorrow. What if I bring you a book and you one to share with me? Then we can discuss them as we wait to get inside."

"Let's," Kim agreed, thinking there wasn't anything better to do.

"Good. Tomorrow then," and with that he pivoted on his heel and moved forward a few inches. They both waited until the attendants

February

came out with the numbered tickets sending the crowd home. Kim's ticket was number 1432. Tomorrow would be a long day and there was talk of sleet.

MARCH

Sarah's Invitation

Sarah turned down her street in the quiet West Side neighborhood, her apartment nestled between Ninety-fourth and Ninety-fifth Street on the Pomander Walk. She collected the mail from her mailbox, then trudged upstairs and set her groceries on the kitchen table.

The ivory vellum envelope with deckled gold leaf edges seemed out of place with her bills. She opened the fancy envelope, enjoying the sensation of sumptuous paper beneath her callused fingers.

> *March 3, 1939*
>
> *Dear Miss Karofsky:*
>
> *It has come to our attention that you are an accomplished musician of considerable reputation. We would be honored to count you as a member of our family.*
>
> *It is our pleasure to offer you an apartment in the Waldorf Astoria Towers at a deeply discounted rate. We would like to have you stop by and consider our offer sometime before*

Sunday March 12th. If you are interested, arrangements will be made regarding your current lease and moving you from your present address.

We look forward to seeing you soon.

Sincerely,

Adam Lewis

Manager, Waldorf Towers

Sarah sat back and thought, 'this must be a joke'. Why her? She might play for the highbrows, but to live with them? She wasn't even sure she had the right clothes to wear through the lobby. And then she figured it out – it was the harp. The Waldorf wanted a live-in harp player. Someone they could call at the drop of a hat. A wedding is taking place and the piano player calls in sick? Try Sarah. The Cattlemen's convention is in town for tough negotiations and the beasts need a little soothing? Give Sarah a call.

She almost threw the offer in the trash, but couldn't quite let go of the beautiful paper. Then she thought, 'Why not? It wouldn't hurt to take a peek.'

Sarah noticed another piece of mail that had fallen to the floor. She stooped to pick it up, an illustrated invitation for an art exhibit at the Labor Club, a retrospective of works from the Harlem Renaissance.

Bill at Bergdorf Goodman

Since the Remington robbery, Bill Curran had been feeling pretty good about himself. Money hadn't been a problem for a few weeks, yet it was time to start considering the future. At forty-five, attracting older women was not as much fun, because now they were a lot older. It was one thing to be in his twenties going after forty-year-olds, however, the idea of luring sixty-year-olds was pathetic.

Yet women were women and Bill knew how to get them. He needed a meal ticket and where better to find one than a Fifth Avenue department store? He emerged from Central Park at Fifty-Ninth and Fifth. Despite the cold there were skaters and people on bobsleds out having a good time. He was glad for his galoshes, since the city parks crews had been busy spreading the streets and sidewalks with rock salt to ensure visitors didn't slip on icy paths. 'Nice for the out-of-town saps, but hell on a good pair of shoes,' thought Bill.

As the Park Plaza rose up before him, he recalled staying there a time or two, first with a blonde and then a redhead. The hotel embodied a magical world that lived up to its reputation. The poor chumps out on the street had no idea. Intricately embroidered yellow silk bedspreads, thick towels large enough to wear, soaps carved into swans and the subtle scent of exotic flowers. Best of all the staff treated each guest like royalty. Even Bill, because he could pay the price of admission. He had found it intoxicating. He recalled a fancy store next door with some Jew name. He'd go there.

He strode down Fifth Avenue and stopped in front of the display windows at Bergdorf Goodman. Throwing his half-smoked cigarette to the ground, he entered through the revolving door.

Three attractive young women rushed up to him, spraying lilac perfume on their wrists and placing their delicate skin beneath his nose.

He breathed in deeply, brushing each wrist with his lips. They giggled and blushed. 'If only they had money,' thought Bill.

"It's called Spring Time," said the lithe blonde in a white dress standing close beside him. "Would you like to buy some for your wife or girlfriend?"

"Don't have either, but if you come along with the perfume I'd be happy to buy it." He gave her a crooked grin. She and the other girls backed away, still giggling.

"It's $1.95 at the Spring Time sale counter," she said pointing to the right. Meanwhile, another pair of victims had come through the door and the young women launched themselves upon the unsuspecting couple. Based on their duds, Bill guessed they had just arrived from Iowa. 'No doubt the king and queen of corn,' he mused.

Bill slowly maneuvered his way into the heart of the store. From there he rose through its center on the new metal escalators. He was surprised at the racket they made clicking and clanking with every inch traveled. The old wooden ones were quieter, but not as sleek. A pianist was playing, a captivating melody that could be heard throughout the store. He went towards the music, dismissing the sales girls trying to foist their wares on him at each landing. The young women were half-hearted at their profession, 'not hungry enough,' thought Bill. 'They need a lesson or two from the working girls downtown.'

At the landing marked 'Formals' he spotted a gorgeous woman slipping an elegant gown onto a mannequin. She was neither plastic nor hard like most women. She was 5'6", her white blonde hair expertly coifed, tight on her head in a sculpture of curls and braids. Her face the color of cream, set off by her dark blue eyes and luscious red lips. She wore a simple gray dress with a pleated skirt and black belt. The tight-fitting bodice revealed an ample bosom. Bill found her exceptional.

"Excuse me, Miss, do you sell men's hats?" he asked.

Miriam looked up, sincerely interested in helping a customer. As soon as their eyes met she recognized Bill's faux interest and dismissed his request with dexterity.

"You'll find them on the third floor." And, so as to ensure he would leave she added, "We're having an excellent sale on men's hats today, thirty percent off. I suggest you hurry, we'll be closing in a few minutes."

"Since I'm here," he said, "maybe I should get something for my mother." He lifted the hem of a dress suggestively. "She's a saint. There isn't anything I wouldn't do for her." He smiled a beguiling smile.

"What type of evening gown would your mother like? Does she go to formal occasions often?"

"Oh yeah, once a week I'd say. You know, teas and stuff." He paused, unsure if women wore gowns to tea. "Besides, she likes the opera. Yep, a big fan of the opera, my mother."

"Lovely. What size is your mother? Oh, and I should remind you that if you're still in need of a hat we're closing in five minutes. Men's hats are on three."

Bill took the liberty of giving Miriam a thorough look up and down. "That's all right, I like the view on this floor just fine. About your size I'd say."

"Excuse me?"

"My mother. She's built a lot like you."

"Isn't that nice." She walked over to a rack of matronly garments decorated with lace and flowers. "Perhaps she'd like one of these."

Bill was way ahead of her. He didn't even follow her to the rack. Instead he stood near a collection of sheer, close fitting dresses with scooped necks and diving backs. He pulled out a red dress that was held up by a single silk ribbon over one shoulder. The skirt was slit to the hip.

"I think my mother would be a vision in this. Would you mind trying it on for me?"

"I'm afraid that dress wouldn't be fitting for an elderly mother," said Miriam. "Older women tend to get chilled and she would be miserable in that number."

"Are you an artist?" he said, placing the dress back on the rack. He knew she was running out the clock on him and he'd have to take another tack. "I don't mean to pry, it just seems obvious that all of this," he waved about the store, "is not really you. What rings your bell?" And as if by magic, a series of bells rang throughout the store.

"What was that?" He asked peering around.

"Closing time."

"You write poetry don't you?" All women her age did. "Would I have seen your work anywhere?"

"Doubtful. Now if you'll excuse me, I need to get my books in order for the evening. Maybe you can come back tomorrow for your hat." Miriam didn't work on Fridays and felt safe asking him back.

"Will you come out for dinner with me tonight?" He knew he'd lost her, but he had nothing to lose in keeping the pressure on.

"No, I'm a married woman." Just at that moment, a man stepped off the escalator. "Here's my husband now." She went up to Jason and gave him a light kiss on the lips.

"How sweet of you to come walk me home, dear. I just need to close out my sales book."

Bill was surprised that her husband was so handsome and well heeled. He wondered why she worked when she already had a feed-bag.

"I'll be off then, M.R." Bill said pointing to the initials on her dress pocket.

"Miriam Rothman." She remained busy closing the counter and didn't look up at him.

"Oh, a Jew," he said under his breath, "Good day to you Miss Rothman. I'm sure we'll meet again."

And with that he left, empty-handed. He hadn't even flirted with anyone worthwhile. Then he realized that when the store closed, many of the women shoppers would go to the Palm Court next door. They would chat and enjoy coffee or hot cocoa. He'd go there.

As Bill departed, Miriam returned to Jason's side and gave him a quick hug. She had never been happier to see him.

He handed her a small bouquet of flowers. "How was your day, my sweet?"

"Dreadful, darling, until you showed up. Give me another moment to get my sales ledger in order. I'll be right with you." She sniffed at the flowers and handed them back to him. "Freesia. You're such a lamb."

"I'm here to make your day sunnier," he said, smiling broadly. She threw him a kiss and stepped back behind a display area.

Jason browsed through the collection of fancy evening gowns. They were resplendent in every color and texture imaginable. There were crepes, suedes and thickly beaded outfits that were actually heavy to lift off the rack. Others were sheer enough that Jason could examine his hand through them. There were dresses with exquisite embroidery so delicate and flawless that he was certain someone went blind sewing them. The dresses were an exhibit just by themselves.

"Miriam, these dresses are stupendous."

"What dear?" she said with only partial attention, as she buttoned her gloves.

"These dresses. They're works of art. I think they're inspiring."

She peered at him for a moment. "Tell me dear, did they serve champagne at this opening you attended?"

It took a moment for him to recall where he had just been. "They did, but I didn't have any," he replied never registering that she was teasing him. "But dearest, you'll never guess who I met – Zora Neale Hurston. She's brilliant. She shared stories with me from her new book. And guess what? She's a Jacob Lawrence fan too. I told her about our beloved Lawrence painting. Zora said she never buys paintings since they'd feel neglected and unappreciated because she travels so much." He smiled at the memory of meeting the talented writer.

"The Harlem show was excellent. I wish you had come with me. I'll tell you all about it over dinner. Let's go to Rueben's."

Miriam would have preferred to head home but reluctantly answered, "Yes dear, just two more minutes." Christine, her manager, appeared and Miriam turned over her sales book with a flourish. "Read'em and weep Chris." When Christine, a woman several years younger than Miriam, registered that Miriam had sold over $2,500 in dresses, she gave a long slow whistle. "Sister, you and I are making some sweet music together. Whatever you need girl, you let me know."

"Right now, if you could let me go a few minutes early, my husband is waiting for me."

"I'm sorry. You forgot we have a staff meeting with the big wigs tonight. Just sit in for a few minutes and I'll clock you out later."

Miriam gave a little pout and went to Jason for a kiss and whiff of her flowers. With a sigh she said, "I will meet you at Rueben's darling. I won't be long."

Jason appeared to Miriam every inch the white knight, holding the bouquet of freesia as his sword and his bowler hat a shield. Jason bowed deeply to the two women. "Christine promise not to keep her too long or her flowers will wilt."

"I promise," Chris replied.

And the two women watched as Jason descended out of sight down the escalator.

March

Rueben's

Jason delighted in eating at Rueben's Deli, a New York landmark, always filled with people from every walk of life. Here at one of the long tables a diner might find themself sitting next to a Broadway producer, the head of a bank, or the ticket taker at the Astor. Jason enjoyed the complimentary bowl of pickles and overhearing the conversations of the other patrons.

The maitre d', dressed in a cheap $2.50 suit, greeted each patron as they entered. He took pride in treating his customers tersely, with only a lightly veiled rudeness in his demeanor. After getting a party seated he would toss the menus onto the table and walk away, letting them know who was the boss. He relished giving a new customer a hard time if they had the audacity to make a special request. It added to the ambience of the place and the regulars knew the drill – and came back for more.

Open twenty-four hours a day, half the restaurant's patrons were women. Rueben's was the one of the few places where women didn't put on pretenses. Here the fairer sex felt free to laugh loudly, slouch comfortably and put their elbows on the table while they ate. Rueben's brought out the less guarded nature in everyone.

The walls were covered with photographs and caricatures of the stars of radio, theater and movies including, Cary Grant, Katharine Hepburn, Jimmy Stewart, Groucho Marx, Benny Goodman, Artie Shaw, and Gertrude Lawrence. Jason felt at home here. Besides, they had the best blintzes in all of Manhattan. What was not to like?

The maître d' showed Jason to a table that hugged the wall, which afforded only slightly more privacy. "Will your wife be along soon? Or would you like to order now?" As a regular, Jason's habits were remembered. His portrait hung in the other room.

"Mrs. Rothman will be here shortly. Why don't you bring me a bowl of borscht in the meantime."

"Gladly."

Jason turned in his chair and looked around. The place was three-quarters full at 5:30 p.m. He suspected the current clientele were mostly actors, actresses, stagehands, and various members of the theater, grabbing a bite after mid-day rehearsals. This would be their only sustenance until after this evening's performance.

"Jason! Jason Rothman!" Jason swung around to determine the source of the voice. There in the doorway stood Lillian Hellman and Dashiell Hammett. Jason stood up and waved them over.

"Lillian." He reached across the table to kiss her, European style, on both cheeks. Her eyes danced with genuine pleasure at seeing him. The towering Hammett reached out a meaty paw and nodded.

"Don't mind Dash, he's just coming off one helluva a bender with Faulkner. They've been tight for a week." Dash appeared sheepish or nauseous. Perhaps it was the smell of the food. Jason thoughtfully moved the pickles aside.

Lillian continued, "So tell me, how are you? How's your play going?" her enthusiasm for life was contagious.

"The notices were good and the box office is holding its own, enough so that Max is producing my next play." Jason smiled, knowing Lillian understood the significance of his words. Max Schneider was a producer known for picking winners.

"Oh Jason," she leapt from her seat and gave him a big kiss on the lips. "Congratulations. You're on your way, boy." She reached for a nonexistent drink. Dash motioned for the waiter. Lillian slapped the table with pleasure. "Boy, you are on your way."

"But enough of me," said Jason. "What of you? The Little Foxes is a huge success. It'll run for years. Congratulations to you."

Lillian feigned a mock bow in her chair and said, "It's still something of a shock to me. They keep telling me to tone down my plays, not to make them so controversial and yet I think that's why people come to see them." She lit up a cigarette and took a deep draw. "Call me crazy."

"It's extraordinary, the emotion you evoke between your characters. And Tallulah is magnificent, as always."

"And boy, does she know it," Hellman replied. "You know she's had me banned from the theater?'"

"No."

"Oh yes,'" putting on a snooty voice Hellman added, "She seems to think I disrupt her creative process." She laughed, "Tallulah

Bankhead is a box office draw and God love her, she is the part, but I don't want to hang around with her. Besides, I'm already on to my next play. And what about you? What's next in the line up? Of course, we're all chasing Odets. The man seems to be made of plays." She took a sip of water and made a sour face, then nodded to Dashiell who doctored it with his pocket flask.

Jason frowned.

"Not to worry," said Hellman, "it's that old bathtub hooch we used to drink during prohibition. It needs some watering down." She raised an eyebrow, "Would you like some?"

"No, thank you," Jason replied with a smile.

Hellman continued, "All of Odets' plays seem to be big hits. You know they're calling him the next Eugene O'Neill?" She sampled her doctored water and sighed appreciatively. "And they call me heavy handed with a script. Look at Odets. He has them all but singing the International and waving a red flag with hammer and sickle. They just love him." Laughing she asked Jason, "So what are you working on?"

"I confess, I was working on a piece, or should I say a vehicle for Katharine Hepburn. We had lunch a few months back and she was dying to return to the stage. Ever since The Lake she hasn't been able to find work."

"Big Bad Wolf Jed Harris - what a dreadful director. I won't let him near any of my plays."

"I agree. I like Kate. I think she has a special quality, so I developed a script for her. Then I heard that Philip Barry has already approached her with something and they fast-tracked it. He finished it last month, and they're already putting it into production."

"What? How's that possible? Who's backing it? Where's the money coming from? Do they already have a theater?"

"Howard Hughes is bankrolling it. Rumor is he's asked Katharine to marry him."

Lillian lit a fresh cigarette off of the one she was about to put out. "That stinks. Passing up a first-rate writer like you? She's a fool."

"She didn't turn me down. I never told her about the play. Barry just got there first and I wouldn't upstage him."

Lillian raised an eyebrow in disbelief. "You wouldn't fight for your star?"

"Lillian, it's not like there aren't other actresses. Hepburn's a risk at best."

She laughed a wonderfully unselfconscious belly laugh. "You're right, it's practically raining stars. There are plenty to go around. When did you say this hit would be finished?"

"I'll probably be ready for production in October or November."

"That gives us seven months to find you a Gertrude Lawrence. No problem." Lillian reached for a pickle, then pointed it at Jason as she was struck with a thought.

"Say, you know Dash and I are going to the coast to work on *To Have and Have Not* next week. Why don't you join us? I'm sure we could find you a starlet there." Lillian was taken by the idea. "Do say yes. There's nothing to lose and everything to gain. Come on, it'll be fun."

"Oh, I couldn't leave. Miriam would worry, what with me out in the sun and all." He smiled.

"Bring her along. Last time I saw her I thought she could use a little sunshine." She winked at him.

At that moment Miriam, escorted by the maitre d', came into the dining room. Lillian rushed up to her, "Miriam dear, you're looking wonderful. How sensational to see you." She kissed Miriam on each cheek.

Miriam, never comfortable with public shows of affection or Lillian, returned Hellman's kisses stiffly.

"So nice to see you Lillian. Will you be joining us for dinner?"

"Oh, no dear. We must be on our way. Many more bars to find between here and the Village. Violin players to sing with, etc."

Miriam stared at Hellman with a puzzled expression.

"No sweets, we've just finished. " Lillian knew that Miriam was not a worthy adversary for her sharp tongue and her respect and affection for Jason caused her to remain civil. A chore to be sure.

"Jason was just telling us about his new play and I invited him out to the coast with us. Please make sure he comes, he's looking a little peaked, don't you think? Besides, it would be good for his career." Lillian knew where to set the hook.

"I'm sure Jason and I will discuss it," said Miriam.

Amid much hand waving and good-byes, Hellman and Hammett left the restaurant. Suddenly it seemed empty. Lillian's personality had filled the room.

"Hello darling." Jason stood and leaned over the table to kiss his wife.

"She means well, doesn't she, Jason?"

"Of course, dear. Lillian is one of my kindest friends. I trust her completely and as you know, in the world of theater, that's saying something."

"I know. It's just that I never feel up to speed conversing with Lillian, or Dorothy Parker for that matter."

Jason laughed out loud. "Darling no one is up to speed with Dorothy. That's why she's Dorothy. We all pit ourselves against her now and again, but in the end, she always wins. Come on, let's have some dinner."

They turned their attention to the menu, while Jason's thoughts strayed out west.

Two tables from where the couple sat Alex Bridges showed his plans for a modern skyscraper to a large man, who looked like an overstuffed mattress wearing a suit. The man, clearly more interested in his blintzes, appeared unapologetic when he spilled blueberry syrup on Alex's drawings. However, the man's wife's eyes never left Alex's chiseled face. Jason noted she surreptitiously slipped a piece of paper into the architect's pocket before he left.

Letters from Germany

Upon returning home from an after show discussion with the cast, Jason saw the letter on the hall table as he took off his coat. It was from Germany. Jason had begun reading the letters from Miriam's family first, because their volatile content could leave Miriam depressed for days. He never shared with her that the missives had the same effect on him.

He picked up the envelope and the letter opener beside it while calling out, "Miriam, I see we have another letter." Jason slit the thin translucent paper envelope and began to read.

Walking into the kitchen he found her lifting an apple pie from the oven. The smell was enticing. "The good news is that they are still able to send letters, and they haven't been arrested," he said as he read.

"Good news, yes," she said, nodding with agreement.

He read the letter in silence. Miriam's family had owned and operated a fashionable restaurant in a Munich suburb for twenty-five years. Recently they had been forced to give up both the restaurant and their home.

"They need money," he said when he finished. "The officials have levied a race tax and are demanding cash payments. I'll go out after dinner and wire them what they need."

"Thank you," she said, drying her hands on her apron. She leaned over and kissed him on the cheek, avoiding the letter. "You're a good man. What else do they say?"

He took off his glasses and polished them on his tie. Jason formed his response carefully. "They've been forced to move into town to work in a local factory. They're living with three other families in four rooms. Everyone's well, but many people have come down with dysentery due to fouled water."

"Did they receive my sponsorship letter?"

"Yes, however, they've been told that nothing will happen until later. There's a new administration taking over emigration and they'll need to process the paperwork."

Miriam's eyes pooled. She kissed him again. "Thank you, husband. I appreciate what you're doing for my family."

"Our family," he said, tucking the letter in his vest pocket, not wanting to share all it contained.

Karl Klyne - A Piece of Advice

The second floor restaurant of the Barbizon Plaza Hotel was basked in the orange light of the setting sun. At a table overlooking Central Park South, Karl Klyne and his companion sat facing the window,

Out of the Dark

by Alan Stipple

Hats off to Mrs. Roosevelt for standing tall and supporting America's greatest opera singer, Marion Anderson. Miss Anderson was recently denied the opportunity to perform at Constitution Hall because the Daughters of the American Revolution do not allow colored entertainers in their facilities. Mrs. Roosevelt quit DAR and had Miss Anderson sing at the White House instead.

News flash: the hottest Tinsel Town eligibles are married - Clark Gable and Carole Lombard tied the knot last week in Kingman, Arizona.

THEATER:

★★★★☆ *Little Foxes*

Lillian Hellman's *Little Foxes* is a tour de force offering Tallulah Bankhead her first vehicle to stardom in the U.S. after years of success in London.

MOVIES:

★★★☆☆ *Jessie James*

Shot in the back by a coward. It seems un-American despite the fact that Jessie James robbed trains for a living. Tyron Power is cast as the famous Jesse James and Henry Fonda as his brother Frank. The movie is a classic western, complete with gunfights, horses, villains and beautiful sweethearts. It was filmed in Technicolor, which means all you black and white purists might just as well stay home.

★★★☆☆ *Pygmalion*

Leslie Howard plays a cad in the classic tale of the teacher whose student surpasses him. Wendy Hiller plays Liza Doolittle and steals every scene away from the sophisticated Mr. Howard. But in the end, when he tells her to fetch his slippers, we in the audience can't help but wish she'd respond back, "Get your own damn slippers."

with their backs to the occasional guests who entered for tea. Few came to the Barbizon, since the Park Plaza's famed high tea was served next door. In this quiet room the thin intense man and the elegant woman conversed softly as they watched the Saturday afternoon shoppers heading home with their packages.

The tables that flanked them were occupied by serious looking men who did not blend in with the genteel décor. These men neither indulged in conversation or tea; instead their dark eyes monitored the room. Karl paid the bodyguards little mind, transfixed as he was on Mrs. Roosevelt.

"Karl, how are your parents? I haven't seen your mother in years. Is she well?"

"Very well. Thank you for asking. Father's grand. He retired this year, finally accepting the fact that I'm not going to take over the business. He's become a golfer. I hear he's quite good at it, then again, I'd expect nothing less from father."

"Please do send him my best. Your father spent so much time with us during the worst of the strikes in '37. He's like family. Such a good man, and a great help to the President and Miss Perkins."

"He'd be pleased to hear that. I'll make a point of letting him know."

The tea arrived and with great aplomb the waiter served it as if to any other guest. The Barbizon Plaza was where the truly famous came when they did not want to be seen.

"And you Karl? How are you?" Mrs. Roosevelt asked, holding the cup daintily with her pinky raised.

"I'm fine," Karl said, without conviction. Mrs. Roosevelt waited for him to collect his thoughts.

"Thank you for meeting me," he began again. "I knew you were in town, and I do have something to discuss with you. I want to share with you what I'm doing these days and see if you can offer me any guidance."

Eleanor's smile held no sarcasm, only the wisdom of experience. He could see that she wanted him to succeed. Karl believed he possessed the fire and passion of the great men of history. Unfortunately, he also knew he was apt to acquire the role of the martyr.

He met her eyes and now spoke with conviction. "All my life, I've been working to improve the conditions of the unfortunate, first in Europe after the Great War and then in New York, during the Depression. My goal has always been to help decent people get the basics: housing, food and a job. I've worked with scores of relief organizations and most recently with the unions. As each organization becomes a living, breathing entity, the work becomes political. Now my activitiess have become less about direct accomplishment and more about working with the various people within these organizations. There's more compromise, trading favors and catering to egos."

He paused and shrugged. "I thought you might have some advice, because you started out like me, a person from a privileged background looking to make things better. Your success in improving living conditions in the Bowery has always been an inspiration to me. Somehow you were able to cross over into politics and continue to make a meaningful impact. Can you tell me how you did it?"

Eleanor gave a nod and pursed her lips. She was a woman who had seen much of the world and knew how it worked. "I wish you could share your sentiments with my advisors, Karl. They would be the first to tell you that I am a dreadful politician." She laughed, her trademark high-pitched laugh, that sounded like it came from a woman half her size. "To respond to your point regarding getting things done, it does help to be married to the President of the United States."

Karl blushed at the magnitude of his arrogance, putting himself on the same level as the First Lady, and then he laughed with her.

Mrs. Roosevelt touched the back of his hand. "Karl, what you describe is the same demon I deal with every day. I've not learned how to overcome it. Everything moves too slowly for me. I want to get so much more done. I see the tools before me, yet feel powerless to use them."

She sighed. "One thing I've learned is, 'You're either a politician or you're not.' Look at the President. He's a born politician, as was Coolidge before him. Men of compromise. They know when to give in and when to stand firm. My uncle TR, on the other hand, God rest his soul, never learned this. He charged around like a bull in a china shop, always upsetting someone. It was his way. The people loved him, yet they could just as easily have burned him in effigy. One thing you can count on as you grow older is that your skin will thicken. You'll learn which fights to turn away from and which ones to see through." Mrs. Roosevelt smiled sympathetically.

Karl paused for a moment before responding. "I understand what you're saying, yet I just can't seem to take it in. For instance, I recently returned from the Appalachian coal mines. The strikers there simply can't get ahead. Some of them, and their families, will die of starvation before the strike is over, and yet they hold out for a measly fifty-cents-a-day pay increase and the ability to work at least thirty hours a week. My heart bleeds. I see the sooty children and the wives without hope and I want to scream."

Again she reached out to him. "Karl, weren't you a teacher? Why don't you go back to teaching?"

"I would, but there aren't many jobs for history teachers. Everyone has more important things on their minds, like how to get food on the table. Besides, if I can help just one person then I'll know I'm doing the right thing."

Mrs. Roosevelt pushed her cup of tea away and spoke with authority. "Young man, I have your answer. Stop trekking around the country and work right here in New York City. Limit the scope of what you're trying to accomplish. Stop attempting to save the world. Focus on an orphanage or a reading program for adults, something where you can see your success in the eyes of the people you want to help."

Staring at the half-eaten cucumber sandwich on his plate, Karl contemplated her words. At first, he thought taking her suggestion felt like admitting failure. Then he recognized that his own logic betrayed him. He had bitten off more than he could chew and was suffering from the indigestion of his best intentions.

"You're right. That makes good sense. " He sat back and took a deep breath. "Yes. I feel better already. That's what I'll do.

WAR CORRESPONDENT

Nancy Ames - Prague

This month war has begun for the people of Czech-Slovakia and Austria, with the invasions by Hitler's armies.

Perhaps this move is simply to steal the gold reserves held by both countries, but this reporter believes it's only the beginning of an expanding cancer across the European landscape. With Hitler's insatiable appetite, one can only assume Romania and Poland are next on his list.

Silver-shirt fascists in New York are gaining in popularity as citizens begin to lose faith in the current administration. These fascists believe that the Jews are behind our economic woes, and that Roosevelt and his secretary of labor, Francis Perkins, are both Jews.

Sometimes the news I gather from our own shores is as distressing as what I am witnessing here. If you are not active politically and are reading this column, it is time to take action against the purveyors of hate.

If not you – who?

Thank you."

"It's my pleasure." Mrs. Roosevelt signaled to her security men and rose. "Just remember the feeling of relief you're experiencing right now. It will not last for long. You must hold onto your resolve, so you don't lose your compass in the future."

And with that she was off, a grande dame sprinkling the fairy dust of goodwill and hope. Karl shook his head, honored and moved to have shared a few thoughts with this truly remarkable woman.

Alex's New Profession

Alex spent his days in the park, teasing the squirrels and half listening to the quasi-politicos standing on milk crates and giving speeches. All of the speeches seemed to be the same: jobs, peace, freedom. He could almost recite the key messages. With the right list of phrases you could go to any party, activist group or women's tea and fit right in, no matter what part of the political spectrum the organization was aligned with. At the moment, he was eyeing a beautiful blonde with pouty red lips who appeared to be in need of rescue.

During Alex's first six months in the city his only paying job had been with a woman who lived on East Sixty Third Street. While her husband was in South America drilling for oil, Alex had been hired to do a little drilling of his own.

He hadn't meant for it to be like that. It hadn't started out that way, although in his mind he could easily reduce himself to the whore he had become. He had been studying the architecture of the apartment building from the street. The Babb, Cook and Willard edifice was a classic made of red brick with a limestone base. It had been built to withstand the test of time, combining the romance of Camelot with the fancy of Max Fleischer. Sort of 'Snow White meets Betty Boop.' He found it enchanting.

"Hey, buddy, you like the building so much, take a picture and get out of here," the doorman shouted.

"Excuse me?" Alex responded. He'd never before been mistook for the rabble that wandered the streets of New York.

"You heard me, get out of here or I call a cop." The doorman approached him somewhat menacingly, his size alone enough to intimidate.

Alex pulled himself up to his most stately height. "Excuse me, sir, but I do not know what you're talking about. I'm here to visit a resident of this building, and I assure you I'll let my friend know the treatment with which I was greeted at her front door."

"Oh yeah? Who are you here to meet?" The doorman eyed him closely, certain this was a ruse, however, unwilling to press the point and be fired. He moved closer to Alex and let his full height of six feet plus weigh in against the younger man's five-foot-eleven.

"Sir, intimidation by a man wearing an organ grinder's uniform is ineffective. Moreover, it's comical. If you will retreat to the premises, I'll enter and you may announce me."

Alex tried to discern if his words were penetrating and thought he saw a flicker of doubt pass over the bruiser's face. Alex continued, "If you would step inside, we'll pretend this ghastly incident never took place and return to our positions as dictated by heaven."

The doorman relaxed, now certain that Alex was an impostor. "Oh brother, I've heard some whoppers in my day, but yours takes the cake." He brushed past Alex and went to the street corner.

"What are you doing?" demanded Alex.

"Finding an officer to have you hauled downtown. I think the air up here has gone to your head, you pie-faced lout."

"Eddie." The stern voice dripped of honeyed steel.

The doorman spun around and doffed his hat to the regal being in front of him. "Mrs. Shirling, how may I help you? Do you need a cab?"

"No, Eddie. I've come down to see what has become of my friend here. I had anticipated him some few minutes ago, and knowing he would never keep me waiting came down to determine the trouble." She smiled at Alex, and then turned back to Eddie with a stone face. "Imagine my surprise to find you detaining him with trivial questions and in a manner quite unfitting to his station. Do you know who this man is?"

Eddie paused, willing to concede that he might have made a mistake.

"This is Count Prestoff," Mrs. Shirling said. "We met during the crossing last fall." She turned to Alex. "It was the Rex, wasn't it, Count?"

Alex never missed a beat. He realized this middle-aged woman desired him. She carried an extra twenty pounds and the powder hiding a poor complexion denied her the title of 'beauty queen', yet she was regally ensembled. Her Madeleine Vionnet, bias-cut rayon dress had an exotic print of maroon and black. On her feet were a pair of black suede Salvatore Ferragamo heels.

"And a beautiful crossing it was." Alex bowed slightly, clicking his heels together as he did so. She held out her gloved hand and awaited his kiss.

Both ignored Eddie, who stood to the side with his hands on his hips.

Alex continued. "My lady, where would you like to go to today? Would you like a ride in the park, or is there an exhibit you wish to see?"

"Foolish man, today's the opening of the Masterworks at the Pierpont Morgan Library. You offered to escort me."

"Of course, of course. It's such a beautiful day. Would you care to walk?"

The doorman's face revealed renewed suspicion. Alex sensed he'd erred. A woman like Mrs. Shirling probably never walked anywhere.

Eddie sneered at Alex, signalling he knew the score. Alex was confident that Eddie would never say a thing. There were undoubtedly plenty of goings on in the building to which the doorman routinely turned a blind eye. A discreet silence was always rewarded with a little something extra around the holidays.

"Let me get you a cab, Mrs. Shirling," Eddie said with exaggerated politeness.

"Thank you."

She stepped forward, slipping her arm through Alex's. Eddie gave out a loud whistle and waved as he saw an available cab approaching. The taxi pulled up and Eddie opened the door for the couple. Alex assisted Mrs. Shirling into the car.

As Alex got in, the doorman leaned over and whispered into his ear. "Count, my ass. You aren't fooling anyone, and if I catch you out of Mrs. Shirling's sight, we'll share more than words." And then in a louder voice, "Yes sir, Count, you are in for a spectacular day."

It had been that simple. Mrs. Shirling took him around to the openings and exhibits of prestige.

Each morning Alex would find a modest roll of bills in his pants pocket and usually a new item to add to his trousseau – a watch, a hat, shoes, a belt – until eventually he became quite the dapper man about town. Nothing was ever said regarding payment for services rendered. But he felt himself sliding down a slippery slope of self-loathing.

At first, he thought he might meet the important and influential men of architecture at parties he attended with Mrs. Shirling. And on a number of occasions he did speak with the giants in the field, including John Mead Howells, Raymond Hood and the master McMead. Mrs. Shirling always introduced Alex as Count Prestoff who designed the most innovative buildings in Europe. The conversations would start around children, dogs, or the exhibit at hand, however, when the focus turned to architecture, they would find a reason to excuse themselves.

Months later he realized that these men knew exactly what he was and were being polite to Mrs. Shirling by not calling him a fraud to his face.

He was scorned by the very society to which he had hoped to gain acceptance. Alex lost his dignity and in the same stroke misplaced the compass of his ambition.

While some men drowned their sorrows in liquor, Alex chose to imbibe in women. Mrs. Shirling had helped him realize he had a gift, and she was more than willing to share him. She didn't like having him underfoot every day, so she ensured he was kept busy with her bridge partners, fellow committee members and even her neighbors. She must have been applauded in her circles for her beneficent nature.

As his self-respect evaporated Alex began to expand his conquests to non-paying admirers. These were younger women, less jaded and still mystified by men. And Alex knew just how to keep them mystified.

APRIL

The Hoofer's Club

Bill emerged from a whorehouse on One Hundred and Thirty-Fifth Street in Harlem. Despite his disdain for blacks he liked his women with some color. The one he'd just had was a polite, sweet young thing around fourteen.

Bill felt good. The future looked bright. He floated above the pavement, above the cares of those around him. He always felt more alive on the streets of Harlem. The neighborhood seemed more vibrant and real than midtown. Here people congregated in small groups, vendors hawking, kids swiping stuff, women yelling at their men or each other. It reminded him of an earlier time in New York.

He was about to light a hand-rolled cigarette when he saw the Hoofer's Club sign. Despite its modest presentation, every dancer alive knew about the legends that had performed there. Bill tucked the cigarette back into its pouch and strode up the stairs to the third floor.

Behind the heavy door, once used to protect a famous and popular speakeasy, a crowd pressed up to the bar and parked around small tables. 'Quite the collection of riff-raff for the middle of the day' thought Bill. He was the only white man in the room. But he blended in with the smoke and noise as he made his way to the bar.

"Got any dancers in this joint?" He asked, laying a five-dollar bill on the bar. The bartender eyed the money warily.

"What you think you doin' with that? You be wantin' some whiskey?"

"Nah, maybe later. Right now I want to do some dancing." He pulled the fin back into his waistcoat pocket.

"We's got some young fellas in back and a couple of smart old guys. You thinkin' of joinin' 'em?"

"Yeah," said Bill.

"Waits here. I'll tell 'em you're comin' in."

Now Bill wanted that drink. He turned his back to the bar and looked out over the afternoon regulars. 'Deadbeats' he thought. A woman snapped her head around to look at him and then quickly looked away.

"Hey Mista, come this way." The bartender lifted a hinged section of the bar and led Bill into a large backroom that contained only two pieces of furniture - a tired upright piano and a stool.

Half a dozen negroes of all ages stood about in shirtsleeves, some wearing waistcoats, all were wearing taps.

Bill hadn't brought his taps. He preferred soft-shoe, although he could tap. Tap his heart out if he had to.

The bartender began introductions. "Mr. Er…"

"Curran, Bill Curran," Bill volunteered.

"Mr. Curran, this here is Fayard Nicholas, Leonard Reed, Ralph Brown, Flash McDonald and Mr. Willie Covan. "Everyone kept their eyes to themselves. The bartender spoke up, "I guess I'll leave you boys to it." Bill reached into his pocket and palmed the five off to the man with a handshake. The man looked back over his shoulder and shrugged at the dancers.

"You'z a dancer Mr. Bill?," asked Flash.

"So I've been told." He shifted from foot to foot in a soft-shoe dance.

The black men relaxed a little. Their instincts told them not to trust this man, but there was an undeniable brotherhood among hoofers.

"We just messin' around. You care to join us?" said the youngest man of the group. He was in his early twenties and long legged. He began to tap out a military march with his shoes.

"Yeah – that's what I had in mind," said Bill.

Feeling more comfortable, the men resumed their earlier conversation. "Hey Flash, show me that two-step you got goin' on."

Flash was tall and lanky, in his late thirties, with deep scars on his face, scars that had not been put there by nature. He nodded to the request and moved to the center of the floor. Then Flash began a complicated step with arms flying and feet kicking wide to the sides. He looked like a windmill. Meanwhile a syncopated rhythm came from his feet. Bill realized there was no accompaniment from the piano – he'd never seen dancers dance without music.

Bill strode over to the rickety upright and took command. He began banging out; "She'll be commin' 'round the mountain when she comes." Flash stopped dancing and the others went silent. The tune was an odd choice for a dancer and unquestionably a white cracker's song. The beat was simple and yet staccato enough for the clicking of feet. The men prided themselves on being able to dance to anything.

Len was the first to take up the challenge. As Bill sang, "She'll be driving six white horses when she comes." Len began to mimic a horse, racing towards home clippity clop, faster and faster. Roy could hear it and joined Len; then Fay, Ralph and Willie did too. Once the dancers were in sync, Bill picked up the tempo. "We'll all come out to meet her when she comes," he sang, beating the notes from the piano. Bill was moving those horses down the mountain with the devil right behind them.

The black men were working up a sweat, captured by a new song, a new rhythm. After four more stanzas of the song, all were showing signs of exhaustion. Thoroughbreds that had run a fine race. Bill finished and they all clapped and smiled at each other.

"What about you, Mr. Bill?" Willie stepped over to the piano and

Bill moved to the middle of the floor. "Let's try a little boogie woogie. You up for it?"

"Give me what you got, boys," said Bill. Willie started slowly with a ragtime shuffle. Bill found his feet and the rhythm. Then Willie picked up the pace to a romping stride piano melody.

Bill Curran was transported. His feet moved to the tempo, his body became the instrument upon which the music played. His limbs knew where to go and how to touch the notes lingering in the air. He danced a combination of tap/ballroom/modern, something the hoofers had never seen before – not in movies or on the stage. There wasn't a single step they couldn't recreate, yet the combination of steps was hypnotic.

The music stopped and everyone stared at Bill, not knowing quite what to say. Finally, Fay made an overture. "You got somethin' new there, Mister. What's it called?"

Bill had never thought to name it. "I don't know. Dance."

"But where's you seen it before? Who taught you?"

"No one, it's just in me."

The men all nodded appreciatively. "You ever try doing that stuff with a partner?" asked Len, his head lowered, not wanting to give offense. "I mean, I see a woman as part of that dance. You know, in one of them long fancy dresses with feathers or somethin'. I think it'd be mighty pretty."

"Yeah, you'd sure beat out any Rogers and Astaire routine," said Fay.

"No, I haven't tried it with a partner," said Bill. "It's just sort of something I do – I feel good when I dance. It's like..." He trailed off, not willing to expose himself.

Then he clapped his hands and said, "What else you got, boys?" They spent the afternoon going back and forth. Despite the natural camaraderie of dancers, the black men continued to be wary of Bill. Their discomfort was not simply sustained by the color of his skin. Bill's presence seemed to broadcast an impending disaster. The hoofers handled him carefully, in the hope that he would leave without incident.

Out of the Dark
by Alan Stipple

Remember Josephine Baker? Who doesn't? Unfortunately you won't be seeing her anytime soon unless you plan to go to South America. As things heat up in Europe, Josephine, now a French citizen, has decided to fly south until things settle down across the pond. Why did she not return home? It's a little matter of Jim Crow.

Now, while we might love Mr. LaGuardia I'm sure that many in New York would just as soon he minded his own business when it comes to exotic dancers. During the World's Fair the mayor has mandated that the city's nude dancers cover up with G-strings and thongs. Sorry, boys.

I'm looking forward to seeing AT&T's new videophones at the World's Fair. These will enable you to see the person you're speaking with. Watch out, ladies. No more talking to your beaus with curlers in your hair.

THEATER:
★★☆☆☆
Ladies and Gentlemen
A vehicle brought to the stage for Helen Hayes. The producers are depending on Miss Hayes to pull in audiences based on her recent success with *Regina Victoria*. Alas, this one is a rather light, non-penetrating bore.

MOVIES:
★★★★☆ *Dodge City*
Any movie with Errol Flynn and Olivia de Havilland is worth seeing. And it's in Technicolor, which at times, is a little distracting, but works all the same.

★★★☆☆ *Dark Victory*
A real tear jerker. Bette Davis plays the wild devil-may-care playgirl to a tee. When it ends up she's losing her vision, she takes life much more seriously and falls in love with something of a wet blanket, George Brent. If I were Bette I would've stuck with playboy Ronald Reagan, but what do I know? Definitely worth the time in the dark.

April

Ernestine Robertson on Ice

The cold spring wind was thwarted by Ernestine's full-length sable coat. With her head tilted back, she tasted the light mist. She glided around the small rink at Rockefeller Center, enjoying the ice with only a handful of other skaters. Ernestine found the effortless motion intoxicating. On skates she moved with grace and speed, the way she always imagined she could on stage. And the best part was her feet didn't hurt, a great relief after eighteen years in toe shoes – a fact she admitted to no one.

Ernestine Robertson had studied ballet since she was three. Stepped into her first toe-shoes at nine. She'd been born in the central coast region of the Golden State of California. Despite Hollywood being a mere four hundred miles away Ernestine always knew her true home would be the stage.

There were no unaccompanied women dancers in Hollywood except Ruby Keeler. Women were forced to partner up. Even Ginger Rogers didn't get any respect without Fred. But Ernestine was born to be a dancer. New York called to her, the city where Agnes DeMille, Martha Graham, Katherine Dunham, and Ruth St. Denis performed and thrilled audiences as solo artists. Ernestine was willing to do whatever it took and she knew she would succeed.

By the time she graduated from high school, she had saved enough money for the journey to New York, four months rent and one meal a day. When Ernestine arrived in the Big Apple, the depression held the city in a vise grip. She could smell the desperation in the air, but it didn't dissuade her. She knew there were dancing jobs to be had. The wealthy still demanded their entertainment.

Ernestine spent some of her precious savings to observe George Balanchine's choreography for the Metropolitan Opera House. During intermission she found herself standing in the lobby beside Lincoln Kirstein, a founder of the recently formed School of American Ballet. During their short conversation Ernestine's wit, charm and California beauty won him over. He invited her to audition and she pirouetted her way into the troupe. Within five years Ernestine owned the number-two spot in the line up, with frequent solos of her own. She had become a draw for the company and was appropriately compensated.

At twenty-four she looked thirty-four. The demanding schedule, travel, late nights, lack of food and chain smoking were wearing on her 'star-quality' features. What's more, a new crop of nineteen-year-olds waited in the wings for their turn. Ernestine's days in the ballet spotlight were coming to an end. Her brutalized feet wouldn't carry her through another season.

Ernestine had to move forward and evolve. Her vision of the future did not include teaching ballet to a bunch of Upper East Side brats. Her destiny would have to be majestic and original. She resolved to discover a new school, a new dance, which would enable her to continue to entertain and headline. Miss Ernestine Robertson was preordained to be the next great choreographer of Gotham.

Miriam's Poetry Contest

It had been a hard winter and Miriam was ready to experience something besides gray. Gray skies, gray trees, gray earth. The monotones of March made her sullen and now, they lingered into April. She found relief going to work at Bergdorf to be among the brightly colored taffeta dresses covered with billowing clouds of pastel chiffon. Sometimes she would just run her hands lightly over the fabrics to soak up the colors.

Today at home, Miriam sat at Jason's desk. She had dipped his favorite pen in the inkpot and let it loom over the white page like a brooding cloud. When Jason was ready to write, he would sit down and stream out pages. Miriam on the other hand, had to fight for every word. Writing was a struggle that she always came away from exhausted.

These days she found herself questioning her chosen 'profession' more often. If you are not paid for whatever you call yourself professionally, are you allowed to lay claim to the title? Is an author an author if unpublished? A painter, a painter without the recent sale of a canvas? It was a conundrum Miriam hadn't solved.

Every time Miriam tried to write, a virtual flood of other things that she should be doing came to mind instead. Feed the cat, sweep the floor, or research the newest appliances that had come on the market. At present, vacuum cleaners intrigued her. She noted her growing predilection for the duties associated with being a house-wife. The role suited her. She felt greater satisfaction cleaning the silver than slaving over a lopsided poem.

She forced herself to stay seated. Miriam needed to concentrate. Her mission was to write a poem about the World's Fair and submit it by the end of the week. She had given this goal to herself and decided to shed her title of poet if she couldn't do it. She wasn't as interested in the prize money as in the affirmation of her skills.

As she placed pen to paper, the phone rang.

"Darling," said a breathless Jason. "I have just finished a meeting with the producers and was wondering if you were free for lunch? Want to meet me at Rueben's and we'll share a giant pastrami sandwich?"

"Would I? You're on. Give me fifteen minutes."

A reprieve. She could finish the poem this evening. She capped the pen, put the top back on the inkpot and dashed for her coat and hat.

Sarah's Therapy Session

"Doctor, I just don't know what to do with myself. I'm all over the place," Sarah whined like a poorly plucked note. "Nothing is bad, actually everything is great, but life seems inescapably random. Can there be any planning involved? Or are we all just silver spheres in a pinball machine?"

Sarah had taken up therapy because it seemed the thing to do. Every movie, magazine, and cocktail discussion had a shrink in it. Her psychiatrist was a carbon copy of Sigmund Freud who, sadly, had just died. But her little man stroked his goatee, wore thick horn-rimmed glasses and spoke in a faint Austrian accent, although he was from Brooklyn.

WAR CORRESPONDENT
Nancy Ames - Milano

No pomp or circumstance was left behind in the celebration of Herr Hitler's 50th birthday. All of Germany was invited to the party. Even Archbishop Orsenigo exalted Hitler by declaring the Fuhrer a good Catholic.

This week Prime Minster Neville Chamberlain stood tall and alerted Hitler that if he invaded Poland, Britain would go to war. Britain has distributed gas masks to all British citizens including children. The U.K. recognizes war as inevitable.

And where is the U.S. in all of this? Roosevelt is constantly warning the American public that Hitler's desire to dominate the world does not end in Europe. In a desperate attempt to do something Roosevelt has written to Hitler and Mussolini urging them not to start a war.

Meanwhile Mussolini celebrates 20 years of fascism by invading Albania. And it gave this reporter a chill when France ended its democracy and gave Premier Daladier dictatorial powers. More worrisome still is Mussolini's attendance at Daladier's coronation.

Still, no one in the States seems to be taking notice. Why isn't anyone paying attention while thousands die? The world is a dangerous place and the wolf is at the door – will no one pick up arms and protect themselves? The only bright spot on the horizon is that Stalin has signed a pact between the USSR, Britain and France keeping the big bear on our side – for now.

April

"Tell me more about how you feel. This lack of planning, does it make you anxious?"

"That's it. I mean, here in New York everyone is out of work, right? And here I am, with more gigs than I can shake a stick at, being paid exceedingly well."

"And the problem is?"

"It isn't part of a plan."

"What plan?"

"That's just it Doctor, I don't have one."

"You're not too old to marry. Isn't that what you really want? To marry and raise children? After all, isn't that what makes a success of every woman?"

"I suppose, but I'm not any closer to being a success there either although I did meet a very nice man at an art exhibit a few months ago."

"Tell me about him."

"There isn't much to tell. He's handsome, a nifty dresser and an architect without a job. I don't mind, but I suspect it's important to him."

"Why don't you ask him to accompany you somewhere? Tell him you have free tickets to protect his pride."

With that, she sat up and spun around to face the doctor, who she found doodling on his pad.

"What are you doing?" he asked flustered. "Please try and relax."

"Doctor, that's a brilliant idea. I can do that. This is why I like coming to you. All of my friends say that their therapists never give them any good suggestions. Never really say anything. Only ask questions and grunt. You're a real advocate. Thank you Doctor."

"Now, now, lay back down." Pleased that he might be helping her, he still felt guilty because he was not following the norm as dictated by his colleagues. Like Sarah's harp playing, psychotherapy was a lucrative profession during these hard times. The doctor wanted to avoid any practice that was non-standard and that might jeopardize his continued success.

"Tell me about your dreams."

Karl's Rescue

At three in the morning there was a knock on Kim's door.

"Miss McIntyre, Miss McIntyre, there be a phone call for ya." Kim roused herself from a dreadful dream of being chased, to wonder what terrible thing would cause someone to call her in the middle of the night.

"I'll be right there." She would be chewed out over this. Her Irish landlady didn't like being woken from her much needed beauty rest. Even though Kim paid extra to ensure she could receive phone calls at night, the service was offered grudgingly.

Who in the world could it be? She pulled a scarf over her dark curls, slipped on her mules and wrap then hurried down the three flights to the phone.

The earpiece lay dangling against the wall. Kim had to stand on tiptoe to speak into the mouthpiece. "Hello, who is it?"

"Kim, dear, it's Karl."

"Karl? Are you all right?"

"Kim, I'm at the Sixth Precinct. Could you please come and bail me out?" There was a long pause. "I'm really sorry to ask, but my life is in danger. Otherwise I wouldn't have called so late. Please, Kim."

With frustrated resignation she said, "Oh, all right." She started to hang up. "Wait a minute. How much do I need to bring?'"

"Twenty-five dollars." Kim remained silent. "Kim, don't worry. I'll get it right back to you."

Her shoulders slumped. "Okay Karl, I'm on my way. Stay alive until I get there."

She hung up the phone and shook her head. The hall was quiet, yet Kim knew Mrs. Murphy was listening.

"Good night, Mrs. Murphy. Sorry for the disturbance," she called out. As Kim began walking up the stairs, Mrs. Murphy burst from her apartment and began hissing at her.

"Ye ain't tellin' me you be goin' out in the middle of the night? What type of lass are you?" She didn't wait for a reply. "I run a respectable boardin' house here – I can't be havin' people runnin' in

71

and out at all hours. You'd better shape up missy, or nothin' but trouble is comin' your way."

Her voice softened for a moment. "It be chilly out there. Remember to bundle up. I'll be callin' you a cab."

"Thank you Mrs. Murphy." Kim was grateful. She was also tired. Tired of always picking the wrong men. She just couldn't seem to get it right. Her artwork was never appreciated, the men she picked were losers – there seemed to be no getting ahead. She didn't know where she belonged in this world. Perhaps she'd just marry the butcher down the street and get it over with. Have lots of kids and stop worrying about being someone or something.

She went upstairs and dressed, putting on her only pair of pants and two sweaters, which just barely fit under her thin coat. Kim reached under her mattress and pulled out the envelope where she kept her money.

She had saved almost fifty dollars by scrimping and going without. She had accumulated a nest egg for herself, insurance against a rainy day. Kim was dreadfully afraid of being poor and on the street. She saw the apple sellers and the girls down near the police station, where Karl now sat in jail. She wouldn't want to live if it came to that.

What had happened? Why was he in jail? Did she care enough about him to be making all this effort? They had only been dating for a few months and she already saw the bulls-eye painted on his back. Karl's destiny was full of pain. She decided, in that moment, that she didn't want to be around to experience it. No, after tonight, she'd break up with Karl no matter how sweet a man he was. She wanted something more than the limited future he could offer.

• • •   • • •   • • •

At the station, the sergeant behind the high counter simply asked who she had come for. After reviewing his register, he demanded the twenty-five dollars. She handed the cash up to him and he gave her a receipt. A little later Karl emerged in handcuffs, escorted by a large Irish policeman.

"Here he is, Miss. What you want with the little Red bastard I couldn't guess. It takes all types."

"Thank you, officer, I'm only a friend."

"With friends like that..." He turned without finishing the phrase and removed the handcuffs.

Karl stepped forward cautiously, afraid she would begin yelling at him. He had been beaten; his lip was bloody and both eyes blackened.

"Thank you, Kim, you're a lifesaver. I mean it. You're peerless among women." She just stood looking at him. "I didn't know who else to call," he added.

Kim wasn't sure she wanted to hear this story, yet she was curious what her twenty-five dollars had bought her. Besides, this was as good a time as any to breakup.

"Let's go around the corner and get some coffee," she said.

Karl winced, knowing the suggestion to be ominous. The desk captain chortled. He had seen it all before and knew what came next.

The dingy diner smelled of rancid grease. The other patrons were creatures of the night: prostitutes, pimps, gamblers and drunks. Karl and Kim sat at a booth. The table was sticky.

"Coffee and donuts?" asked the waitress. Kim nodded.

"So Karl, what's this about? Why do you think someone wants to kill you?"

"Kim, it's true, I swear."

"Yeah, but on what do you swear? You're a communist Karl, you don't believe in God and you can't swear on your mother's grave, she's still alive."

"I swear on my love for you, Kim."

At that she guffawed, "You'll have to do better than that." Karl sputtered and Kim held up her hand, "Skip it for now and tell me why they arrested you."

"I was organizing this group of couriers – you know, the guys who go from the courthouse to lawyers' offices, etc."

"Yeah, I know who they are." The waitress set a plate of donuts and two cups of steaming coffee in front of them. Karl began pouring sugar into his cup like it was a full meal.

"Hey Karl, ease up on the sugar."

"Huh? Oh yeah." He looked up at her.

Kim could see his sincere fondness for her in his expression.

"So anyway, this one courier alerted me that 'my kind' were in real danger."

"What kind?" asked Kim.

"Those of us who organize the workers. He said that Roosevelt was giving new powers to the Committee on Un-American Activities."

"Oh that. Everyone thinks Martin Dies is an idiot. Why would that change?"

"Because Roosevelt needs political backing in order to carry out the next phase of the New Deal. You've seen the papers. The press is taking potshots at his programs by saying that the relief funds are slowing down the kick-start to the economy. Corporations are leaning on him. He's giving more latitude to the Committee so big business can break up the unions."

"Oh please, haven't we been here before? There's been ten years of this finger-pointing nonsense."

"But there hasn't been a war looming before, a war that will propel us out of the depression. And it comes complete with a race of people to blame." He dropped his voice and looked about furtively. "This courier told me that Roosevelt has given his blessing to go after the communists and the Jews."

"What? That's ridiculous. Communism and the Popular Front represent millions of votes. Is he planning to arrest everyone? And why the Jews? Aren't they having a hard enough time in Europe? Karl, you're crazy."

"Maybe so, but you just bailed me out of jail."

"Touché. By the way, what was the charge?"

"Conspiring against the government of the United States."

"What!?"

"That's right. The long hand of the Committee reached out and decided I was worth toying with. I doubt they think I'm a kingpin or anything, but the police, who are working for the committee, figure I know the right people and they want me to pass along names. They told me if I couldn't find a way out tonight they'd kill me, to spread the word and scare the next patsy they scoop up."

He examined her face to determine if she believed him. He could see that misgivings still lingered there. "Kim, they meant it. They're out to bust us this time and no one, not even Roosevelt, can save us. A dark time is coming. Darker than hunger, a darkness of the soul."

"Karl, you're so melodramatic." She had made up her mind.

"Listen Karl, it's over between us. I don't think you and I have the same values or goals and it's time to break it off."

"But Kim, I love you."

"Oh please. You love Stalin. It's time for you to find out what you're searching for, because I think the police are right. This life is going to kill you. I'm sorry Karl, I've had enough, you're a nice guy, but we're through."

She stood up, dug around in her purse, pulled out two bits for the coffee and donuts and set it on the table. "I hope you find your heart's desire."

"Kim, let me take you home."

"Don't bother, I'll grab a cab."

"Kim, please stay a moment. I know you share my ideals. I'm working for the freedom of every man, woman and child."

"That's nonsense Karl. Most people aren't worried about freedom. They're happy just to have a job. Wake up and smell the coffee." She put on her coat and bent down to kiss his cheek.

"Good luck, Karl. Take care of yourself and don't forget to repay me the twenty-five dollars."

With that she left. Karl remained staring into his coffee. He knew it was useless to go after her. He had suspected for a while that they were not right for each other. Yet it made him sad. He asked out loud, "What does it mean to be an American?"

No one responded.

MAY

World's Fair – Ernestine

Ernestine splurged and bought an overpriced first day ticket from the concierge at her hotel. She paid seventeen dollars for a two dollar ticket and felt it well worth it.

She took a cab to the fairgrounds, wearing a fiery red dress that clung to her sculpted body. Her outfit stood out in dramatic contrast to the popular, loose-fitting pastel rayon dresses the other women wore. She arrived an hour after the official opening to avoid the crowds waiting at the turnstiles. She felt only slightly conspicuous being there unaccompanied. As far as she could tell, she might be the only woman at the World's Fair solo, which didn't bother her one iota.

For a moment Ernestine stood agape, awed by the sheer magnitude of the Fair, everything was scaled larger than life, all shiny and modern. Even hard-boiled Ernestine, the star of the stage, was taken in by the grandeur of this make-believe city. The newness appealed to her. She had always disliked anything old, anything with curlicues, dark woods, or fragility. She liked the cool slick lines of art

Out of the Dark

World's Fair Special Edition
by Alan Stipple

Today the New York World's Fair opened with the theme, *The World of Tomorrow*. Over 175 countries are represented; Westinghouse, GE, Ford and other major companies have pavilions showing off their newest technologies.

RCA presented for the first time *RadioVision* with several hours of broadcasting. The Fair sports gardens, three pools, an ice skating rink and five dance floors, one so large, it can hold 1,000 people. During the day the park will be full of ice cream and children. After the sun goes down, the dance floors will steam.

Mayor LaGuardia himself has ensured that the World's Fair will be the greatest show on earth. Two trains, three buses, four subways and a direct line from Penn Station deliver the attendees to its gates in Queens. Millions will enjoy this fair.

The image of the Trylon and Perisphere has been seared into our brains for more than two years. To finally see them in person and will not disappoint.

deco and the 'get to it' attitude of today's modern furniture.

She waited in line at the GE pavilion to ride what seemed like an amusement park car. The ticket taker started to put a small child with an ice cream cone and a bottle of Pepsi in the seat beside her. Her glare convinced the Fair employee to reassign the little boy to a different car.

As the ride progressed. Mannequins spoke to Ernestine as her chariot wheeled by, each telling her what to expect from the future. They showcased long thin bulbs called fluorescent lights, dishwashers and other inventions.

But of the many things Ernestine saw that day at the Fair, what impressed her the most were the dance palaces. She wondered if the Fair management hired popular stars to draw audiences.

She waited out the May Day park activities until dusk. Then she saw a big band assembling. Tommy Dorsey was the evening's headliner, along with the all black cast of the Hot Mikado, featuring Bill Robinson, one of the world's finest hoofers. He would certainly bring in the crowds. Ernestine had heard rumor that the dance team Yolanda and Veloz were in attendance. She hoped to catch a glimpse of their routine to figure out how to improve upon it.

Her eyes scoured the crowd to find a suitable partner.

World's Fair – Bill

Bill won his ticket at a poker game. Actually, he had lifted the ticket from a man he had beaten to a pulp. The fool had accused Bill of cheating at cards.

He liked the idea of going to opening day. Bill resented the fact that it was on a Commie holiday, because he assumed the Red bastards would be dancing around with flowers in their hair and between their teeth. Given the chance, he'd tell them where to put their flowers.

Entering the gates he experienced a burst of elation at the sight of the Trylon and Perisphere. They seemed like friends. He saw children wading in the pools. Bill thought it would be grand to have half a dozen little brats to do his bidding and call him Papa. But that was for later. Whenever he wanted to settle down, there were always a million sappy girls to marry. Right now, he didn't want any ties. He didn't really believe that marriage would limit his range, only that there lingered an assumption he would show up at home, occasionally.

Another thing that really grabbed Bill's attention was how many pretty girls there were wandering around. They were fresh, young, dolled-up things, which looked ready to be plucked. But he'd leave that for when the dancing started.

He spent the day visiting the exhibits. He bought himself a pennant that said the New York World's Fair, its top decorated with a dog's head. A beagle.

'I'm gonna get me one of them dogs when I settle down,' thought Bill. 'Nothing better, and they always obey you the first time.'

As night descended and the music began, Bill spied a striking woman in red across the dance floor. She was his type, a dancer, long and thin. What's more, she didn't walk, she prowled. He strode purposefully over to her and introduced himself. "Bill Curran at your service."

"Excuse me?" Ernestine couldn't help, but smile. She knew what Bill was after, now and later.

"Dance? Would you like to dance?"

"I would. I'm Ernestine Robertson."

"Bill Curran. A pleasure, Miss." He deftly removed his hat and kissed her hand at the same time. Then Bill and Ernestine began to dance.

Other dancers stepped back as they entertained the throng with steps like the Lindy Hop, the Black Bottom, the Yam and the SuzieQ. Many in the audience believed Ernestine and Bill were paid entertainers. Even Fair employees thought management had forgotten to inform them about the new performers.

Ernestine and Bill floated in each other's arms. The appreciative crowd cheered them on. Both dancers recognized that their future was intertwined.

Out of the Dark
by Alan Stipple

The Pulitzers were awarded this week. Marjorie Kinnan Rawlings won for her novel, *The Yearling* and Professor Carl Van Doren received the award for his biography, *Benjamin Franklin*. Also, Robert Sherwood takes home the prize for his play *Abe Lincoln in Illinois*.

THEATER:
My Heart's in the Highlands - by William Saroyan left this critic a little confused. Now, I know I'm supposed to like what I don't understand and don't get me wrong, I'll recommend the play. It's just that it was a little over my head. It seemed more like Nietzsche. I found myself wanting to yell up to the stage, "Could you repeat that last line." And then, have a minute or two of silence to digest it.

MOVIES:
★★★☆☆ Bachelor Mother - Ginger Rogers, a clerk in a department store, is mistaken for the mother of an illegitimate baby. Things get out of hand as the son of the storeowner (David Niven) is accused of being the father. This is Ginger's first starring role without Fred, and I, for one, wasn't looking for him. Nor did I feel any desire to have Miss Rodgers break out in dance. Bully for you Ginger.

★★★☆☆ Union Pacific - Thanks to Ulysses S. Grant and Barbara Stanwyck the trains run unobstructed across the expanse of this great country. Cecil B. DeMille produced and directed this film (some of it from a stretcher after surgery). Many of the scenes are shot at the actual locations and the golden spike is the real thing. We'll forgive DeMille for nepotism allowing his new son-in-law Anthony Quinn a small part. Come on Cecil, let's see a little more of Quinn. It looks like the boy can act.

May

The MOMA

Sarah threw open her window, letting her red hair be blown about by the fresh air accompanied by the sound of traffic on Park Avenue. The morning was cool and full of promise. 'Spring in the city. There just isn't anything better.' Looking out the window she admired the cascades of tulips planted along the meridian, each block pulsating with colors – red, yellow, purple, magenta, such a refreshing sight after months of uninterrupted gray.

She began her morning exercises with deep knee bends. 'Hey what am I doing. It's spring. Time to take a turn in the park and check out the cherry blossoms.'

Sarah felt great. She had played her harp last night at a private function of swells uptown. However, Sarah had been scaling back her gigs, hoping that she would be able to figure out her plan. Her shrink had said, "Only do what you must, until you determine what you really want to do. Then you should dedicate yourself to it – body and soul."

She chose to believe that this meant a little less personal savings and a lot more living. On a morning like this, she felt like anything was possible. Then she remembered that the Museum of Modern Art was opening today. Maybe she'd run by Saks and see if she could find a new frock for the occasion. She had a VIP ticket (which they'd given to her, knowing they'd want her to play eventually) and maybe she'd meet herself a Mr. VIP.

She had hoped Bud Rawley might be that special someone, but he hadn't called in months. She hadn't seen him since the Plaza. She liked him. Buddy made her feel warm and jazzed at the same time like a good cup of coffee. If life were a matter of chance meetings, who knew? Maybe he'd be at the opening.

Jason at the MOMA

"Miriam, why don't you come with me?"
"What?"
"Come to the MOMA opening."

WAR CORRESPONDENT
Nancy Ames - Madrid

Whenever anyone thinks of Nazis, good, bad or indifferent, they have one man to thank - Herr Joseph Goebbels, the German Minster of propaganda. He is despised by most of the leaders in his own party, but adored by Hitler. Goebbels has a club leg, so based on Nazi laws he should have been euthanised. But his deformity has been overlooked because he's able to spin such powerful messages. An entire country stands and cheers at his will. The phrase 'Heil Hitler' is his trademark creation.

N.Y. and Hollywood press agents should take their cue from Goebbels, who always makes sure that his client is seen only in the best light.

Even with 99% of the vote, he fought on for the last 1% for Hitler. Ah, but it's the artists who should worry, since he has censored all film, fine art and music that is not first approved by his office.

Goebbels is credited with the idea of identifying Jews as an inferior race and then pitting all the pent up anger of the German people toward them. Let us hope God's chosen will be able to withstand Goebbel's premeditated wrath.

The first concentration camp exclusively for women has been opened outside of Berlin. It's to be a model for future camps being built throughout occupied Europe.

"What dear? I'm in the shower."

"You should come with me." He knew she didn't hear. He didn't shout because this was an old argument. When Miriam had reached her eligibility limit for the Federal Writers Project, she started to teach poetry to school children. She seemed to enjoy it. Jason remembered with a wince his discomfort of learning poetry as a young boy. The fact that students liked Miriam was a miracle and a testament to her skill with kids. Nevertheless she started to find more and more reasons not to join him at social functions. He wondered if it was because she had stopped writing.

Jason attended so many events stag these days that he wouldn't be surprised if there were whispers of their separation. Of course, they'd be wrong. He and Miriam were more in love today than the day they were married. It had been eight years this month since they wed and to him she remained the most beautiful woman in the world. More than that she was steadfast and loyal and always there for him one hundred percent. He smiled at the thought of Miriam and decided that he would pick up a gift for her on the way back from the museum.

"Darling, I'm going now." He stepped into the bathroom to say goodbye, the steam fogged his glasses.

She poked her head out from behind the shower curtain, her hair protected by a plastic bathing cap. "Are you leaving, dear?" Her moist lips touched his and it was enough.

"Yes, my love. Are sure you won't reconsider and join me?"

"No, I don't want to disappoint the children," she said, speaking now from behind the curtain. "But you have a wonderful time. Bring me back detailed descriptions."

"I will, dear, and you have a good class."

Jason stepped into the hall and removed his glasses to polish off the beads of water with the back of his tie. Then he buttoned up his vest, placed his homburg on his head and went off to explore New York's newest museum.

When he arrived at the MOMA, a line had formed that stretched out to Sixth Avenue, snaked around the corner past the Wellington

Hotel and went on up toward Central Park. He didn't know for sure if he was meant to stand in the line or not. If so, he would leave and just go for a walk. He went to the front of the building on Fifty-Third Street. The brushed silver entrance gleamed. A liveried doorman stood beside the revolving door and inspected the invitations. Jason noticed that there were two entrances and certain individuals were shown into one with a minimal line. Jason handed the man his invite and was grateful to be shown to the VIP door.

He did, however, feel for all those poor souls whose lives had been reduced to waiting in lines.

Entering the MOMA he immediately sensed something fresh – a new way to think about architecture and public places. The concept of a museum dedicated to modern art was unique. "The New Artists" had been around for less than fifty years. Very few people, beyond those who traveled in Jason's circles, knew about these progressive creators. Jason was surprised that so many waited outside, perhaps without even knowing what was in store for them.

His keenest interest was in the photography exhibit. Previously there had only been a few places, mostly in Greenwich Village, where one could go to view photographs. The MOMA was the first museum to fully recognize photography as an art form. Jason had heard there would be a number of Steichens and Man Rays. He liked both men's work, despite the dramatic differences in their subject matter and exposure.

"Jason?" A woman's soft voice came from behind him. "Jason Rothman?"

He turned to meet a woman of society, a resplendent work of art in her own right. The fashionable dress she wore consisted of many layers of purple and lavender silk. On any other woman the frock might look like a massive bruise, but on Mrs. John D. Rockefeller, Jr. it evoked the impression of a delicate flower.

"Mrs. Rockefeller, how are you? What a pleasure to see you." She held out her hand to him and he shook it, later realizing she had anticipated that he would kiss it. Mrs. Rockefeller spent a great deal of time on the continent. "Have you had a chance to examine the exhibits yet?" he asked.

"Why no, shall we see the first one together? I'm to meet Peggy Guggenheim somewhere upstairs. She has a new discovery she wants to introduce me to."

Jason was always impressed by the social graces of someone like Mrs. Rockefeller. She knew how to make conversation with anyone.

"Please." He held out his arm. "Shall we first try this newfangled metal escalator?"

"Let's brave it," she said with a smile.

They enjoyed the view into a perfect garden to their right, as they waited in a short line.

"Brilliant, don't you think?" she said, turning to Jason.

"I do, yet isn't this architecture just catching up to the atriums of the great art centers in Europe? Haven't the grand museums always had a separate area to ponder the beauty within?"

Mrs. Rockefeller gave a soft high laugh without guile, a laugh of friendship. Jason took mental notes.

"You're right. It's always been one of my complaints about the Metropolitan. It does have the enclosed atrium in the hall of statues, however, it's not the same as being able to step outside on a warm spring day, full of the emotions evoked by the great masters, now is it?"

"Quite right, Mrs. Rockefeller."

They stepped onto the escalator single file. She grimaced slightly.

"You know, I just don't like these things and they are everywhere these days. I'm always afraid I'm going to step on to it at just the wrong moment, fall and get my skirt caught in the gears." She gripped the handrail.

He knew she was serious, dropping her guard for a moment. He was glad to be in front of her so he could help make her transition off the mechanical device easier. "I feel the same way, Mrs. Rockefeller." At the top he stepped aside and offered her his arm, which she grabbed like a shipwrecked woman. He noted that if they were still together by the third floor, they should take the elevator down.

The landing they were on was a bit of a disappointment. They faced a long white wall on the left. Presumably there were treasures hidden behind it. In front of them a sign pointed toward the American Artists. "Oh good, I am sure Peggy will be in there," said Mrs. Rockefeller.

Jason would have preferred to head for the Impressionist works the museum boasted of purchasing. However, he wouldn't leave Mrs. Rockefeller's side until safely placing her in someone else's care.

The entrance to the room continued to open up, with each passageway being slightly wider than the one before, until they came to the main room with a surprisingly low ceiling. It was generally the habit of grand museums to give art abundant vertical clearance. Here a very tall person might be able to place his hand upon the ceiling, or so it seemed. Jason thought the room felt cramped and stuffy.

Mrs. Rockefeller turned to Jason, evidently thinking the same thing, "You must give them credit for being novel."

"Indeed."

A massive painting, almost forty feet long, dominated the far wall. It was a dark canvas with splotches of color. There were hints of recognizable images, a wheel, a bird, it left everything open to interpretation.

"Ah, there's Peggy with her new discovery. Let's go over."

"Peg dear, how are you?" Mrs. Rockefeller and Miss Guggenheim kissed continental style and Jason stood waiting to be introduced.

"Miss Guggenheim, you know Jason Rothman, don't you? He's the playwright with one hit on Broadway at present and another scheduled to come out this fall. We all have high hopes for him."

The balding man standing next to Peggy Guggenheim said, "I thought the Joe's name was Audets."

Peggy laughed and touched his arm with her gloved hand. "Why no, you silly man, that is Odets and he does seem to have the corner on the genius market right now. Mr. Rothman here is going to give Mr. Odets a run for his money. How do you do, Mr. Rothman? It's a pleasure to meet you."

"The pleasure is mine, Miss Guggenheim." Jason knew that if he kept his mouth shut, these two ladies of society would take care of everything, unfortunately he couldn't resist.

He pointed to the work on the wall. "Is this your new discovery Miss Guggenheim?" He regretted it the moment he spoke, because he realized what the next question would be.

"Yes," said Miss Guggenheim, "it's my good fortune to introduce Mr. Jackson Pollock's work. Do you like it?"

Now he was in trouble. The artist standing beside Peggy twitched nervously. The epitome of the man the phrase 'ants in your pants' described.

"To be honest with you, I still don't understand modern art. I'd be very appreciative if you could explain this piece to me."

The man almost leapt at Jason and it was only Peg's hand that held him back firmly. The twitchy man spoke in an uncomfortably loud voice.

"What's there to explain? Do you like it or not? That's all there is to it. There's no magic. I paint, that's all. This other shit is for the intellectuals, for you snobs to be able to justify your purchases. You either like it or not." Spent, he shoved his fists into his pockets, hung his head, and stepped away from the small party.

"Forgive Mr. Pollock, he's rather keyed up today. He's a great artist. Do you know his wife? Lee Krasner? Also a very accomplished artist, I believe she has a piece or two exhibited here as well. Let me explain this work of Mr. Pollock's to you." Miss Guggenheim went on to breathe life into the dark canvas. Jason would never again look at random splotches of paint in the same way.

Meanwhile Pollock had begun to case the room like a wild animal stalking prey. Jason was certain he would find it.

Alex and Sarah at the MOMA

Alex entered through the VIP door with Mrs. Van Horne. He was having a bad day. Most of the time Alex could ignore what he had become. After all, he had a plan. His vision was to build skyscrapers. Somehow he allowed this dream to justify his humiliation. Hell, at this point he'd be happy just designing a boathouse. Servicing these society women had become excruciating.

Perhaps if he had a pimp, he'd have an excuse, someone who

spent all of his money. A cad who left him with these dreadful people who cared not a whit for his aspirations. Instead, he had only himself to blame and a job to do. A job that, thanks to one of his aunts, he did with great artistry.

"Alex, I would like you to meet Colonel Brighton." Before him stood a man in his sixties, robust and smiling, who made it clear he would enjoy taking Alex's place with Mrs. Van Horne. Mrs. Van Horne was obviously interested. The idea of engaging in sex with an equal would be a novelty for her. Unfortunately, it could only be for one night. That was all their social strata would permit. And what a glorious night it might be. Alex was the only witness as these two society leaders mentally weighed the pros and cons of such a tryst.

"Alex is an architect, Colonel," Mrs. Van Horne said, as if holding out a brooch for his inspection.

"What buildings have you worked on, son?"

"None sir." This was not the first time he had been introduced as a working architect. Alex had his response down pat. He knew he need only utter one sentence. No one ever asked to hear more from him.

"I have drawings in at several firms right now." Most people would nod and drop it at that, then continue their conversation with his society maven.

"Why are you hanging around here, son? Why don't you go to Europe? After the Great War, entire cities needed to be rebuilt. This war, it appears, will be a humdinger. They are already dropping bombs of a magnitude we could not even have imagined. A lot of buildings will need to be replaced." The Colonel winked at him, nodding towards Mrs. Van Horne and held out his arm to her. He maneuvered her onto the escalator and Alex watched them ride up to the next floor.

Behind him a voice called out, "Alex, isn't it? I'm Sarah Karofsky. We met this past winter at Kim McIntyre's art exhibit. How nice to see you again." Sarah smiled an open and honest smile her bright red hair shown like a halo.

Seeing Sarah made Alex realize more acutely that in a few short months he had become someone else. It was difficult to look into her freckled innocent face.

"Sarah, you're as enchanting as ever." It was his working-self talking. He wondered if he had lost the capacity to be real anymore.

"Why, thank you." She glanced around. "Are you here alone?"

"Hard to say. I might be."

She contemplated his answer like the RCA dog, Nipper, her head tipped to one side.

He laughed. "I'm sorry, I don't mean to be so cryptic. I came here with someone, however she has met an old friend and gone off with him. I'm not certain whether or not she'll expect me to take her home later."

"Would you care to join me in touring the museum?" She smiled and held out her arm, not in the practiced way of the women he spent time with, but in the mimicking way she had seen hundreds of times before in her own profession as harpist. As he considered that, he realized she might not be as innocent as he assumed. After all, how many times had he gone to tearooms like the Palm Court to be shown off by his latest mistress?

They rode up the escalator and turned left since the crowd seemed to be streaming ahead towards the American Artists exhibit. Behind a plain white door at the end of the corridor the world opened up. There a photographic exhibit took their breath away. Neither had ever seen such a large display of photographs in life-size formats.

"Do you know these artists by sight?" asked Sarah without guile.

"No, not really. I probably could pick out a Brady because there are Civil War soldiers lying around in the foreground. But beyond that..."

"Then, perhaps you're in for a treat. I do know these prints. I believe I'll be able to share a variety of tidbits with you." She paused. "If you'd like."

"Very much. It'll be quite something having my very own docent tour."

"Here we have the king, Mr. Edward Steichen." They were standing in front of the photographer's famous portrait of John Pierpont Morgan. Morgan's eyes were fierce and penetrating. Sarah continued.

"Steichen's vision of the Flatiron building brought him fame. But what he's best known for is his protégé, Edward Stieglitz. Stieglitz started the landmark magazine Aperture, where he single-handedly turned photography into an accepted art form. The photos here," she gestured to a dozen prints on the wall, "are already his best known, but it's this collection of Georgia O'Keeffe nudes that put all of us women to shame." They both laughed, "Did you know he and Georgia are an item?" she added.

"Actually, I did know. They've lived together for years over at the Holleran House on Lexington and Forty-Ninth. Right?"

She grinned. "Yes. Stieglitz *discovered* Georgia when she was nineteen." She suppressed a giggle. "Actually, Stieglitz pays the bills with the photos he takes for Vanity Fair, Cosmopolitan and a variety of advertising agencies in town. I like his work, but I'm not crazy about the man."

Alex didn't know whether Stieglitz or Steichen were great photographers or not, yet he was certain he preferred drawings of buildings to photographs. He had seen the original design for the Flatiron Building and no photographic rendition could compare.

"Here we have Man Ray," continued Sarah, "a Frenchman who also has a penchant for younger women."

'No wonder all the middle-aged women flock to me,' thought Alex. 'Men their own age want pubescent girls.'

"Man Ray is considered avant-garde. That's the new term given to the modern photographers." She paused. "Actually some of the painters like Pollock, Duchamp and Cornell are also using the term."

She turned to him mid-step and he almost ran into her. "Did you go to the film *La Cartomancienne – The Fortune Teller*, a couple of years ago?"

"Why, I don't think so."

"Not surprising. It didn't last long in the theaters. It was very avant-garde. All imagery and metaphor." She quickly turned back to the photo at hand. Alex realized Sarah plucked at ideas and thoughts like the strings on her harp.

"This is my favorite Man Ray, The Woman with Pearls." Alex studied the photograph. A delicate young woman held up a string of pearls that hung below her navel. The black background and the woman's dress melted into each other so that only her white face, hand and pearls stood out, giving the photo the ethereal feeling of having captured an apparition.

"Over here we have a newcomer, Ansel Adams. If you see a mountain man wandering the halls complete with beard, hiking clothes and a broad-rimmed hat, that's Ansel. He works as a forest ranger or something out in California and takes these beautiful shots of the wilderness. TR and Muir would have adored him. He showed up in New York a few months ago, portfolio under his arm, hawking his wares to the galleries. Several have picked him up simply because the curators hadn't been west of the Mississippi. It's a novelty. Sort of like the craze for pictures of Indians."

Sarah lost interest in the subject and moved on, Alex lingered, he liked this work; it was fresh and clean. He wanted to stand in this great valley at the foot of the sheer rock face called 'Half Dome'. He promised himself that he would go there one day and then hastened to catch up with Sarah.

They roamed through the rest of the exhibits, admiring the Stickley furniture and feeling equally confused by the abstract art. They adored the Impressionists. Alex wanted to visit the places depicted in Monet's paintings of Notre Dame and the Champs Elysee. He easily imagined himself working in France and told Sarah.

"Then why don't you go?"

"Because the country is on the brink of war," he responded logically.

"All the more reason to be there when they need to rebuild. A war hero is bound to secure commissions. How many could you ever hope to get here?"

"How odd you should say that. Earlier someone else said the same thing to me. I had never thought of it. I suppose you're both right." Alex recognized that the universe might be showing him a way out of his predicament. "I'll give it serious consideration. In the meantime, are you free for dinner later this week, or perhaps lunch? I presume you work during the dinner hour."

Sarah was thrilled to find a man who understood her schedule. Most men just assumed she would skip work to be with them. Alex was different he thought ahead. The change that had come over him in these few short months was not lost on Sarah. His dignity had been damaged. Nevertheless, she knew instinctively that he was a decent man. The depression had done terrible things to many good people.

"That would be swell, Alex. How about lunch and a matinee? I have tickets to a new Hart and Kaufman play opening this week. Would you care to join me?"

"I'd love to. What's your number?"

"Circle 3-4777. Does Wednesday work for you?" asked Sarah.

"I'll make it work."

"Spectacular. I'll see you then." She held out her hand for a shake. He found himself turning it over to kiss it – pleased that this was a hand he wanted to kiss. Sarah blushed, producing the loveliest effect on her freckles.

"Until Wednesday then." They waved to each other as she left. Alex turned back to the escalators to determine if his services were still required.

Kim and the MOMA

Kim waited in line for three hours to get into the MOMA on opening day. To return on any other day when it wasn't quite so fashionable would have made more sense. However, the VIPs would be in attendance today and she wanted to mix with them.

Once inside, beyond the ticket takers, she dashed for the escalator to get into the main galleries. She passed clusters of people standing around talking. Kim could never grasp why so few people came to an art museum to actually look at the art. She headed for the largest gallery, the one with modern geniuses like Rothko, Guston, Kline, and deKooning. As she walked into the room she couldn't miss the sprawling Pollock. She was drawn to it like a lover, entranced by its depth, like a thick blanket on a cold day. She was snared by its complexity. She loved the work.

A man approached her from behind. "What do you think of it?"

"I love it," she said flatly, assuming him to be a masher.

"Is that the best you can do? What do you love about it?"

"First, the movement." Kim gazed at the painting. "The yin and yang of it. The playfulness. The ability to convey the colors of the rainbow with shades of black. The portrayal of all of life's possibilities." She turned to stare at her inquisitor.

He was of medium height, balding and a bit disheveled. "What do you see?" she asked.

He hesitated. "The rantings of a child."

"Nothing else?" She wondered why he bothered being in a room of abstract art. She knew it didn't run to everyone's taste.

"Nope, maybe some spilled beer." He pointed to the upper right hand corner of the painting and Kim noticed the discoloration. She spun around.

"Are you Pollock?"

"At your service, and how best can I service you?"

She could smell the liquor on his breath and knew he was drunk, yet she welcomed the chance for conversation. "So is it true what they say? Just random splattering and drizzling of paint? Nothing behind it?"

A cloud passed over his face. His voice went up a few decibels. "I didn't say that. This is my child. I give birth to each piece of art. This represents days of work." He calmed for a moment, pulling on the ends of his coat. "What's your name?"

"Kim McIntyre."

"Are you an artist?"

"Oil pastels." She looked up at his massive canvas. "On a much smaller scale."

"Don't be ridiculous. Naturally they're smaller, unless you live in a barn." His voice lowered. "Hey listen, what're you doing later?" He moved closer and put his arm around her in a lascivious way. "Maybe you and I could sneak out of here and I could show you my technique."

She gently slipped from his hold and turned to face him. "That would be an honor, but I must return to my easel. I work on

Wednesdays. Sorry, perhaps a rain check?"

"Yeah, yeah, it always rains in the summer and makes those flowers bloom." He had already dismissed her and moved off to find a fresh victim. Kim headed in the opposite direction to enjoy the other paintings in the gallery.

After a few moments she heard a voice behind her, this one a woman's.

"Excuse me, may I have a word with you?"

Kim wondered if it was another painter. She turned to find a refined woman, dressed with impeccable style. She wore a flowing sari made of the finest Indian silk and a single string of mid-length pearls about her neck. She held out her hand.

"I'm Shirley Price. I saw how you handled Mr. Pollock. I haven't seen footwork like that since I last attended the ballet." She smiled a warm and open smile.

Kim grinned. "Thank you. He's just a little drunk. He didn't mean anything by it."

"No, he didn't and you knew it. Are you this good with all temperamental artists?"

"It takes one to know one."

"I see, a painter?"

"Of sorts. Oil pastels."

"Ah, Picasso's creation. The combination of oil paints with crayons. Very nice." She paused, studying Kim. "I would like to discuss a proposition with you, if you don't mind."

Kim's heart leapt. This woman must be with the museum. Maybe she'd consider Kim for a show.

"Let's go downstairs to the café and talk."

"Gladly."

"Have you been out to the World's Fair yet?" Shirley asked, as they walked.

"No, I was planning on going in a few weeks, once the crowds thin out."

"I wouldn't wait too long. I believe the crowds are going to pick up. At least we hope so. We've only had half the expected attendance, which is another story. I assume you've heard that we invested thirty million dollars in a museum on the property to house the great works of art from Europe?"

She waited for Kim's reply, as they navigated the cafeteria line. After choosing their refreshments they walked over to an out of the way a table.

"I've seen the write-ups on the museum. I applied for a position back in March. I never heard from anyone."

"Consider yourself notified. I would like you to work at the museum as an assistant curator. Because of the war, many European artists are coming to the U.S. for refuge and they find themselves standing before their paintings like Pollock a moment ago. I would like your help in managing them."

Kim was excited and disappointed at the same time. Chagrined for not being acknowledged as an artist; excited because she was being offered a job that would allow her to use her expertise. It would be far more satisfying than sitting behind the glass of a vending booth, selling tickets at the Ziegfield Theater.

"I'd be thrilled."

"I realize you maybe frustrated that the position does not directly reflect your own talent. However, I can assure you, it will call upon all your skills, including your knowledge of art." Shirley raised her bottle of *Coca Cola*. "Shall we toast to it then?" They clinked the necks. "Then it's done. Take my card." Shirley wrote on the back Monday, May 22, 10am. She handed the card to Kim.

"I don't know what to say. Thank you."

"It's my pleasure. I'm looking forward to working with you. I promise the job will not be dull."

With that, Miss Shirley Price was off, clutching her Coco Chanel patent leather bag. Kim sat back as though drifting into in a dream. She began to wonder what would become of the artwork she was to curate in Queens, should America go to war.

JUNE

Sarah and Alex

When Alex awoke, a sliver of moon greeted him. A mere fingernail clipping. The moon was so fine and so clean, renewing itself month after month. The dark, smeared clouds that appeared below it reminded him of himself; smudged with the lies and deceit of his trade; each falsehood further staining his soul. Tomorrow there'd be no moon, yet it would still be there, simply lacking enough light to shine. He feared that this too would be his fate.

He called the freckled faced Sarah.

"Hello?"

She sounded groggy.

"Oh Sarah, I'm sorry to be calling so early. You must have worked late last night."

There was a soft murmur of acknowledgement into the phone.

"It's Alex. I want you to go back to sleep and dream of beautiful tropical fishes swimming in coral reefs. Meet me at the Battery Park Aquarium at noon today."

Out of the Dark
by Alan Stipple

Thank God and Mr. Roosevelt for the creation of the WPA, or I guess now, the Federal Works Agency, the consolidation of several organizations. This program has ensured that the history of our country will be captured for posterity. Zora Neale Hurston has given us a collection of southern negro stories in *Mules and Men,* while John and Ruby Lomax have ventured into the backwoods of the Appalachia and brought us folk music the world might never have otherwise known.

The World's Fair giveth and taketh away. It appears several producers have decided to close popular plays on Broadway, stating that the number of choices will be too great for visitors to our town. More likely the promoters fear the Fair will draw patrons away from the Great White Way.

MOVIES:
★★★☆☆ *The Private Lives of Elizabeth and Essex* - If you're a fan of Bette Davis or Errol Flynn you'll not be able to resist this lavish period piece. Both actors were given the budget, script and roles to make up for not being allowed off the lot to do *Gone with the Wind.* I certainly hope *GWTW* delivers considerably more. Both actors give fine performances, but the material is thin. And to imagine Errol choosing to stay with dried-up Elizabeth over the adorable handmaid is more than this critic can believe.

★★★★★ *Mr. Smith Goes to Washington* Another vehicle in which Frank Capra lets us know that all is not right in the world; that democracy is a privilege and should be cherished. Comedy, drama, and politics come together as Capra takes on political corruption and business bullies. Claude Rains as the 'Silver Knight' brings in an excellent performance as the compromised hero. Jimmy Stewart and Jean Arthur make this film one that shouldn't be overlooked.

A groggy, "Swell." drifted back to him.

"Sweet dreams." He hung up, pleased with himself.

Ernestine's Vision

Ernestine was driven. What drove her, she didn't know for sure. She had already become a famous ballerina. What more did she want? She left ballet and its accolades without a backward glance. Did she want more fame? Probably. She never lost sight of the fact that in order to get anywhere in this world, one needed to work hard and be lucky. She had already put in the work. Now she was feeling lucky to have found Bill Curran.

However, she wasn't entirely sure about Bill. Like her he was driven, but motivated by a dark force; something Ernestine didn't recognize and preferred to ignore. She intuitively knew never to ask Bill where he had been before meeting her for rehearsal. There was a barbarous, somewhat frightening quality to his manner.

In just a few short weeks she and Bill had perfected an original routine full of complicated, syncopated steps and mid-air turns. The fantasy was made complete with several beautiful flowing gowns. Ernestine began setting up auditions. She realized that they would have to start in the smaller venues and work their way up to the hot spots. The club owners would talk about them as they became popular. Success was always dependent on grassroots publicity.

This was the beginning of Ernestine's vision to create a new art form. She anticipated combining ballet, ballroom and African dance into something never seen before a combination of Dunham, deMille and Graham. Ernestine relentlessly practiced no less than four hours a day, testing, perfecting, trying new moves before her studio mirrors, like a pianist playing the same tune over and over until all of the notes flowed together.

In the afternoons she met with Bill and practiced for an additional four hours. He was as much of a perfectionist as she and so the routines gelled much faster than she had expected. He also added to the choreography. Bill spent time at the Hoofers Club in Harlem and contributed Negro dance moves, new to Ernestine. He had wanted to add tap, but she resisted, believing tap was too lowbrow. She knew the society crowd, having danced for them for years. The rich wanted their entertainment like their sex, smooth and quiet.

Bill was strong and tall, capable of managing the more strenuous dance moves with ease. She had longed for powerful arms like his when she was on stage in Swan Lake or the Nutcracker. While the smaller beautiful gay male dancers might be able to jump higher, they struggled with lifting a ballerina. Mishaps were common.

As Ernestine practiced alone she considered how Bill's motives were a mystery to her. She knew he had secrets. She stood at the ballet bar and held a grand plié.

As though he had been conjured by the devil, Bill stood in the doorway.

"Hey, I thought you were having some fancy new floor put in." Like most dancers, he was not modest and proceeded to strip out of his street clothes in front of her in order to get into his workout clothes. There had never been any romantic sparks between them, although they did have sex.

"I was," she replied, "but the architect was a fool. He brought me this ridiculously expensive bid, and I sent him packing. I had someone lay this oak floor for practically nothing."

Bill eyed it carefully going to one of the corners to inspect the seams. "It's a good job. I'm impressed."

"I was too. You know how slow all these union types are these days. I got a couple of colored fellows. They put the whole thing down in one day."

"Good for you. So what's on the schedule?" asked Bill, clapping his hands.

"I've identified the five most popular songs. Let's start with some improvisational dance to loosen up."

"Perfect. And where are we on your timeline?" He gave her a sly smile. "I assume you have a timeline?"

She laughed. "We are ahead of schedule. We should start setting up auditions in two weeks. Do you feel ready?"

Bill stood his full height and puffed out his chest. "Miss Robertson, you and I are going to make history. Yolanda and Veloz, watch out."

Ernestine put a record on and went to Bill's arms. She could swear she smelled blood, but chose to ignore it and concentrated instead on dancing.

The Aquarium

The Aquarium, built in 1896, sat at the end of Battery Park, built inside a fort from the early 1800s. The fort had been the location of the immigration station, prior to its move out to Ellis Island in 1892. The Aquarium had a huge fish tank at its center housed by a large, round turret that rose up and could be seen by passing ferries, tugboats and ships as they entered the harbor. It also made the architects McKim, Mead, and White famous. Everything built by the trio after the Aquarium was measured against its success. Alex spent hours studying it from all angles.

He liked going to Battery Park. It had been such a mess just after the Great War, full of derelicts and thieves. LaGuardia had taken it upon himself to clean it up, before successfully tackling the rest of the city. The mayor's goal was to make it safe enough that a six-year old girl could play there without her nanny. LaGuardia arranged for truckfulls of daffodil and tulip bulbs to be delivered there every year to ensure that Battery Park was the beauty spot of lower Manhattan.

The Aquarium stood in the center, hosting over 5,000 visitors a day and as many as 50,000 when the fleet was in town. While the lines were sometimes long, the facility could handle it.

Sitting on a bench in front of the entrance, Alex waited patiently for Sarah. A half-hour later he began to wonder if she had forgotten or had not been awake enough to register the call. Just as he stood to find a phone, she came running up in a blue and white polka dot summer dress, a delicate straw hat perched on her coppery red hair, complete with a stuffed songbird.

"I'm dreadfully sorry," she panted. "I woke late and grabbed a cab, thinking it would be faster than the subway, but the traffic was frightful getting downtown. I can't wait until they finish the Eastside Highway."

"It's fine," said Alex, "you're not so late. The fish are still here." He smiled.

"Alex, I don't usually sleep in so late, even after a performance, except last night..."

"Do tell." He motioned for them to sit on the bench.

"Did you know that King George and Queen Elizabeth are in the country?"

"The first English monarchs to visit America. It's all over the news – I couldn't miss it if I tried. Did you meet them?"

She bobbed her head up and down like a small child. "Not only did I meet them, I played for them. They're staying at the Waldorf, after traveling from Washington, where they suffered through dozens of formal engagements. The queen had a headache and called down to the front desk asking for a harp player. Can you imagine? It seems there's a philosophy on the continent that the sound of the harp has healing properties for all sorts of ailments, including headaches."

"What were they like? The king and queen?"

"Very nice, truly, very nice people. Different, because they've been famous since the day they were born. To me they were pleasant, polite and very respectful. I played in their parlor. They're in the grand presidential suite, which I believe has twelve rooms to accommodate all the servants. The king and queen sat in armchairs, dressed casually. They didn't acknowledge me as I played. The queen kept her eyes closed and the king was reading documents.

I played for about half an hour. At the end they offered a polite applause and the queen told me she felt much better. As I left the butler handed me a fifty-dollar bill and thanked me. "Can you imagine, fifty dollars? I'll treat today."

"It's not necessary. I have money," he said defensively. This was a subject they did not discuss. Alex always had money even though he didn't have a job. "Only fifty dollars? No diamond tiara?" He poked her in the ribs to lighten the mood and to show he was teasing. "Come on, let's go visit the fishies."

"No jewels, however, she did write me a sweet note this morning thanking me for playing and telling me that it was the most pleasant time they had spent in New York."

"Goodness, you're practically royalty. Perhaps they'll adopt you. Princess Sarah. It has a nice ring." He laughed good-naturedly as they entered the aquarium. It was cool and dark inside. Sarah felt the thrill of having her career, her love life and even the weather a resounding success.

About an hour later, Sarah had to leave, to pick up her laundry before her concert at Carnegie Hall. This concert had been on the schedule for months. She was playing with a virtuoso new pianist, Arthur Schnabel. He was so full of himself that Sarah could barely stand to be around him.

"I'm disappointed that I have to leave, but I've got to do these errands," said Sarah. "You should stay and enjoy the aquarium."

"No, no, I'll take you home."

"I insist. We practically just got here. You haven't even seen the sea lions. Please stay." She leaned over and kissed him on the mouth, in public. Alex reciprocated.

"Are you available tonight after the concert?" he asked.

"I don't think so, it's going to end late. How about tomorrow? I'll make you dinner at my apartment, if you're brave enough to try my cooking." She grinned.

"It's a date."

She took his hand and squeezed it. "Have a peachy afternoon."

He kissed her hard upon the mouth. Then he let her spin free and watched her as she swished away.

Alex liked this woman. She was smart, upbeat and pretty. Yet he felt dirty and dishonest by not telling her what he did for a living. He was certain if she knew she'd never see him again. The relationship was doomed. He decided he simply couldn't get emotionally involved with her or any woman. They had already slept together twice, he registered that the time had come to end it. He studied the mammoth tank above him and imagined the sixty-eight tons of water breaking free and suffocating him beneath a tidal wave.

"Excuse me?" He heard a gentle voice behind him and then felt a hand touch his shoulder. "Aren't you Alex?"

"Why yes, yes I am." Before him stood an attractive petite brunette, dressed in Greenwich Village bohemian clothing. A hand painted scarf pulled back her luxurious dark hair. Her cornflower blue eyes sparkled as she spoke. "We've met," she said. Alex couldn't believe he'd forget a beauty like this.

"If you say so."

"I'm Mailou's friend. We met at the Negro Art Exhibit back in February. I think I also saw you at the opening of the MOMA." She realized he didn't remember her.

She held out her hand. "I'm Kim McIntyre, an artist. Or I guess I should say 'curator' these days."

Alex paused recognizing the name. Then snapped his fingers and said, "Of course. I've seen your artwork. You have an eye for architecture," he recalled her exhibit, where he had met Sarah. He pushed Sarah from his thoughts to focus on the beauty in front of him. "What do you mean, curator? Where?"

"At the World's Fair. It's a fluky thing. One of those right time, right place, situations and the next thing I knew I was in charge of a thirty million dollar exhibit."

Alex stared at her, awed by the fact that she would blurt out details of her life to strangers. The women he 'went' with had many secrets and one paid dearly for each piece of information you wheedled out of them.

Kim misinterpreted his stare. "Oh, I'm sorry. I don't mean to brag. Like I said, it wasn't something I expected, it was handed to me. Have you been to the Fair yet?" she asked, trying to restart the conversation. A crowd of fourth graders began to stream through. Alex took Kim's elbow and moved her away. The children's voices were a cacophony of sound and their damp hands smudged the glass.

"No, not yet. I keep meaning to. I figure I have a couple more months."

"You should go sooner rather than later. The architecture is magnificent. They say it's not as good as the San Francisco Exposition, but I wouldn't know. I think it's very inventive."

"Then I'll gladly undertake the journey to Queens. What days do you work?"

"I didn't mean to see me. I meant for you to see the exhibits. I work six days a week. I get free passes and I'd be happy to leave one for you at the gate."

"What day don't you work?"

"Monday. Which is actually awful, because so little is open on a Monday. In town, that is."

"Today is Wednesday. How did you get away?"

"Oh, I start later this week. I'm really looking forward to it. I've been unemployed for some time now."

"I hear you," said Alex. "Hey, have you seen the sea lions and penguins here?"

"No, I haven't."

"Let's go. They're a riot."

"Terrific. I'm glad I ran into you."

"Same here," said Alex, who was off and running like a dog at the track.

At the Theater

Jason and Miriam went to see a new play. They had missed opening night, because Miriam had the flu and Jason wouldn't leave her side. She never forgot how lucky she was to have found Jason. He hadn't been a success when they met, yet she'd known he would be. Her mission in this life was to contribute to that success, acting as a touchstone for his creativity. She found keeping Jason buoyed sometimes proved a challenge. His extraordinary ability to empathize with others sometimes left him susceptible to extreme emotions. Her job was to provide him with a safe haven in which to live and work. She generally took pride in her role while harboring occasional self-doubt.

It rankled her that although she no longer thought of herself as a poet, Jason still saw her as nothing else. In his mind a 'housewife' was someone to make fun of on stage, a woman of limited intellectual capacity without ambition and full of petty concerns. But Miriam had already set aside her poetic aspirations to raise a family. She feared that one day Jason would look upon her as he did one of his two dimensional characters. Miriam worried that if that day came, his attention might drift, roused by one of the ambitious actresses who nightly tried to spirit him away with the ruse of discussing a play.

Instead of fretting, she turned her attention to that evening's play, *The American Way* by Kaufman and Hart, a musical and the perfect summer tourist venue. The play skyrocketed across the stage, each scene and dance adding to the last until the audience felt they were riding to the finish line on a galloping horse. Jason made notes in the little pocket folio that he always carried in order to capture moments of inspiration or dialogue for future plays.

Miriam knew that Jason didn't care for musicals, although he did enjoy the complexity of the staging required to accommodate the vast number of cast members and sets. At intermission they went to the lobby and ordered champagne.

"So what do you think?" asked Jason.

"Dear, you know I never comment on a play inside the theater. Too many ears about." She scrutinized the crowd to determine if any of the critics like Alan Stipple or Walter Winchell were within earshot. "I'll say that they're doing an amazing job with the sets. How many change-outs have there been, five?"

"Six, actually, and I agree, the back wall of the stage must be in New Jersey. Where are they storing all of this?"

"I do like Marlene Dietrich's performance and Mr. March seems to be enjoying his part. Have you seen Fredric since he's been in town?"

"Once. He was at the Saroyan play, *My Heart's in the Highlands*. We stepped out for a smoke at intermission." Jason remembered the night vividly. There had been a cool breeze, a relief after being cooped up in the stuffy Lyceum Theater. March had explained that it was imperative for Jason to move to Hollywood, and not just for the money. Broadway, he said, would dry up and blow away if a war should come. Hollywood, however, would flourish, promoting patriotism. The future was out West.

Jason suspected March was right and had decided to go to California the following month. He and Carole Lombard had been talking about his new play. Lombard had wired him, "I want to act on Broadway once before I die. But you must come here to convince me."

The only problem was he hadn't told Miriam yet. He was certain she'd be angry. He decided to take the plunge and tell her now.

"And you didn't go pub crawling with him after the show?" asked Miriam knowing March's penchant for drink.

"You know I would always rather come home to you." He hesitated a moment and then went on, "Fredric suggested that I need to go to Hollywood and make films. What do you think?"

His words hit her like a slap. Her voice cracked as she spoke. Her hand instinctively went to her cheek and then moved up to ensure that none of her light blonde curls had fallen out of place. "But why? We live in New York. You like it here. There's nowhere else with as much theater, except maybe London, and now with the war..." she trailed off. She didn't know for sure why this made her so anxious, the thought of leaving New York was like jumping into the middle of the ocean without a life preserver.

"We must prepare for when the war comes," replied Jason. "You remember Bernard Shaw's preface to *Arms and the Man*? How the theaters shut down during the Great War both here and abroad?"

"I do," she said. "But we've made a commitment to New York. It's our home. How could we leave?"

"It's just for a visit. Come with me and see for yourself. Everyone says it's beautiful. Sunshine all year round. You could swim at the beach every day."

She studied him with her hands on her hips. All traces of compassion had vanished from her soft face, her red lips were set and her violet eyes pierced him. "When are you going?"

"I was just saying we should think about it. I didn't say anything about a specific date."

"Jason Isadore Rothman, I know you. I know when you have set your mind to something. I wouldn't be surprised if you had the tickets in your pocket." She reached over and pulled back the lapel of his evening jacket. Luckily, it was empty. However, she was right, he had talked to a travel agent that afternoon.

"Okay, okay I'll come clean. You win. I confess."

"That sir, is a line from the *Philadelphia Story*. A play you did not write."

"Touché. You're right. I want to go to Hollywood to meet with Lombard and Gable regarding my play. Someone showed Lombard an early version of *The Cat's Pajamas* and she's interested. The only hitch is she wants to meet me to discuss it." He cajoled. "Please come with me."

"You know I can't do that. There's my work and the children's poetry class."

WAR CORRESPONDENT
Nancy Ames - Santo Domingo

Last month a ship with 937 Jewish refugees left the port of Hamburg, Germany for America. The *St. Louis* found no welcome from the great lady that stands in our harbor. Instead of greeting the immigrants with, "Bring me your tired, your poor, your weary," she denied them port. The ship never reached shore.

A Cuban naval vessel escorted the St. Louis back to Europe. The episode has become known as the *Voyage of the Damned.*

What I want to know is when will America amend the plaque on the Statue of Liberty? How much more dire does the situation have to get for refugees to be allowed on our shores?

These passengers were fleeing certain death at the hands of the Nazis. Yet we in the United States have determined not to accept any new immigrants despite the fact that Hitler has stated in no uncertain terms that any Jew left in Europe will be annihilated. Is America condoning this behavior?

Fortunately the rest of the world is not as heartless. The refugees on the *St. Louis* were parceled off to Belgium, Holland, France, and Britain. But the solution is only temporary since these countries have also ceased to accept immigrants. The plight of the *St. Louis* brings up the thorny issue of where are millions of dislocated Jews to go?

"Nonsense," he said hastily, "you're a store clerk and your teaching job is practically volunteer. They'll both be here when you get back." He felt the extreme discomfort of his foot in his mouth. He had never meant to diminish the value of her work.

"Miriam I'm sorry. I didn't mean that. I just know I'm better with you, than away from you."

She turned away wordlessly to return to her seat, her emotions ready to overcome her. He had said it. Said it out loud. He didn't find her contribution to their marriage to be of any importance. How would she ever be able to explain that she wanted to be a mother?

When the play ended and they were leaving the theater, she thundered, "I won't be going with you, but I would appreciate knowing how long you'll be gone, so I can line up my lovers in your absence."

Several people turned to stare at her as she walked by. Jason increased his stride to catch up to her.

"I love you," he whispered. "Everything you do is perfect and makes my life possible."

"I'm glad you realize that you're nothing without me, dear. I trust you'll be home soon."

He tried to hold her hand as she continued marching home. "Darling, I disappear a little every minute I'm away from you. I'll fly to the coast and come back in just a few days so I don't become invisible."

She turned and looked at him. "Good."

There was an 'or else' that hung in the air between them.

Karl at the World's Fair

Karl sat in the shadow of the Trylon and Perisphere. Despite his growing cynicism as to the survivability of the capitalist state, he couldn't help but be moved by the optimism expressed at the World's Fair. It suggested there would be plenty for everyone, a clean, well-lit future where all of the manual tasks of day-to-day life would be accomplished by machines.

Washing machines, vacuum cleaners, faster cars, planes, super highways for a speedier life. Not like today, when most people barely got by, never having enough to eat and lacking the necessities, month after month, year after year.

With two-thirds of the country living below the poverty line, he found it difficult to ignore the rhetoric he heard from his fellow communists and the union leaders. The vision that the forefathers had believed in, freedom for all, equality for the workingman, had not come to fruition.

Karl believed in America; his family had thrived here. The union organizers, with whom he worked assumed Karl came from a poor immigrant family that lived in the tenements, a myth he chose not to dispel. In truth, his family lived in a palatial estate outside of Chicago.

The abundance he was brought up with made him feel obligated to give something back. To simply amass wealth without contribution negated one's success.

He had been taught that character meant everything; achievements only mattered when they benefited the greater good. He strove to live up to that dictum. He was determined to make a difference with his life and as long as he could remain anonymous among his peers he believed he had a chance.

A student of history, he knew how this chapter would end – with the world at war, a war which the average man would pay for.

Karl had come to New York five years ago, after spending three years on the continent during the darkest days of the depression. His heart was permanently scarred by the poverty he'd seen. Starving children's bulging stomachs, rickets, polio, scarlet fever and cholera were part of everyday life.

He'd gone to Europe full of light and optimism, but every day he stayed, a gloom descended upon him. The Europe of his fantasies, full of beauty and grandeur, was reduced to want. The talent and genius of Europe were fleeing. It would forever change the balance of power. He knew there was nothing he could do, yet he held on to his belief that he could make things better.

Karl came home to America desperate to find hope, only to discover a widespread depression of spirit. He wanted to bring his excellent education to bear. But everywhere he turned the world was perverted by poverty and corruption.

He wished for a partner, a soul mate, someone with an equal depth of commitment. He was losing faith, his confidence seeping away like the air from a punctured tire. A tire Karl was no longer certain he could repair.

He tried to stay focused, and follow the advice of Mrs. Roosevelt by remaining in New York. So far he felt his accomplishments were minimal. He had set up a food drive for workers no longer eligible for the WPA. He had been instrumental in launching a clinic staffed with volunteer doctors that provided children with basic healthcare. He also raised funds for the Green Street Orphanage.

But it wasn't enough. It wasn't nearly enough. He worked day and night in his dank little apartment, using candles in the wee hours after the electricity was shut off. He gave away his monthly allowance to the needy, a dollar at a time. Ultimately he had nothing left for himself. He barely ate. He lived on black coffee and donuts.

Karl was meeting with the head of the communist party labor union that evening, the head of the CIO the next day. He needed to make a difference. It meant so much to him. It took little to move him to tears these days. He felt time running out.

"So much to do, so much want. If the body is willing the heart is inspired." He pulled his tattered coat closer as a cold wind began to blow. His head cluttered with obligations, he dug in his pockets and uncovered great wealth in the form of a fifty-cent piece. He decided to go back into the city and treat himself to a real meal and perhaps a movie. Karl needed a break, he knew that the endless work was wearing him down and he required a new perspective.

He considered going to see his high school friend Sarah Karofsky and perhaps hear her play the harp. Karl realized his shabby clothes would not permit him into the venues where she worked. Instead he chose a happy mindless movie downtown in order to avoid his thoughts. As he watched William Powell and Myrna Loy on the screen in their beautiful outfits, living their sublime lives, he recognized that the audience around him enjoyed their short reprieve. He decided not to focus on the negative and just experience the comedy unfolding before him.

After a wonderful dinner of corned beef hash complete with potatoes and cabbage, he strolled about the city streets that shimmered with mica. Streets paved with gold.

By the time he reached his hovel he knew what to do – he would align himself with Mrs. Roosevelt. The next day he would go to her office in New York and offer to help her efforts in any way he could.

Bill and Meyer Lansky

A person's true nature is written all over his face. Bill thought he had heard that somewhere. He was surprised when a member of Dutch Shultz's old gang approached him about doing a little work on the side.

"Hey buddy, my boss would like to talk to you."

"Who's your boss?"

"You don't need to worry about that. Just get in the car."

A regular Joe would have argued, kept on walking, ignoring the big maroon Buick crawling along the street. Only to be whacked on the back of the head and dropped into the trunk unconscious, or tossed over the axle hump on the floor of the backseat. Bill, just got in.

"Meyer said you were smart."

"He was right."

Bill knew it was useless to ask these thugs any questions. They were on a need-to-know basis, only given enough information to do their job. Bill remained silent as they crossed over the new Triborough Bridge and headed for Connecticut.

During the ride he took in the sights, including the car, which was almost as large as his apartment. This machine had to have some serious horsepower just to lug around the tonnage of its own frame. Bill appreciated the quality of the car's radio. He'd wanted a portable radio since seeing them at the World's Fair. As the car barreled onto the Merritt Parkway, he considered how a good radio could entertain you during the tedium of driving on these new highways.

Willie "The Lion" Smith was banging out a tune on the piano, *Jumpin' Down Blues*, sweet and full of bounce. "Hey, is that a colored man playing on your radio?"

The driver and co-pilot were startled to hear Bill speak. The man who had approached Bill said, "Yep that's Willie all right. I saw him at the Apollo once when that place was a happening thing."

The driver added, "That boy could smoke."

"That's nothin'," said the other. "They're going to put that Negress Ethel Waters on that new RadioVision in a couple of months."

"Think of that," said Bill.

He sat back and watched the scenery pass by, broken up by the occasional overpass built in that unmistakable WPA style. 'At least all those taxes paid for something,' he thought.

After about forty-five minutes they arrived at their destination. Bill had never been to Connecticut before and was astonished by the lush green vegetation. There was a pleasant scent of the countryside in the air and a sense of calm that emanated from the landscape. Bill decided then and there he'd retire here; get himself a wife, a few horses and call it home. No wonder Dutch Schultz couldn't resist the place. Even after the Connecticut legislature told him if he crossed the state line he'd be arrested on racketeering charges. And he was, but Schultz died in a gunfight before they could put him in jail.

Bill took off his grey felt hat. He'd heard that 90% of the men's hats worn in New York were made around here and thought that under other circumstances, maybe he would do a little shopping.

The car had pulled into a large estate, sort of White House-esque, complete with a circular driveway. A massive maple stood just off center in the circle's manicured lawn, dappling the driveway in shade. Bill, with keen perception, noted that every blade of grass, tree branch and hedge about the house were meticulously trimmed and pruned. Someone cared deeply about this property.

At the front door a butler acknowledged the men. Inside the foyer a grand staircase led to the second floor.

"Mr. Lansky will see you in the library," said the butler. He escorted Bill to a door just off the foyer. Bill walked in, expecting a grand room based on the movies he'd seen. Instead it was a modest library with only two chairs, a handsome globe, and a few thousand volumes. The books were carefully displayed in floor-to-ceiling bookcases, with a rolling ladder that hung from a high railing in order to reach the highest shelves.

Bill held his hat by the brim and was inspecting the titles of the books when Meyer Lansky walked into the room, smoking a large cigar. Judging by the aroma, Bill guessed a Cuban.

"Good afternoon Mr. Curran. Thank you for joining me on such short notice." Meyer sat in one of the over stuffed chairs.

"A great place you have here. Had it for long?" Genuinely interested, Bill discovered something that a mobster had, that he wanted, besides money.

"I bought it from Dutch Schultz's widow three years ago." Lansky paused. "Sit, make yourself comfortable. Did anyone offer you a drink? Would you like a cigar? The tobacco is grown on my property in Cuba."

"I'm not much of a smoker, but I'll take you up on that drink."

Lansky pulled a long tapestry cord that hung from the ceiling. There was no sound, but Bill suspected a buzzer went off somewhere in the house alerting the servants to his request.

"I'm sure you're anxious to return to the city, so if it's all right with you I'll get down to business," said Lansky.

Bill sat back in the chair and stretched his long legs out in front of him, crossing them at the ankle. He dropped his hat on the floor beside the chair. "I'm in no rush. Take all the time you'd like."

Lansky noted that no one was ever this calm in his presence. He wasn't sure if he had misread Bill. Maybe he was already a wise guy or simply a wannabe.

"So, Bill – do you mind me calling you Bill?" Bill shook his head no. "Good. Bill, we're always on the lookout for friends who travel throughout the social strata of society. It's pretty easy to find people who live at the lower levels. These scum are all around us. But you, Bill, you seem capable of mixing with the elite. Which is a good trick for a boy from your background. Not easily done. You maneuver in and out as if there weren't a class war going on in this country." Lansky took a big pull from his cigar and slowly let out the smoke to see if Bill would respond. Bill kept silent and Lansky continued.

"I admire this because I know you have no formal education," he continued. "When you were perusing my books, could you read them? Do you know what they're about?"

"Let's assume I do," said Bill with a poker player's expression.

"Good, very good. No small feat, pulling yourself up from nothing and now you're about to launch a very successful career with that ballerina, dancing at the watering holes of the well to do. You'll have access to them in a way we could never dream of. At some point you'll be on ocean liners and at private parties. You'll have the ear of the wealthiest men in this country and I would like to pay you to carry some messages for me. You'll find I can be very generous."

Neither man spoke for several moments.

"I'm listening," Bill finally responded, as the servant entered with a scotch.

"So you're out there dancing, everyone sees you, it kind of makes you famous like these rich folks and they're comfortable with you, eating at their table, sitting at the bar with them and so on. Now some of these folks are my best customers and getting close to them without raising suspicion can be difficult beyond the use of doormen, concierges and the like. You, I believe, could engage them in longer discussions and be more motivating, if the need should arise." Again he paused, watching Bill.

Bill decided what this library needed was a window. He knew as soon as he thought it that it would spoil the books. He had grown bored with the conversation. All of this could have been said on a New York sidewalk. Finally, just to get the ball rolling, he asked, "How much?"

"Don't you want to know what first?"

"Nah, let's determine the floor of this deal first."

Meyer smiled. He liked this guy. He wouldn't live long, but he liked his chutzpah. He needed someone like this on the payroll.

"How about a hundred dollars a week, with the caveat that you keep dancing. I'm paying you for your access, after all."

"We're still talking straight transfer of information, no rough stuff, right?"

"That's right. If we should require more persuasive measures you would be appropriately compensated." Meyer eyed him carefully. Bill gave nothing away. "Is it a deal?"

Bill reached out his hand and said, "It's a deal, but I got to tell you, we don't even have our first dancing gig yet."

"You will by the time you return to the city. Don't worry about that. We'll be able to keep you and the ballerina hoofing into the next decade."

"Do I get to keep the money I make dancing?"

Meyer appreciated Bill's exacting nature, a quality one wanted in a numbers runner. Perhaps he had underestimated Bill. He'd have to keep a close eye on him.

"What you make you keep. We've also taken the liberty of getting you a room at the Waldorf Towers. You should live among the swells." He saw the question form on Bill's face. "Yes, we'll pay the rent. Consider it part of our bonus plan." Meyer raised his glass to Bill. Bill stood up and clinked his against it. With Bill hovering above him, Meyer realized that the man could be menacing. There would be many occasions where Bill could be useful. Meyer would have to bring him along slowly.

"Would you care for a tour of the place, Bill? I can ask Gerry to take you around."

"I'd like that, " said Bill. "Do you keep horses? I'm partial to horseflesh."

Lansky couldn't control his smile. "I do have a small stable out back. If you can wait a minute I'd be happy to take you around myself."

Bill's mood actually changed to that of a young man. Meyer had found the special thing that brought Bill joy. 'It's always good to know a potential weakness in a friend or foe', thought Lansky.

A servant came in and whispered in Meyer's ear. "I'll be right back. In the meantime, you might like to know that I've secured your opening at the Rainbow Room in two weeks."

As Meyer stepped out of the library Bill began to consider his future. It was one with money.

JULY

Sarah's Decision

Her mother and grandmother had always warned her that it 'only takes once' and they were right. Sarah knew before she went to the doctor that the stork had been sticking his nose where he shouldn't. The fact that she had gone from being a healthy person one day, to a perpetually sick one the next, confirmed her suspicions.

While the sex with Alex was excellent, that did not make him husband material. There wasn't anyone else on the horizon, so the decision was simple.

She would have an abortion. Luckily she had the cash. The going rate for a clean, professional, safe abortion was thirty dollars, of course, money wasn't the issue. She wanted a baby someday, just not now.

If she tried to keep this baby and her clientele found out, she'd lose all of her commissions. She'd have to leave town and start over. And that wouldn't do any good because this sort of thing always caught up with you. Besides, what kind of life could she offer a child? With her current work she slept until midday and was never

117

Out of the Dark

by Alan Stipple

It sure has been hot lately with temperatures topping 100 degrees so you're going to want your entertainment with air conditioning. Make your cool escape and get thee some entertainment.

We have a new songbird in our midst. Harry James has recorded with an *Amateur Hour* winner named Frank Sinatra. You'll be hearing him soon, singing *Melancholy Mood*. I predict this young man will capture attention and hearts.

Since July 1935 the Treasury Relief Art Project (TRAP) has had the following goal:

To commission art from unemployed artists to decorate existing federal buildings.

Today is a sad day. TRAP is no more. Now that economic recovery is in sight, the administration has ended the program, leaving it up to private business to continue the good work. Artists, take it from me, don't hold your breath.

MOVIES:

★☆☆☆☆ ***Winter Carnival*** - with Ann Sheriden, the Oomph girl, who doesn't hold a candle to Harlow no matter what her press agent says. It's only been two years and none of us have forgotten the Harlow siren. *Winter Carnival* was to be Sheriden's coming out party and while she does a fine job with the contrived plot I'd say Miss Sheriden is looking at a short career.

★★★★☆ ***Juarez***
What can I say about *Juarez* beyond the fact that it stars Claude Rains and Bette Davis? I'm beginning to think Miss Davis has devised some clever way to duplicate herself. It seems there are always two successful Davis movies running at any one time. What will she do next, take on theater and juggling too? No expense was spared. And unlike the Franz Werfel play where Juarez is kept off stage, Paul Muni has a substantial role as Juarez. The movie premiered to rave reviews in Mexico City amidst much pageantry.

home at night. No, this wasn't the time to have a baby.

Life wasn't fair. They'd been careful about using condoms and spermicidal jelly. It seemed so unreasonable that abortions were still illegal in the States. All of the other civilized countries allowed women to terminate an unwanted pregnancy. What was the U.S. looking to do, repopulate the frontier? She knew the answer to her own question. The reason abortion was illegal in the U.S. was fear that immigrants would overpopulate the country, since it was only the well heeled whites that could afford to end a pregnancy. This was the legislature's attempt to keep the population in balance.

Luckily Sarah cared less about such outdated views and had several places she could go: Europe, Puerto Rico, Mexico, Canada, or even an illegal operation here in New York. She chose Canada because it was an overnight train ride. She'd go to Montreal for a three-day vacation and take care of it. She treated the whole process as if she were preparing for an out of town performance. Deep down she knew this to be a crossroads, a decision she would return to over and over again. Still she had no doubts, no second thoughts, as to the correctness of the decision.

She'd been thinking about breaking things off with Alex anyway. His careful avoidance about the source of his income left her uneasy. She suspected it might be better not to know, since it was probably illegal.

She wished she could tell a girlfriend, but decided to keep the pregnancy to herself.

Jason Goes to Hollywood

It felt wrong leaving Miriam. Jason had begged, shouted, pleaded, even whined, trying to convince her to join him, but to no avail. "I suppose," he said to her back, which was suggestively covered by a seductive nightgown, "I'll just have to get home all that much faster," and he kissed the nape of her neck. He knew the nightgown was an effort to get him to stay.

In order to keep to his promise of brevity, he decided to fly out to the coast on one of the new Clipper planes. He had flown before, but

July

never across the country. Jason boarded the plane at the new North Beach airport.

There was already talk of naming it after mayor LaGuardia. Jason marveled at how easy it would now be to fly, with an airport so close to Manhattan. The plane seated twenty-five people and looked like a dining car on one of the new streamlined diesel trains.

His seat was equipped with all the comforts of home – it reclined and had a lamp, footrest and big pockets on either side to hold all his books and papers. It even had a special holder for women's knitting needles: a necessity to attract today's modern woman. Jason tried to recall the last social function he had attended where a woman hadn't pulled out her knitting or crochet work. The woman's social standing or age didn't seem to matter; the practice was as natural as breathing or blinking. Most men found it irritating, but Jason enjoyed the industrious nature of women. They always seemed to be in production, a virtue very few men possessed, including himself.

Jason was planning to use the flight time to polish up the script for Lombard. The second act needed a little more slapstick. Lombard was such a great physical comedienne and he wanted the play to be a comfortable venue for her, as it would be her first time on stage.

He also wanted it to be something Gable would be proud to see Lombard in. Clark was the linchpin in this deal, given the couple's newlywed status. Yet something gnawed at Jason, causing him to wonder if this was a fool's errand. Was there really a chance he could pull the deal off? Max Schneider had committed the money; he felt the play a 'sure thing.' Lombard's agent had confirmed Carole was open to the possibilities of a theatrical role – especially one that showed off her talents.

The script needed more wit, more screwball comedy.

Just before takeoff, Charlotte, an attractive stewardess with a slight southern accent, took Jason's briefcase with a smile. Then she secured him into his seat, letting him know she would return his briefcase as soon as they were airborne.

As the plane was readied for takeoff Jason pulled a letter from his jacket pocket, a note from Miriam's parents in Germany. As he read the correspondence a second time, Jason realized that should he stay

1

longer in California, he would need to have Miriam's letters forwarded to him. He didn't want her to face them alone.

"News from abroad?" asked the tanned, middle-aged man seated across from him.

"My wife's family is in Germany. It's not good. The news is always a strain."

"Yeah, some big things are shaking over there. It's no taffy pull. I'm glad to be in the movie business in a land of make-believe." He paused, considering Jason. "You're looking pretty peaked. You all right?"

"I'll level with you. This war situation is weighing on me. These letters sound like science fiction, something H.G. Wells might write. Citizens being deprived of their livelihood, homes, education, all in the name of racial purity."

He suddenly realized his flying companion might be on either side of this issue. Most people in the U.S. leaned toward isolationism. With the dramatic impacts of the First World War and the depression few people were willing to take on any additional sacrifices.

"Forgive me,' Jason said. "Of course, I don't know where you stand on the war." Jason tipped an imaginary hat, not being able to get up and shake hands, "Jason Rothman."

"Billy Wilder, friend." Wilder took a deep breath. "I appreciate your candor. Most people skirt the topic, even though it's probably what's at the forefront of all our minds. The truth is, like you, I've reached a place of comfort. I have everything I need. I'm safe. I left Germany when Hitler made himself Chancellor. I try to give back enough so that I don't feel guilty. But the rumors, the stories I hear, it's so much worse than when I left, so unbelievable. I don't understand man's inhumanity to man. Nowadays I've got to pay attention to this Un-American Activities Committee. It seems they're looking to put most of us in Hollywood out of business."

"Tell me more about Hitler's Germany, and the Committee," asked Jason.

Their discussion continued well into the night.

Just outside of Chicago, the plane was hit by lightning. The jolt upset the passengers and a few minutes later an announcement was made. There was engine damage and they would have to land for repairs. Even without the lightning Jason had found the trip fatiguing. The noise and vibration from the propellers made his teeth chatter.

In the end, the trip took thirty-two hours, due to bad weather and plane changes. Jason decided to take the train home.

At the Los Angeles Airport, Lombard's agent ushered him into a cream colored convertible that gleamed in the bright Southern California sun. Jason was whisked away to the Mondrian Hotel, where he checked in and promptly fell asleep, fully dressed on top of his bed.

Central Park

It was a beautiful summer day. Central Park was full of people from all over the city. Women strolled the pathways wearing light rayon summer dresses and men wore straw hats, their jackets tossed over their shoulders and shirtsleeves rolled up to the elbow.

Since the Queen's visit last month women had taken to carrying parasols. The landscape was dotted with colorful domes of red, yellow, paisley, and blue. Japanese paper parasols were particularly popular, being delicately painted and light to carry.

Some men were playing baseball on one of the west fields and a women's team had drawn quite a crowd on the north field. At the zoo, children of all sizes were dressed immaculately for their day out. They could be seen eating cotton candy and marveling at the polar bears.

Across the river, in the house that Ruth built, Lou Gehrig was being honored in his last appearance as a Yankee. Struck down by a disease without a name, The Iron Man reminded people that life is a precious gift.

A day so beautiful was a rarity in New York City. The sun allowed the children in the wading pond to feel refreshed by the water that sprayed across their faces, yet didn't cause their mothers to swelter under its glare. The flowers were pert and the leaves flickered with gentle breezes. A day like this held the promise of a beautiful summer night full of fireflies.

On the east side of the park near Seventy-Second Street, a group of stern young men stood about in work clothes. Their faces glowered in anger, in contrast to the smiles of most of the park visitors. An older man of significant girth stood before them shouting.

"You must rise up," he yelled. "You must stand on your own two feet and say, 'No More!'" The men looked at each other and nodded in agreement. "The AFL will not protect you. Walter Reuther has no interest in you, except for your dues. Only the CIO can give you what you're looking for." He paused and regained the attention of the men around him. He saw that he was collecting a crowd of onlookers and raised his voice.

"I'm John Lewis, and I tell you, with the CIO you can expect a regular paycheck, an eight-hour work day and job safety."

Since most of those in the assembled throng had none of these things, it sounded pretty good.

A petite woman watched from the edge of the crowd. A cigarette hung from her red lips. Karl was standing beside her. She cursed out loud, "Damn commies. Looking to bleed the owners dry."

Karl glanced over at her and saw an aging woman with an intensity not seen on the face of a mother.

"Excuse me Ma'am, were you talking to me?" Karl removed his hat as he addressed her.

"Only if you were listening young man," she looked Karl over. "If workers understood what they were doing to the machine maybe they'd stop. Do you agree with that rhetoric?" She asked jutting her chin toward the CIO spokesman.

"Not exactly. I believe it should go further than the unions, that the unions will only get fat on the backs of the workers and then the worker will be carrying the weight of two parasites. The owner and the union bosses." He knew that would startle her. Karl could tell her perspective was not in alignment with his own.

She stamped out her cigarette on the ground while pulling out another, which Karl lit. She took a deep drag blowing the smoke out through her nose, as if preparing to go into battle. "You're so wrong, on so many levels, I hesitate to even begin to tell you the truth of the matter."

WAR CORRESPONDENT

Nancy Ames - District of Columbia

The Senate and the House seem to agree with the publishing moguls that there will be no war. The Neutrality Act still holds, despite a recent vote. America will continue to sell small arms to belligerent nations although there is a provision against more 'Lethal Weapons.'

It's hard to understand why Roosevelt is fighting so hard for a third term. Now that he has lost all support in the House and the Senate, every step he takes is thwarted. Why bother? With a war looming in our future why not take some time off, Mr. President?

Instead he is doing his best to prepare. Roosevelt has begun a new program to teach college students to fly airplanes.

I will leave you with a quote from my good friend Dorothy Thompson:

Peace is not the absence of conflict, but the presence of creative alternatives for responding to conflict – alternatives to passive or aggressive responses, alternatives to violence.

> *Dorothy Thompson,*
> *Journalist*

Karl hid the amusement he felt. He loved being incognito. By donning the clothes of a worker his ignorance was assumed. His advanced degrees remained invisible beneath blue denim.

"Please enlighten me," he said.

As she began to speak, a tall man came and stood behind them. He was listening to the union leader. He towered above Karl and Ayn and they ignored his presence like the nearby high rises.

"Young man, the workers are the parasites. You have it backwards. If it were not for the industrialist there would be no workers." She paused waiting for some acknowledgement. "Can you see that?"

"Please continue."

"It's upon the brains and energy of the creative person that all workers suckle. Each great company owes its allegiance to the one man or woman with the original dream. The individual, who went without sleep, sustenance and idle pleasure, dedicating their lifeblood to the materialization of an original thought. Workers are merely a natural extension of a great idea. They're the cogs in the wheel of inspiration. That they should make demands is absurd."

Karl was enjoying this, but maintained his poker face.

"So, are you saying that workers are nothing more than slaves and should be treated as such?"

"Not slaves, I didn't take free will out of the equation. But they have a choice as to which idea to follow and support. They should feel honored to have the opportunity to work with a person of such ability. Instead, the workers and the government believe they have a claim against the very individual who makes their meager lives possible."

"Ah, there you've said it - their meager lives. Why can't the owner share more with the workers? Why must the owner live in the palatial mansion while the worker barely makes enough to feed his family?"

Ayn stepped back for a moment and took a long hard look at Karl.

"You're a communist aren't you?" she asked. Karl nodded in agreement.

"Ah then, my assessment of you was correct. I am no fool. By your speech patterns and confidence I'd wager you were educated in an Ivy League school. I'd say Yale or Harvard. Your costume suggests you believe that all of the production should be shared evenly among the masses, that all men are created equal and each should receive an equal share in the spoils? Do I have your attitudes, misdirected as they are, about right?"

Karl removed his hat and flourished it with a bow to Ayn, "Karl Klyne at your service Ma'am." He arose with a smile on his face and a mischievous glint in his eye. Here was a real adversary. She rarely had the opportunity to argue politics with anyone trained in the art of debate.

"You're correct Ma'am....," he began. She interrupted him and held out her hand. "Ayn Rand. Drop the Ma'am stuff."

"Mrs. Rand I studied music at Yale and Juilliard. Yes, I was born with a silver spoon in my mouth and have dedicated myself to the sharing of the spoils."

"Based on your wardrobe I dare say you are no longer a musician. What then Mr. Klyne, do you create? What great notion, idea, invention have you offered the world to date? More precisely, what have you developed that someone would want to buy?"

"Nothing, but that doesn't mean..."

She interrupted him, "Exactly so, what right have you to talk about anything? How can you offer an opinion? Without the men that you vilify there would be nothing. You would all be sitting in the mud and catching squirrels for dinner."

"Ah, but you can't keep a good capitalist down. They emerge in every society and the first thing they do is exploit the worker," Karl responded.

"You're so naïve. I'll agree with you that it's impossible to eliminate men of vision. You can kill them, round them up and isolate them like Hitler's doing right now, but you cannot eliminate them. They make the earth spin and make our lives interesting and full of color."

"That may be so, but the color I'm familiar with is black and blue. Administered from the batons of the police, whom your men of vision employ, to wield against their workers."

Ayn's smile was wry, "Oh I see. And a poet too." Her chuckle turned into a smoker's cough. When her hacking subsided she continued with vigor, "since these owners are so evil, let's say I remove them, take them to a place where they cannot trouble your workers. What then Mr. Klyne? What becomes of your beloved society?"

Karl pondered this for a moment. A world without landlords, industrialists and factory owners. A world of the worker.

"I suspect you have reached a peaceful place in the equation," she said. "Now carry it a little further. No bosses, no one telling anyone what to do. Nice right? All right now there are no factories, no buildings, no trains, planes, transportation, machinery, communication comes to an end. What have you now?"

Karl considered that for a moment. "An agrarian society. Back to the farm where each family is responsible for their own plot of land and happiness."

"Oh come now, I expected better from you. Is that really what you want? Is everyone better off as a farmer, than as a mill worker, or a middle manager in a large corporation? Shouldn't everyone have the choice of where they wish to live on the ladder?"

Karl did not respond. He looked down at the dirt where he stood. He had never followed this line of logic before. He was certain it was flawed, but he needed more time.

"Must everyone in your Utopia be a good farmer? Do you believe that's the natural state of man?"

"Hell no." Came Bill Curran's booming voice from behind them. The tall man continued, "My family were piss-poor farmers. They took to stealing horses. It was easier. To hell with the boss man, to hell with working." He laughed.

"Ah, but stranger, you're more like the worker than you think, since you do not create anything either. Making your theft only a variation on what the worker carriers out."

"Now you're being ridiculous," claimed Karl.

"Am I," asked Rand. "Listen to your CIO friend Mr. Lewis there." Karl held up his hand in protest. "He's not a friend of mine."

"To Mr. Stalin then," continued Rand. "Both say that you should, as a worker, have more of the owner's share of the profits." She turned pointing to the tall man. "The thief also wants to take a portion of the spoils. Now granted, he doesn't give anything back." She paused and bit her lower lip, "Wait, that's not completely true. A thief causes the creator to think of ways to prevent the robbery. Causing the creation of new industries in theft prevention. Take insurance, for example, the goal of which is to protect against loss. In a way, the thief is perhaps even more of a catalyst in society than the worker."

"Amen sister." said Bill. Karl rolled his eyes.

"All I know," Bill added, "is that the owners have lots and I want some of it. I don't need it all, I don't want to break anyone's spirit, because I want to keep feeding from the trough."

"My point exactly," said Ayn enthusiastically turning to Karl.

"He," ventured Karl, "is not contributing anything. He's willing to go to jail, take risks, and live without integrity."

Bill spoke up, "Are you suggesting there's not a bond between thieves? If so, you're dead wrong. The structure is very rigid." He paused, "Pardon me, my name's Bill Curran." Bill removed his boater and bowed slightly to Ayn. Then he turned and shook Karl's hand roughly. Bill continued, "I realize that my sixth grade education makes the two of you a lot smarter than me. But I've got to tell you, you guys sound lost. You seem to lack the *doing* part of the equation."

Ayn tilted her head back and laughed with joy. Even Karl chuckled.

"Mr. Curran," said Karl, "You may not be that far off. I've spent most of my life theorizing, only lately have I been trying to put it into practice. It's the practice I find difficult."

"And you, sir, have me pegged too. I'm a writer and while I spew my ideas out on the page, and defend them vehemently, my only creation is ink on paper. While you," Ayn quickly looked Bill over, a handsome sensual man built for sex. "While you, I suspect, inspire a great many," she said suggestively.

"I'm not sure what you mean by that, but I get around. Could I take you two for a drink?" asked Bill.

"No, I need to get back to my thoughts on action," said Karl.

"I'd be happy to join you for drink, Mr. Curran," said Ayn.

The trio disbanded and left the union leader collecting his members. With each new face he saw in the crowd he could feel money in his pockets.

Miriam, Auden and Isherwood

Miriam hummed as she prepared the apartment for her lunch guests. She had invited W.H. Auden and Christopher Isherwood.

She was at her best serving others. Turning fresh eyes on the flat she was pleased to find everything in good order. Tidy, yet still possessing that lived-in look, a book here, knitting there. Only the flowers were on their last legs. Petals from a stargazer lily lay scattered on the coffee table. She would have to pick up a fresh bouquet at the store.

Miriam always felt it odd that in the middle of summer it seemed harder to find beautiful cut flowers than in the dead of winter. She suspected this was because so many people neglected to buy them in the summer, so the vendors only stocked carnations and roses. Perhaps she could find a farmer's stand with sunflowers from New Jersey.

She grabbed her purse and the ivory handle of a little green parasol that set off her yellow and wisteria purple silk dress.

As she stepped out of the artificially cooled confines of her building she met a dense ocean of moisture. New York felt like a steam bath and it was only ten in the morning. Miriam sensed her yellow curls drooping.

'I'll buy another oscillating fan for the living room' she thought, as she picked up her pace despite the heat.

Crossing the threshold of the corner store, she called out, "Good morning Sammy. How are you today?"

"Mrs. Miriam, what a pleasure. What are you doing here on a Monday? Especially when the rest of the world is working or hiding in their air conditioned buildings?" Sammy had been flirting with the neighborhood women for sixty years. He was a little white haired man that possessed a twinkle in his eye that caused every woman to adore him. Sammy stepped out from behind the counter wearing a long green apron tied neatly around his slim waist.

"It's a good day, Mrs. Miriam. We have lots of supplies today. I had success at the market this morning. Come look, fresh bananas, guavas and pineapples, a ship from South America must have made it past the German blockades last night."

"Sammy, I have two guests coming for lunch. What do you suggest?" she knew he would give up his finest treasures if they were his suggestion.

"Men or women?"

"Men, but they're not big eaters." During the height of the depression the phrase meant her guests were having trouble making ends meet.

"Ah then, they'll be hungry. Let's you and I look in my deli section." He took her by the arm and pointed to his suggestions. "I have wonderful brisket that just came in today. I know if it were women I would never suggest such a thing, but men, they like to feel full."

She smiled? Both of these men always seemed full to her, full of ideas, motion and life.

"You're probably right," Miriam agreed. "What do you have for desert?"

"We have a delicious strudel. They'll love it. The crust is so light." He walked off pleased to have it to offer to her.

W.H. Auden and Christopher Isherwood while being respected poets were also known to be homosexual. This was only openly acknowledged in literary circles, where everyone's sexual escapades were fair game.

Dorothy Parker had once said to Auden, "You, sir, are a better poet than I, but since we cannot sleep together I have little use for you because you'll not share your essence. So be off and I'll chat up another man who cannot write as well, but whose pencil has lead enough to fill my blank sheets."

Auden loved that story and repeated it frequently. Miriam always blushed with its telling. Auden and Isherwood together provided an endless supply of one-liners. Miriam rarely got a word in edgewise.

At the end of one of their visits her stomach hurt from laughter. She needed some prolonged laughter now. Her heart contracted at the thought of Jason.

Mrs. Sammy, a plump eastern European Jew, emerged from the back of the store and held out her flour-covered hand. "Miriam my dear, how are you? Is Mr. Rothman back yet? You must miss him so. Papa tells me you're having a lunch for some young men. Who are these men? Should I be worried?"

Nothing went unnoticed in Miriam's neighborhood. If she ever had the inclination to cheat on Jason, she would have to do it at least twenty blocks away.

"No, Mrs. Sammy, these young men are artists."

"Ah, I see, friends from the Village?"

"Exactly."

"You artists, always looking to learn more about life." She paused and her face became serious. "But you'll not learn of life completely until you have a child. And how's that going to happen with Mr. Rothman thousands of miles away. When is he coming home?"

Miriam fiddled with a bunch of grapes, trying to regain her composure. "I don't know exactly. He's working on a play with Carole Lombard and Clark Gable." She looked up into Mrs. Sammy's worried eyes, "But he calls every day."

"Every day? He must be getting rich like those movie stars. Clark Gable, you say? You tell him I say hello. Mr. Gable, I think, is very handsome." In a conspirator's whisper, she added "But don't tell Papa, he'll be jealous."

They laughed together as Mr. Sammy came to the counter and put her purchases into a used bag. "These too, Mr. Sammy," said Miriam, as she held up the grapes. He worked out the purchases on her account. Mrs. Sammy walked her to the door, "The next time you talk to Mr. Rothman you tell him we miss him and he must hurry home."

"I will." For both of us she thought, and stepped out into the sweltering summer day.

Ernestine and the Dance

It was coming too easy. Ernestine had been in the dance business too long not to realize that something was amiss. A new dancing couple should expect to be hoofing it in second and third-rate joints for several months before establishing a name for themselves. Reputations grew via word-of-mouth and eventually the club owners would hear about you. They would come down, see your act, and invite you to fill in one or two nights a week as the warm-up act. That's the way it was always done.

In Ernestine and Bill's case, things happened overnight. In less than two weeks they were the headliners at the Rainbow Room and the Starlight Club.

They were good, but not flawless. The routine needed a lot of work and now Bill hated to practice at all. With so much early recognition, it was impossible to get him into the studio for rehearsals.

Ernestine loved her studio. When she entered its welcoming space she felt inspired, prepared to take on the world. She felt that within these four walls she would discover the magic of movement. She would create something new here. Ernestine continued practicing three to four hours a day, even without Bill.

She couldn't blame him. He had told her that he had friends in high places and it appeared to be true. Bill produced the money for costumes, secured the best venues and had a tireless publicist ensuring their praises were sung in every major media outlet in town.

One day Ernestine picked up a copy of The New Yorker and began reading about herself dancing in a beautiful shimmering silver gown at the Rainbow Room. It was a good trick, because she hadn't danced there on the night they mentioned and no one but Bill and her dressmaker had ever seen the silver dress.

Bill had come to the studio a few weeks earlier with a photographer and the publicity photos seemed to be everywhere. Posters at bus stops, on trash cans, in every subway station. People recognized her on the street. There was something odd about being a star and not having worked for it.

Ernestine believed in her talent and knew that she would outshine this faux publicity and secure the fame she truly deserved. With or without Bill.

Karl Under Surveillance

Karl was becoming too popular. He had hangers-on and this made him suspicious. Not that he was an unlikable guy, however, people had lately been inviting him to dinner and asking for his opinion on socialism, communism and the state of the American government.

At first he felt flattered and pleased there were more hands to help. Then he realized the attention was focused a little too closely on him.

He was being watched. The once piffling Committee on Un-American Activities was gaining traction. The organization that Eleanor and Franklin Roosevelt had ridiculed for years, had now been given free reign and a budget to root out terrorists. Someone had identified Karl. He imagined some poor wretch turning his name in for a few dollars, so the informant could feed his or her family. Seven hundred and fifty thousand jobs had disappeared overnight, with the elimination of the WPA. People were desperate, but Karl didn't hold it against the neighbor that turned him in.

Karl had never fit in with the downtrodden. With his precise grammar, he would always be seen as the other. His confident stance alone could have him served up to the Committee, add to that his political activities and he was a prime candidate.

Once the Feds found out his family's background, and he suspected it would not be long now, he would be the ideal patsy.

He knew he should leave New York and settle out west in Oregon or Washington State. Stay away from politics. But Karl was committed to the ideals of being an American. He felt the need to shoulder the responsibility by helping as many people as he could, no matter what the future held.

Kim's Good Fortune

Kim could not believe her good fortune. It was as if she had awoken in someone else's life. In less than a month she had become the curator of the International Art exhibit, the most influential exhibit at the New York World's Fair. Before she set foot in the building she knew the history of every painting by heart.

Each day she would take pleasure in spending time with a different canvas, appreciating its strengths and weaknesses. She knew where Picasso was making fun of his audience. When Monet lost interest in a subject, perhaps in a hurry to go in for supper. She could feel Van Gogh's madness in the thickness of his paint strokes. She recognized the slow destruction of Manet's mind, as exhibited in the ever-increasing predominance of black on his canvases. Kim felt as if she knew these men, for the majority of artists in the show were men. There were very few women, not as many as had been in the Harlem shows or even the WPA exhibits. Oddly, she was being pressured to replace even the few on exhibit with lesser-known male artists. She wasn't quite sure why and until someone could explain it to her she continued to feature Cassatt, Vallayer-Coster, Valadon, Bonheur, Hosmer and Beauclerk's work.

Kim herself had stopped painting. The muse of hunger having left her. Looking at paintings all day sparked a desire to explain them, rather than duplicate the brush strokes. She turned into one of the most loathsome of creatures, a critic. Someone who conjures up stories based on what they, the talentless, believe an artist might feel. She would have to live with it, at least for now. If the depression had taught Kim anything it was that nothing was permanent.

Besides, it was July and the Fair would close at the end of October. A few months couldn't strip her of her artist's badge – could they?

George Whalen entered the building and immediately the guards and staff began to buzz. He was a tall, handsome man with a trim mustache. Whalen had dreamed the dream of the World's Fair. Like a magician, pulling a rabbit from his hat, the Fair lived where once there had been nothing but a dumpsite of ash. His associates considered him a genie and within the walls of this fairyland he was deeply respected.

"Miss McIntyre, could I have a word with you?" Kim knew her

stock had gone up with the rest of the staff. Mr. Whalen knew her name.

"Of course, Mr. Whalen. What can I do for you?" Kim strode over, to reduce the distance between them. They ended up in front of an erotic Picasso. Whalen didn't even notice the painting.

"Miss McIntyre, could we retire into the exhibit offices for a moment? I have a favor to ask you." Sex crossed her mind for a fraction of a second. The too-good-to-be-true circumstances of her employment might now be presenting her with an invoice. But she shrugged off such seedy thoughts and followed him into the inner recesses of the museum.

Thanks to the forethought of the architects Harrison and Fouilhoux, a little conference room had been designed for visiting dignitaries. The small space was constantly in use.

Mr. Whalen shut the door behind Kim. "I've been meaning to thank you for making the trip to Washington D.C. last month to oversee the Italian Renaissance exhibit."

"It was my pleasure," said Kim. "Most of the paintings I'd never seen in person, only as reproductions in books. It was an honor."

Mr. Whalen looked uncomfortable. Kim wondered if she was about to be fired. He cleared his throat.

"May I get you a glass of water, sir?"

"No, no. I'm fine Miss McIntyre. I'm not sure if you're aware that Randolph Hearst, the media giant, is broke."

"I've heard rumors sir. I didn't put much stock in them."

"Well it's true. He's liquidating all of his priceless antiquities at Sotheby's and remarkably, the preview is at Gimbels. I'd like you to attend the Sotheby's auction for me."

"It would be my pleasure. What shall I do there, sir?"

"I'd like you to carefully review the lots and determine if any of the paintings should find their way into this exhibit."

Kim was speechless. The enormity of the request overwhelmed her.

"Perhaps you are aware that the Fair is not pulling in the attendance we were hoping for. Ticket purchasers tend to be highbrows and while they have the money to pay for all the attractions, there are just not enough of them. The committee and I have decided to position the Fair into more of an every man event next year, but that means there'll be no further purchases of fine art. If we're going to do it, we must do it now."

Kim was at a loss. "Why me, sir?"

"You're an artist, you have a good eye. You are able to enter these works. While the rest of us see only flat surfaces, you see emotion. That's a rare talent young lady."

Kim was taken aback. Not only surprised that he knew all this about her, but she believed everyone experienced paintings as she did.

"You will have a two million dollar budget at the auction. Choose your paintings wisely. They'll become American treasures."

She knew she shouldn't ask, that she should keep her mouth shut and enjoy the incredible opportunity. Still she couldn't stop herself. "Mr. Whalen, where will the paintings reside once the Fair is closed?"

He stiffened and glared at her.

"That's really none of your business Miss McIntyre. Just find the right art." He flushed in response to the veiled accusation.

In an attempt to keep her job Kim continued, "Please sir, don't misunderstand. When choosing art I imagine the artistic environment of its future home." She hesitated giving him time to understand her meaning. "Each painting will have a relationship to the art surrounding it and its overall presentation in the room." She dared not press too hard. Although she already suspected that these precious paintings might be divided between Fair patrons. Kim didn't want to believe it, refused to believe it of Mr. Whalen, but his answer would tell all. "It does make a difference sir," she said in her defense.

George Whalen relaxed visibly upon hearing her explanation. "Ah, I wasn't thinking." He paused for a moment. "Consider the Frick's smallish rooms, works of the masters hanging side by side. Also imagine one grand viewing gallery in the truest sense, where painting are stacked three high along the walls."

As she imagined the space in her mind's eye Kim refused to let his answer disappoint her. She didn't know whose house she was standing in, however she suspected it faced Central Park.

"I'll see to it, sir. When is the auction?"

"The viewing is today and tomorrow and the auction itself is this Thursday. I assume you can find someone to cover for you?"

"Not a problem." The opportunity was glorious. "Shall I report back to you after the viewing?" He looked at her, puzzled. She added, "To go over my choices with you?" His features cleared and he smiled.

"I hadn't thought of that, an excellent idea. How about over dinner tomorrow night?' He looked at her closely for the first time. "The Starlight Club?"

"That would be very nice sir. However, I must admit I haven't the clothes to suit the establishment."

He frowned, deep ridges forming across his brow. "Poppycock. I'll have something sent over to your house. Size six?"

Good eye, she thought. "Yes sir, I wear a size six but please, we could go to the automat. It would be fine by me."

"But not by me, Miss McIntyre. I look forward to seeing you tomorrow at eight at the Starlight Club. I'll have your ensemble delivered to your home."

And with that he was gone. Kim felt dazed.

Carole and Clark

Jason had hoped that his trip to Los Angeles would be speedy, so that he could return to Miriam as quickly as possible, but fate dealt him a different hand. Lombard and Gable were in a movie together, *No Man of Her Own*. It was being shot on a back lot in Studio City and going badly. They were both terrific, everyone agreed, the script, however, proved to be a stinker. Between each scene new pages were written. A week had passed before Jason finally drove up the long driveway to the Gable's big home in Beverly Hills.

Jason had seen bigger 'homes' in Europe and even in Newport, yet there was something about the elegance of Beverly Hills mansions. They were so manicured and perfect. He wasn't sure if it was because things were newer here, or simply cleaner. All of his memories of New York included grit and dirt. The bright sun seemed to wash the color out of everything in LA, leaving it Ivory Snow white. Sunglasses were a requirement for an out-of-towner.

Brilliant red and yellow hibiscus dotted the landscape as Jason approached. At ten a.m. the temperature was 80 degrees with a light wind blowing in from the ocean. Jason wasn't sure where to leave the car. He decided to pull up to the front door and ask. He rang the bell and a plump Latino woman answered.

"And you are?" The woman appeared to be in her mid-fifties. She struck a pose of pure boredom, making it clear that she ran this house like the Madame of a popular bordello.

"Jason Rothman, I have an appointment with Mr. and Mrs. Gable."

Without acknowledgement, the woman turned and yelled at the top of her voice, "Mr. Rothman's here."

Having lived in NY all of his life, Jason had met many maids and butlers, but no one like this tank of a woman. He was about to object to her method of announcing him when she turned back with a smile. "Hi I'm Liza, please follow me. They're expecting you."

Jason trailed behind her making his way across the polished marble floors and Oriental rugs. Everything was a luxurious white, yellow or gold. He hoped he had wiped his feet well at the door.

"They're out by the pool. I'll take you to them," said Liza.

Jason wondered why all the shouting if they knew he was coming? His question was answered when he reached the backyard. The space was dedicated to a gigantic pool the likes of which Jason had only seen in public parks. The pool and its surrounds were large enough to entertain hundreds of people. Jason could imagine all of Hollywood here for a gala event. Once his eyes adjusted to the brilliant sunlight he saw Carole and Clark in swimsuits waving to him from under an umbrella at the far end.

Clark Gable stood up and approached him. "Welcome Mr. Rothman," he held out his hand and continued, "May I call you Jason? Rothman sounds too much like a bankers name."

"Of course," Jason responded, noting the ethnic slur even though Gable seemed completely unaware.

"Look darling, we have a famous playwright in our midst," said Clark.

"Mr. Rothman, it's such a pleasure to meet you. Clark and I truly enjoyed your script." Lombard's enthusiasm and beauty were mesmerizing. Jason immediately understood the source of her stardom. Now he wanted her for his leading lady more than ever.

"Thank you Mrs. Gable, I'm flattered by your praise."

"Ah, get off it Jason, call me Carole and I'll call you Jason." She gave him a heart-melting smile. He nodded. He couldn't imagine denying her much of anything.

"Swell. How about a drink?" she asked eagerly.

"It's still a little early…" Jason proffered.

"Don't be ridiculous. The warden here won't let me drink unless we have company and you constitute company. How about I mix us up some mimosas?"

"I have no idea what that is, but it sounds wonderful."

"Don't know what a mimosa is?" she shook her head and went to the bar.

While Lombard busied herself with the drinks, Gable leaned over to Jason, "Actually, old man, she's really excited about the script. She wants to do the play, but you're going to have to convince her that she's got the goods. She's afraid of those snooty theater types. I don't mean you, of course, old sport." He looked closely at Jason for the first time.

"Hey, it's too hot for that jacket," said Clark. "Take if off. We don't stand on ceremony here. Go ahead and get down to your shirt-sleeves. Better yet, we have a swimsuit for you in the cabana." Clark started to get up.

"No, no I'm fine," Jason mopped his brow with his handkerchief. He had purchased a taupe linen suit, now a mass of wrinkles. He would never dream of removing his jacket back in New York, no matter how warm the summer day. Yet things were topsy-turvy here and he was melting. It was as if the old rules didn't apply in L.A. There was a thrilling sense of danger, of ignoring tradition and setting out on a new road.

"Alright." Jason stood up, removed his jacket and then throwing custom to the wind, he unbuttoned his waistcoat and rolled up his shirtsleeves.

"There you go. Much better," said Carole as she handed him a drink and sat down on the end of a chaise lounge. She perched there as if ready to pounce, leaning in toward Jason.

"So you really think I can do this part? The part of Amy?"

"Why of course," he hesitated, almost using her formal name, "Carole. You're perfect for it."

"But you wrote it for Katharine Hepburn didn't you? Isn't that why you're out here, cause she went with the Philip Barry play instead?" she turned to Clark. "Didn't Howard Hughes buy that play for her?"

"Something like that, baby."

"Whatever, isn't it her part?"

Jason was a little uncomfortable. He anticipated that Lombard would have heard. "Indeed, I did initially write it for Miss Hepburn. However, I've made significant modifications to highlight your charms and comic timing. It's been customized for you."

"Really? How so?" Her interest was piqued and he pulled the script from his briefcase and thumbed through the dog-eared pages.

"For instance, here on page twenty-eight. I originally had the lead playing this as a stuck-up society woman. I have rewritten the part to be played by you as a charming ingénue who wants to learn more of the world."

"An ingénue." Carole looked to Clark, "Can I still play ingénue roles, Pa?"

"Definitely, my little chickadee, for as long as you like." He leaned over and kissed her. Jason felt his heart contract, thinking of Miriam at home, alone.

"You got a sweetheart or a wife Mr. Rothman?" Clark missed nothing. He winked at Jason.

"My wife's name is Miriam." Jason beamed with pleasure just mentioning her name. His love for Miriam showed in his expression.

"Then you know what a pain in the ass they are." Clark laughed and Carole feigned shock and threw her drink at him. They wrestled for a moment and then Clark tossed her into the pool. He then dove in after her.

Paddling around in the deep end he called up to Jason.

"Sorry, old man. Please don't take it personal. Ma and I have been cooped up in a building without windows for three weeks and we're a little stir crazy. It isn't that we don't want to talk to you about your script." He dove under the cool blue water, pulling Carole with him. When he popped up he continued. "Just be patient with us." He twirled in the pool. "We'll be out in a moment and we can meet properly in the living room." He threw back his head in a Tarzan yell, "Liza."

When she appeared at the sliding glass door, he called out, "Liza, you old pirate. Take Mr. Jason into the living room and make him comfortable."

"Aye, aye sir," she replied and gave him a mock salute. She turned to Jason, "Come along my matey."

Jason realized he had been dismissed. He followed Liza into the house, hearing Carole and Clark splashing in the pool behind him.

AUGUST

Jason and the Script

Jason had found a small apartment in Culver City that he rented by the week. Starlets and would-be actors lived in the slightly run-down complex, having moved to Hollywood to be discovered.

There were a total of eight apartments, four on either side that faced each other across a common area where a few desert flowers grew. The bungalows were efficiency units with a single burner hot-plate, a sink, some dishes and a bed. In an attempt to impart cheer to the rooms someone had decorated them in a red and yellow motif, everything from the walls to the cushions.

Jason never spoke of his own success to the other occupants. He didn't mentioned that each day he drove his rented Chevy to Clark Gable and Carole Lombard's house to work on a script. It would make his neighbors crazy. They would insist upon introductions. Truth be known he didn't actually believe any of them had the wherewithal to make it in the movie business. Most were talkers and daydreamers. All except one, Denise.

August

A young waif of not more than eighteen, Denise worked every night in her apartment practicing scripts before the mirror. She got up early in the morning before most of her neighbors even stirred in their beds. Each day she would stand in long lines at the studio for the opportunity to try out for a part, any part. She worked as an extra whenever she could. She even tried out for roles of old men and young boys because she knew that eventually the directors and managers would start recognizing her face, see her tenacity and want that kind of commitment for their movie.

Jason believed Denise would succeed, with a little luck. He gave her suggestions on which monologues to read, choosing unusual pieces that would grab the attention of casting directors because they were dramatic and thought provoking.

Denise read everything Jason suggested, she visited the public library weekly and ordered hard-to-get books from other branches. She knew her Shakespeare, Euripides, and Marlow as well as Kaufman, Saroyan and Odets. Jason found her charming and frequently took her out for a hot dog. But for all of Denise's sweetness and drive, she was not Miriam.

He had never meant to abandon Miriam for so long. New York was becoming a distant memory, their apartment a far away haven. Jason could see how people got lost in California, forgetting their way home. Be it gold, stardom, success or just plain sunshine, California and its warmth enticed you with reasons not to leave. Everything here focused on the future. In California, the past was erased.

His timeline for returning home was reset every day by the Gables. With each visit, he drove up to the house convinced this would be the last day; today he would see the final edits on the script. Carole would say 'Yes, let's do it,' and Jason would head home on the next plane or train.

But each day she'd identify a new scene to revise or, worse yet, to add. He would spend hours with them and then head back to the apartment and work on the changes to have them ready for the following morning. It had been four weeks and he was beginning to wonder if Carole was using their daily editing sessions to stall, in order to avoid commitment. He was going to have to set a date and stick to it, because in the end, there were other actresses.

Sarah and Harpo

Sarah's days grew dour. She found herself losing vibrancy. While she still dressed fetchingly, she stopped adding the flourishing touches like a permanent wave to her red hair. She ceased accentuating her outfits with the gold brooches she had sought out in the tiny shops south of Canal. Her days proceeded without direction.

Perhaps it was aborting the baby. Or the fact that Alex turned out to be a heel. Maybe if she'd been truly passionate about the harp it would provide solace. Instead, her dissatisfaction deepened despite a wonderful income, a fabulous place to live and a vibrant career. Even her sessions with the psychotherapist left her depressed. She feared becoming one of the empty, painted matrons of Fifth Avenue.

Harry Liam Kelly, who accompanied her on piano, often made fun of these women, who possessed too much money and not enough ambition, who searched for diversions in shopping, therapy and lovers.

Sarah and Harry were playing today at the Plaza. The requests were always the same - *Blue Danube, Ode to Joy, Tales from Vienna Woods*, and other mind-numbing renditions. Harry's Irish temper flared with each request. He wanted to play his own pieces. Having heard them, Sarah felt certain that only the ears of a select audience would ever enjoy his discordant melodies.

Sarah chose to keep her eyes focused on her hands and the strings before her, ignoring the seating of guests by the maître d'. This time she heard the stir too late to look up and determine the source. The famous guest had already been seated behind a large palm, which blocked her view. 'Probably a Hollywood starlet', she thought, since the Palm Court was the place to be seen when visiting New York.

She looked over at Harry and saw that he had noted the entrance of the famous guest and nodded in the direction of the palm.

When the piece was over, fewer people clapped than usual. The

Out of the Dark

by Alan Stipple

For those of you who have not visited the Fair by now, it's time to do so. Go for the exhibits, but stay for the warm nights with fountain light shows and fireworks.

THEATER:
Philadelphia Story - 'Box Office Poison' Katharine Hepburn has made quite a comeback with this year's spoof on the rich and mighty. A classic work by Philip Barry, full of his trademark banter. In a comedy of stereotypes, Barry has given us something that just may save Hepburn's career.

MOVIES:
★★★★☆ ***The Wizard of Oz*** - I, for one, think we have a cult picture here. While it may not have taken the box office by storm how could anyone resist little people called munchkins and a strawman that can dance without a brain? Freud would have a field day with this movie. I think it'll go down in history as an all time great. Me and Toto say, 'See it soon!'

★★★★☆
On Borrowed Time
I admit it, even I wept during this movie. But how could you help it with Lionel Barrymore attempting to cheat death in the form of Sir Cedric Hardwicke? Barrymore plays almost the entire movie from his real life wheelchair. You find yourself cheering for him and in the last scene when he struggles to his feet – a little voice within you cries out saying, "Not for me, don't stand for me – we love you anyway, we'll always love you. Thank you. Thank you. Thank you." A movie bound to move even the most manly man to tears.

room was still abuzz over the unexpected visitor. Sara guessed Katharine Hepburn or Fredric March, both of whom stopped in now and again. The chance to see a celebrity brought people to the Palm Court. However, when one arrived, people were often distracted and forgot to leave a tip.

Sarah felt resigned. She and Harry prepared to begin another piece when the famous guest stood up and everyone began to clap. He bowed slightly and the audience began to call out for him to play. Harry turned to Sarah and spoke in a stage whisper, "He'll be wanting your harp I think."

When the actor turned to face Sarah, she was shocked to see it was Harpo Marx. She had always wondered if he could really play, suspicious that somebody else's hands plucked the strings in his movies. She was about to find out. With a slight bow to the audience he headed for the stage and the room broke into applause.

He stood before Sarah, "How do you do? My name is Harpo Marx."

All Sarah could think was, 'Why would this man with such a sweet voice, so full of warmth and charm, be mute in the movies?'

"Sara Karofsky, Mr. Marx. How do you do?"

"Very well, thank you. Would you mind terribly, if I played a tune on your harp?"

"Please Mr. Marx," she said over the din, "I'd love to hear you play." The patrons clapped as they realized they would get what they wanted most – a great story to go with their visit to New York.

She rose and stood off to the side. The maître d' came over and guided her to a seat near the stage. Harpo leaned the seventy-five pound instrument into his shoulder and plucked a couple of major chords, focusing on the red and black strings. Sarah kept her instrument tuned and her setups taut. She saw the appreciation in his face. Harry sat on his stool, with his back to the piano, indicating he wouldn't interfere. Sarah already knew Harpo was legit, the calluses on his forefingers and thumbs had confirmed this. When Harpo began to play, the smile vanished from his face. He approached the harp as if in prayer.

The piece was haunting and difficult, well beyond the taste of the average high tea crowd. His plucking and strumming formed complex harmonics, something Sarah never bothered with, although she knew how to create them.

She felt transported by the music. Elevated by a man whose passion for the harp was evident in the way he caressed the strings and coaxed the vibrato. He held the body of the harp to his shoulder like a lover.

Now his face shone, illuminated.

When he finished, a hush fell over the audience, followed by wild applause. He stood and took a bow. The patrons begged for an encore. He refused with a smile. Harpo approached Sarah, to shake her hand, as the clapping continued.

"Miss Karofsky, I realize that what I'm about to say might be inappropriate, however, would you permit me to give you a piece of advice?"

She didn't know what to say, she felt exposed and vulnerable. With false bravado she replied, "Please Mr. Marx, feel free."

"I could hear that your heart is not in your playing and I can only hope that it's somewhere else. Please don't get me wrong, you're a marvelous technician, however, you play without passion, without zest. Miss Karofsky, life is so very short, and you are so very fine. Go out and live your dreams." And with that he kissed her on the cheek and waved to the audience.

Sarah drew upon every ounce of professionalism within her to finish the set. She even returned Harpo's wave goodbye. But when the performance was over, in the manager's office, as she and Harry divided up the tips, she broke down.

Harry took her home, feeling helpless.

Sarah was still crying when she stepped out of the elevator onto her floor. Inside the apartment she found a large bouquet of red roses, with baby's breath and ferns. She couldn't imagine who had sent them.

The card inside held only three words, "Be Happy, Harpo."

Sarah slid to the floor and sobbed.

Jason and Clark

The two men sat under an umbrella at the table by the shimmering pool. Carole was doing a few quick laps before digging into the script again.

"Clark, what do you think about the war?" Jason asked, breaking the rhythmic sound of Carole's strokes.

"Aren't you getting ahead of yourself, old man? We aren't at war yet."

Jason paused and looked at Clark, wondering if this was his way of saying he didn't want to talk about it.

"No, not yet, but we will be, any day now. You don't put eleven million men in the field and expect nothing to happen."

Clark's smile evaporated and empathy filled his eyes. "No sport, I don't suppose you do. You got family over there?" he asked as he reached for a cigarette.

Jason nodded.

"I'm really sorry to hear it. I've been working on a little something to pull the studios and actors together once it starts – sort of a traveling Vaudeville act for the troops. All the old geezers I've talked to from the Great War complained about how they didn't feel supported. I'm looking to make sure the boys don't feel that way this time.

"Besides," he said, his jovial smile returning. "My blonde bombshell is one helluva weapon. No one will be able to resist her. Wet or dry." Clark put out his cigarette, stood up, gave a wink, took off his robe and dove in after Carole.

The war conversation was over, Jason was left to wonder about his own plans. What would he do once it began?

Miriam and the Radio

Miriam had succumbed to the habit-forming radio while Jason was away. Half hour heart-wrenching dramas, with heroines from all walks of life: Dr. Susan, Brenda Curtis, Big Sister, and Helen Trent, women facing the challenges of sick children, troubled marriages, unscrupulous business partners, dying friends and cheating husbands. Miriam would turn on the radio for background noise and then find herself sitting in a chair actually listening and worse yet, being caught up in the drivel.

And drivel it was. Jason would be appalled. He would shudder at the quality of the writing, but not Miriam. No, she sat through it, receiving the additional benefit of learning how Palmolive would leave her hands soft after washing dishes, how Ivory Flakes would make her silk stockings last longer, and that Double Certified Flour Bread would enable her children to grow up strong. It went on and on every day. As she listened she became increasingly embarrassed, like she was doing something illicit. There were poems to be written, art to be viewed, and theater to attend, instead she sat there rotting her brain.

Miriam wondered if the new RadioVision would be full of the same pablum. After all, the radio had been introduced as an educational tool, a way to bring people knowledge. Instead, it had warped into something akin to a Marvel comic book. She got up and turned off the large floor-standing radio just as Molly was expressing her love for Sam.

She would go for a walk instead. The weather was magnificent and while Jason might be missing a beautiful summer in New York, there was no reason for Miriam to sequester herself in the apartment, waiting for his random calls. The next time they spoke she would suggest fixing a regular time for his call so she could feel freer to go out.

She went into the bedroom. The bed beckoned, with the thought of a nap. Without Jason, to whom she had wholeheartedly dedicated herself, she felt lost. Again she questioned her desire for a child. Was it because she did not want to face this void in herself? She ignored the temptation to immerse herself in the escape of sleep and changed her shoes, leaving the apartment without a backward glance.

Carole and Clark

"Clark darling?"

150

WAR CORRESPONDENT

Nancy Ames - Casablanca

There is much to cover in this dispatch. It's dirty and dusty here in Northern Africa and desperation hangs in the air like the promise of rain.

In Europe eleven million armed troops stand ready for battle. While Prime Minister Chamberlain may be proven right, that "There will be peace in our time," it will not be realized until a dreadful battle has taken the lives of a good many of our brothers. And despite the PM's optimism, London and Paris are ghost towns. Britain has an added advantage having armed a million of its women for battle. Watch out Hitler!

The cynic in me recognizes that war is only interesting when profits are involved hence the 'cash and carry' policy put forth by Roosevelt is picking up steam in Congress. I believe Roosevelt is appealing to the greedy lobbyists while offering England an advantage over Germany. Since Britain has both the ships and the cash, she stands to benefit.

The Pact of Steel between Germany and Russia is something that the world should heed. Russia is now free to focus on reprisals against Japan while Germany is directing its attention toward attacking France and Britain.

One thing that has come from this deal of two devils (Hitler and Stalin) is that the American communists have all turned in their red cards and joined legitimate political parties. Those left standing behind their communist ideals will be shunned and ridiculed.

How could any U.S. citizen doubt that a war is coming? Look at the pictures of the 500,000 troops Hitler has amassed in Berlin. His air power alone is twice that of the Allies. The entire German economy is based on the manufacturing of tanks, ships, and other implements of destruction. The only thing Hitler is missing is gasoline, which will undoubtedly cause him to quickly invade the Middle East.

August

"My love?"

"Do you think I should do Jason's play?"

"What? What are you saying? If I didn't, would the man be practically living with us? It's a good play and he's been very patient with you, my little minx. Not all writers would cave in to your every whim as he has." Gable sat beside her on the divan where she stretched out pouting.

"What is it sugar? Are you afraid of doing a play? If you don't want to do it, you don't have to, but it isn't fair to lead Jason on. Have you seen how he sometimes looks off into the distance? It's his wife he's thinking about. He misses her terribly, he stays here for you, to meet your requests. If you're toying with him, sweets, you have to let him go."

Carole's eyes pooled with tears. "Clark, I don't know if I have it in me. What if it's a hit and I have to go on stage eight times a week for a year? That would kill me."

"Then define the length of the run. You set up the play, get it going, then someone else will take over."

"But that's just it. What if someone else does it better than me? I couldn't bear it."

Clark pulled her close, whispering softly, "Darling, there's no one who shines brighter than you in person, on the stage or on the big screen. You, my dear, are larger than life."

They held each other. They were equals: lovers, partners, and winners of life's grand prize. Clark knew that Jason had the same good fortune and wanted to see him reunited with his beloved.

"I tell you what," said Gable, "You and Jason make your final edits today. And we'll send him packing for home. Then you and I will go camping up at Big Bear. We'll live like slobs and shoot at things. Better yet I can watch you go skinny dipping in a cold mountain lake and get all goose pimpled." He beamed.

"You dirty old man. Let's go and then I can watch you shrink up...." He covered her mouth with his hand. When she wiggled loose and let out a holler.

"Yippee! Liza, LIZA, where are you? We need our things packed right away!" She danced around the living room. When she came back to stand in front of Gable, she said, "I'm ready, you know. I was just afraid they'd call me a fraud." He started to say something, but she shook her head. "I know it's crazy. But that's how I felt. Now I'm not worried, because I know Jason won't let me fail." She jumped back into Clark's lap with another elated, "Yippee!"

The Last Straw

The first time Bill hit Ernestine she thought it was a mistake. Upset over a missed dance step, the slap came out of nowhere and she didn't want to believe it. The second time there wasn't any doubt.

Having tripped over his own feet, he accused her of being clumsy. Drawing his hand back to hit her in the face, he reconsidered the show that evening and balled up his fist and hit her in the stomach instead. She collapsed to the floor. Then she threw up.

The entire time he stood over her, seething, waiting for her to fight back. Ernestine stayed down on the floor, hoping to gain time to think. She recognized Bill's assets as a dance partner, she might even be falling in love with him, but physical violence and humiliation were not going to be part of her life. Bill was damaged goods.

Ernestine knew he could not be trifled with, especially in his current rage. She would need to maneuver out of this relationship carefully or he might kill her.

Kill her? She had never thought of that. This man was actually capable of murder – why hadn't she seen it before? The good manners, cool temperament, fast wit, he seemed like a Cary Grant knock off. Yet beneath it all there was a man so angry, so abused, that his only recourse was to make someone else pay. Unfortunately, it seemed that he had decided it would be Ernestine.

She should have seen it coming. She had let remarks go by, like, "You've always had it easy – you don't know hard." And, "Stop whining bitch. I'm the one who has to carry you through all these dances." On both occasions she assumed he had too much to drink. Nevertheless, she overlooked the telltale signs and continued to enjoy the fan's adoration.

She remained crumpled on the floor. He would either regain his self-control, followed by remorse or he might kick her silly. She hoped for remorse.

"Get up. Get up, you stinking bitch," he screamed at her. The veins along the side of his temple were distended. His rage had not yet passed. There, with her head in her own filth, she retched again, this time uncontrollably spitting some of her bile on his shoes. She realized this might be it. The vomit might push him into the red zone of no return.

Instead it awoke in him a sense of decency, as though he had just walked through the door and found Ernestine lying on the floor.

"Ernestine, Ernestine are you all right? He bent down and lifted her gently. She knew not to flinch as he laid her down on the red sofa in the rehearsal room. He retrieved a wet a towel and stroked her face and brow. Ernestine watched him. She wondered once again, what breaks a man, causing him to split from his own self? It must have been something hideous. She didn't really want to know. All she knew for sure was that she needed to get as far away as possible from Bill Curran.

SEPTEMBER

Jason Heads Home

Jason decided to take the train home, not wanting to repeat his fateful flight out. There were times when the new Silver Stream diesel locomotive exceeded 100 miles per hour and Jason felt like he was flying.

Giddy from his success with the Gables over the last six weeks, he splurged and bought a compartment for himself so that he could spread out and work during the three-day trip.

Those final days had resembled theatrical rehearsals. Carole would test line after line to weigh its merits, insisting on performing in front of the gardener and maids. Who, for the most part, spoke only Spanish. But none of it mattered now. Carole would be good to her word and follow through. Should she waver, Clark would shore up any doubts.

Jason's current goal was to polish the script so that New York theatergoers would like it. The Gables were experts when it came to movies. They had helped turn The Cat's Pajamas into a wise crack-

155

ing, slapstick jaunt. However, what worked on the silver screen didn't always work in the theater, mostly because the audiences were not the same. Paying five dollars versus a nickel a ticket to see a performance meant expectations were higher.

Every idea would be leveraged in the end. The Gables' input had been invaluable because eventually, Jason would sell the script as a screenplay to one of the movie studios. Once the Broadway play was a hit, Jason would have a package deal, complete with a box office star.

He was certain Carole had struck on the same plan. That way, even if she flopped on Broadway she could reprise the role for the movie.

She didn't have to worry about whether or not the play would be a success. By virtue of her popularity alone, many who had never been to the theater before would want to see her in real life, much like Katharine Hepburn, currently on stage in the Philadelphia Story.

Jason sat back for a moment and watched the desert pass by outside his window. So much open space. So little water. Did anything really live out there? Occasionally a shack or ranch would dart past his window and he would imagine what it would be like to live in such isolation. Maybe there was a play in it, something along the lines of the Petrified Forest.

"Mr. Rothman?" The knock at the door was the Pullman porter.

"Yes Joseph?"

"Mr. Rothman, we be pullin' into Phoenix in a few minutes. You'll be able to stretch your legs if you'd like."

"Thank you Joseph. I might just do that." Jason realized it would be good to step outside and smell the desert air, a respite from his speeding bullet trajectory. He put on his shoes and jacket and straightened his tie.

As the train pulled into Phoenix he was surprised to see how large the town was. He knew about Arizona from the Almanac. It came in second to last in education, population, infant mortality, and literacy (second only to New Mexico). It had seemed a place to avoid, yet standing on the platform Jason could see the beginnings of a real city. The air smelled good and clean. Nothing like New York or

Los Angeles, although the plume from his train's engine stained the sky.

On the platform he noticed an enchanting young woman. She was tall and lean with yellow hair the color of quilted maple. She held a large white hat in her hands and wore a pale green summer dress. White piping accented the hem and a tiny print decorated the background, unfortunately he wasn't close enough to see the pattern. She wore stylish shoes that were surprisingly white considering the desert dust. He suspected she hailed from Phoenix. Jason realized she had caught him looking at her. He blushed, tipping his straw boater in acknowledgement.

She walked up to him and asked, innocently. "Sir, are you on this train?"

"Indeed, I am. Will you be joining us for the rest of our journey?"

"I'm going on to Philadelphia."

He smiled and couldn't stop himself from saying "I hope you brought something warmer for your trip back east." He hated himself the moment he said it. What if this was the only dress the woman owned? She quickly let him forget his indiscretion by laughing, a natural open laugh that made him want to know more about her.

"Oh no, I have an entire trunk of appropriate eastern styled clothing. You needn't fear for me sir."

Jason walked up to her and did something totally out of character. He held out his hand and said, "I'm Jason Rothman. I'm heading to New York. If you haven't any plans, let's have dinner together this evening."

"That would be delightful," she said, bewitching him. Her eyes were green and matched her dress, which he now saw was covered with shamrocks. The little white buttons were four-leaf clovers.

"Terrific. I'll put in a reservation for seven-thirty, if that's all right with you. Miss...?" He realized she had not shared her name yet.

"Betty Stern. Seven-thirty sounds perfect. I look forward to seeing you at dinner. " And as if on cue, the conductor blew his whistle and shouted, "All aboard." Jason helped Betty up into the car and Jason

September

WAR CORRESPONDENT
Nancy Ames - London

September 3, 1939 will be remembered as the day the Second World War began. An unimaginable event, occurring only twenty short years after the war to end all wars. It's no longer a matter of whether America will enter the war, but when. The industrial machine has moved into high gear. Roosevelt, Britain and France are prepared for the fight of their lives. Thank God Roosevelt will not sit back and allow America to encourage the reign of tyrants.

How the combatants measure up:

Units	Allies	Germany
Military ships of all kinds	377	28
Submarine	10	46
Aircraft	3164	3649

GERMANY
• Hitler's Final Solution for the Jews is ghettos
• Jews are no longer allowed to own radios
• South Africa and Canada have declared war on Germany
• Iraq breaks diplomatic relations with Germany
• German U-boats sink Swedish and British cargo boats
• An attempt was made on Hitler's life during the annual festivities at a Munich Beer Hall

POLAND
• Nazis, dressed as Poles, stage an attack on a radio station as an excuse for Germany to invade Poland
• Germany invades Poland. There is little to no hope for its survival
• Warsaw surrenders to Germany September 27th. Germany takes 150,000 prisoners
• Germans and Soviets divide Poland
• The Polish government flees to Paris in exile

EUROPE
• Winston Churchill is named First Lord of the Admiralty
• A German U-boat off the coast of Ireland sinks the British civilian liner Athenia. All aboard die, including American passengers
• Petrol rationing is introduced in Germany and Britain
• Lithuania is forced to come under Soviet control
• German U-boat penetrates English waters sinking British carriers

U.S.A
• Roosevelt declares a 'limited national emergency' in response to the outbreak of war
• Igor Sikorsky develops and flies first helicopter, which could prove useful in upcoming war

returned to his room. He felt as lightheaded as a teenager. Why he would feel this way about any woman, especially after weeks with Carole Lombard who never claimed his attention, remained a mystery to him.

Sarah and Buddy at the 21 Club

He sent a note with a spray of cymbidium orchids. It took a moment for Sarah to remember him - Bud Rawley. She hadn't heard from him since his last visit to the Plaza in February. The card mentioned that he'd just returned from Europe. She suspected he was beating a quick retreat, with the continent at war. He asked to see her. Actually he wrote, 'Love to see you any time, any place – how about lunch tomorrow?'

It made no sense that thinking about Buddy could make her smile. She barely knew him, except that he was rich, funny and a fan.

Lunch tomorrow with Mr. Rawley would work perfectly with her schedule. She wrote a quick reply and stepped out into the hall to ask the bellman to deliver it. Surprisingly the cymbidium delivery boy still stood outside her door.

"Miss is that your response?"

"Yes it is," she said with amazement.

"I'll take it to Mr. Rawley. He asked me to wait until you responded."

"How long were you to wait outside my door?"

He smiled sheepishly. "As long as it took Miss, I wasn't to rush you."

She laughed, "Well you're in luck. My answer is yes and that should mean a big tip for you. In the meantime," she pulled the quarter from her pocket that she had intended to give the bellman.

"Thank you Miss." And he took off down the corridor.

The next day Sarah met Buddy at the 21 Club, considered a trendy meeting place for the elite.

Buddy was already at the table when she arrived. He stood as she approached.

"Sarah, it's so good of you to come." He reached out to take her hand in greeting. "I regret that so much time has passed since our last meeting. I've been away, in Europe." An emotion Sarah couldn't identify passed over his face, quickly replaced by a bright smile.

"Is it as bad as they say?" she asked.

"Worse." He paused, clearly deciding how much he should share. "In fact it is much worse."

"Do you want to talk about it?" Sarah sat down before Buddy could pull out her chair.

He continued, "I know that many people here are repulsed by the notion of going to war, however, if they had seen what I've seen…"

"Tell me, I want to know."

He nodded. "I started my trip in London. The Brits are fully prepared. Their windows are taped or covered. Sandbags fill the streets. And yet people go on living, getting up and going to work, raising their children. Many are in the military. Everyone is already at war." He paused and took a sip of water, realizing that the story could easily get away from him.

"It must be tragic," she said. Despite the words her mood was still light. "People are so resilient. Look at us, we made it through the worst of the depression and at times I thought we'd all lay down and die."

"You're right, my dear. Nevertheless this is different. People in Europe also must consider chemical weapons that threaten their limited amounts of food and water. The population has become numb. If there is a silver lining it is that people are kinder to each other, charitable to strangers and friends, the way we were here during the height of the depression. Of course England went through the depression as well and now the war is what has greeted them just as they begin to emerge from economic ruin."

He caught the eye of the waiter.

"A bottle of Château Margaux, 1932, Brane-Cantenac." He turned again to Sarah. "I should stop my rambling long enough for you to order."

Sarah found herself extremely interested in what he had to say. She liked this man, his honesty, his passion and most of all his willingness to share. He treated her like a peer, despite their age difference. She felt that she could sit there all day listening to him. She ordered her usual.

"What kind of soup do you have today?"

"We have carrot and leek soup today. What would mademoiselle prefer?"

"Carrot please, and a house salad."

"Very good. And for you sir?"

"I'll have the filet mignon, baked potato, and broccoli."

"I'm sorry sir, we're only serving string beans today."

Bud Rawley looked up and remained silent until the waiter lifted his eyes from his pad and took in Buddy's face. Sarah saw what the waiter saw, a man who wouldn't be denied.

"We'll find you some broccoli sir."

"Thank you...and a salad."

"Very good sir." As the waiter ran off to fill the special request, Buddy turned his full attention back to Sarah.

"Please continue," she said her mood more somber now. "I'm very interested in hearing about the war from someone who's been there. I've been skeptical of what we're being told here at home."

"The rest gets pretty ugly. Are you sure you're up for it?"

"Absolutely."

"Well, I went to the continent after Britain. France is steeled against the impending onslaught, but she hasn't a chance. I have firsthand knowledge of her armament reserves and she's not prepared. She believes the Maginot Line, the extensive underground tunnel and bunker system, will save her, but it won't. It's the story of the ant and the grasshopper. Britain has been stockpiling like the ant and may withstand Germany. France has been the grasshopper. Too much good wine and pate." Right on cue the waiter proffered a bottle of wine for Buddy to assess the label. With his assent the wine was poured into both of their glasses and Buddy raised his glass to Sarah.

"To you Miss Karofsky. Thank you for joining me today."

"It's my pleasure Mr. Rawley." They smiled at each other, both noting how remarkably at ease they were in each other's company.

"Please go on, Mr. Rawley." She sensed he was leaving out the most disagreeable parts. "Are you sparing me the treatment of the Jews?"

"I apologize in advance for the indelicacy of this question. Are you Jewish Miss Karofsky?" he appeared chagrined at having asked the question.

"It's perfectly alright. My mother's Jewish, my father a Methodist. They are – were – in love. Religion never got in the way. I was raised to choose the religion that best suited my nature. At present, I've not found one. That is to say, I consider myself spiritual, just not very religious. My mother still has or had family in Germany. We haven't heard from them since the war broke out."

"Then I'm about to give you some sad news. I worked my way into the heart of Europe, what was Austria, Romania, Poland and finally, Germany." He took a deep sigh. "What I'm going to tell you will sound like fiction. That's why I believe most of the American press has not fully reported back to its citizens. They think no one will believe it. They fear that their audience will reject the notion that people could be so cruel to each other."

She offered, "Yet look at how we treat the colored. It shouldn't be such a big leap."

"Indeed there is a difference. Sarah, Jews are treated worse than animals. They're branded, with yellow stars sewn onto their clothing. They're not allowed to work, own property or associate with non-Jews. They've been rounded up into the dirtiest parts of the cities, without food or water and left to starve.

A few are allowed outside of the ghetto during the day to do odd jobs, but they're kicked and spat upon by the populace. It's as if all the anger the Germans felt about losing the Great War and the deprivation they experienced afterward has been leveled at the Jews. It's a frighteningly irrational behavior, emanating from the most rational people I've ever worked with. The paradox is beyond belief."

"Mr. Rawley, how is it you were in Germany?" asked Sarah.

He met her gaze. He knew he would have to tell her eventually. What good would a marriage be without absolute honesty, and marriage, after all, was what he had in mind. He knew it from the moment they had met that one day he would ask her to marry him.

After all these months in Europe, his one goal was to come back and be with her. His mind was made up. He also knew he needed to move slowly so as not scare her. Yet here she was, fearless, with the ability to face the unknown with an open heart and mind.

"I'm an arms dealer Miss Karofsky." He let a beat or two go by so that she could absorb his meaning. "I sell weapons all over the world."

"But I thought the Neutrality Act forbids you from selling weapons to our allies or the aggressors?"

"You're quite right, but as with anything involving business, men are capable of finding a way around such impediments. You see, we're not allowed to sell a plane to the Europeans, yet we can sell them the aluminum, steel, rivets, and all the things that go into the making of the plane. What's more we can sell our expertise and go there to build factories and train their staff to assemble the planes. The treaty is a farce and should be eliminated, because it's hurting our allies. They depended on purchasing ready-made supplies from us and didn't build out their factories in time. The Brits in particular are at a distinct disadvantage. The Germans have quickly converted their manufacturing plants into airplane factories. And we helped them do it."

Sarah's initial reaction was to walk out. This might not be his fault, but someone was to blame. She knew this was how the world worked and that nothing would stop someone from making money. Sarah had lived among the rich long enough to know that. She took a deep, composing breath before she continued.

"Mr. Rawley, did you sell weapons to the Germans?"

He knew the wrong answer would cause her to rise to her feet and walk away forever. Still, he would not lie to her.

"Miss Karofsky, please hear me out." He could see her tensing. "This is going to sound like *Ripley's Believe It or Not*, but please bear with me. Under the Neutrality Act of 1935, if I sell my wares to Britain or France I must sell to Germany. Since I would prefer to sell only to the allies, my only recourse is to sell Germany my low-grade product at a premium price. I sell my highest quality product to the allies at deep discounts. It's the best way I can help without breaking the law."

"Mr. Rawley that is absurd. Why is our government supporting these inane policies?"

"It was not intentional Miss Karofsky. Even today many good senators believe they're doing the right thing. The problem is they rarely leave their little sphere on Washington. They simply do not realize the mess they're creating in Europe."

"Can't you tell them?"

A faint cynical smile appeared on Bud's face. "They won't listen to me. Not for the reasons you might suspect. They won't listen to me because they feel they have given me what I need to get rich, so why should there be any further discussion – except to ask for kick-backs."

"That is crazy." Sarah placed her chin on her hand ignoring the fact her elbows were on the table. She was thinking hard. "There must be something we could do," she mused out loud.

Buddy ached to say, 'There is. You could marry me.' But he knew the time was not right. "On the bright side, a few of us, with the help of the Poles, were able to secure a couple of German Enigma machines. One is in France and the other in Britain. These machines will allow the allies to translate coded German messages." He hesitated before he added, "Miss Karofsky, I've not come to the worst part of my story."

She raised her head in surprise.

"You mean it gets worse?"

"I'm afraid so. The Jews have had everything taken from them, their money, homes and dignity. And yet the Reich continues to levy taxes. Hitler assumes the allies will pay it. There's a hitch. One the Germans have not considered. No one will pay the ransom."

Sarah began to protest. "Why...."

"Hear me out," he interrupted. "It's not because people do not want to pay. There are other issues. Britain and France cannot afford to pay. Nor can any other country except the U.S. And while America could pay or could rally to extend itself to save these poor wretched souls, they will not do so because of their fierce neutrality stance. What's more, anti-Semitism is rampant in this country. There is fear at the highest levels that if our government bails out the Jews we'll need to bring them here. Hitler's edict states clearly that whomever pays the ransom must also remove the Jews and keep them."

The waiter arrived with their salads. Buddy was relieved to have a momentary reprieve. Sarah sat silently grasping the complexity of the situation. She spoke first.

"So if no one pays the ransom, what will become of the Jews? They're not allowed to work, right?" Bud nodded in agreement. "Then what will become of several million people?"

"I'm sorry, Miss Karofsky, I hadn't meant to invite you here to tell you this and here we are, in the first fifteen minutes, discussing the war."

"Mr. Rawley, please answer my question."

"They'll die." He said, trying to gauge her reaction. "Hitler has not hidden his intention to annihilate the Jews, but I don't think even he had a plan to kill millions. He knows that he can't have people dying around the countryside from starvation. It would bring cholera. If he let's them live they might rise up against him. I believe he'll bring German precision to bear on the problem of how to kill millions without damaging his own country through bombings or mass graves. This is a nightmare."

As his words sank in and Sarah grasped the enormity of the situation, she began to cry. She didn't want Buddy to see her like this. She leapt to her feet and ran toward the women's lounge, almost knocking over a waiter in her path. By the time Buddy reached her she was whimpering like an injured animal. What she had heard was beyond comprehension, the coming of an evil so great that it might consume the world. He took her in his arms and stroked her red hair.

Between gasps for air Sarah asked him, "How is this possible? And if people know of it, why can't they stop it?" He said nothing and instead rocked her, murmuring it would be all right.

Sarah realized Buddy knew more and she suspected he had a plan. As her tears stopped and her breathing returned to normal she wanted to know what it was. She wanted to be a part of it. Here was a man with a view from the top of the world and he wanted her. Together they would make a difference. Sarah had found her mission

165

and knew her destiny for the first time in her life.

Jason on the Train

Betty Stern appeared in the dining car precisely at seven-thirty. She was dressed in a chic somber traveling outfit of brown and cream.

"Good evening," said Jason, bowing slightly.

"How do you do Mr. Rothman?"

"Please call me Jason."

"Isn't it a little early for such informalities?" A smile revealed a dimple in her left cheek.

"On trains all formalities are erased. It's only on terra firma these things remain rigid."

"Ah, you're a writer then?" She watched his response carefully, as she sat down.

"You have me in one guess Miss Holmes. Indeed, I am a writer. And you're an actress? I should warn you, Hollywood is in the opposite direction," he parried, while pointing West.

"You, sir, would make a terrible Dr. Watson." She wore her golden hair in a loose fitting snood, the latest rage. "Would you like to guess again?"

"You live on an Indian reservation and teach English to the savages." This brought a frown to her face. Before she could respond he quickly added, "I'm sorry, I didn't mean to be such a beast. I'm truly not a racist, I'm just trying too hard to impress you."

She was more serious now, no longer playing the coquette that he had met on the train platform.

"Are you married, Mr. Rothman?"

"I am, to an amazing woman, Miriam. She's a poet."

"Then why are you flirting with me?" She said it in all seriousness and her face became emotionless.

"In truth I don't know. Maybe because I've been cooped up working for the last six weeks and haven't had any amusing companionship." Jason relaxed. He would henceforth be himself. It had been fun being someone else for a few hours.

"Ah, then, let me enlighten you as to what it is I do and you can decide if you wish to pass any more time with me." She looked over the menu leaving their conversation hanging between them.

Jason assumed she wouldn't pick up the thread until after they had ordered, surprisingly she continued. She simply didn't look up at him.

"I work for a man named Martin Dies," she said. "Have you heard of him?"

Jason racked his brains. He had heard of him, but where? The name conjured up images of Washington D.C.

"Is he a politician?"

She chortled at this and then locked eyes with Jason's. There was actually something viperous about her.

"I suppose he has political aspirations in the future. At present Mr. Dies runs the office on Un-American Activities. He's looking to eliminate the Red element in our population." Then she added with a condescending note, "And no, I don't mean American Indians."

'Oh shit,' was all Jason could think. She was more dangerous than a rattlesnake. This woman could bring down powerful individuals and she knew it. He had meant to learn more about the group and their agenda while he was in Hollywood. Instead the play took all of his time and he had never gotten around to learning the details. Now he wished he could remember anything. It was probably safe to guess that her boss hated Jews and writers.

"How nice for you," he said with equal condescension.

"I thought I should tell you now before you had the opportunity to incriminate yourself."

"What is your employer after?"

"He's just looking to make sure that certain Americans recognize which side their bread is buttered on."

"I see. By destroying the Constitution?"

"Ooh, we haven't had our soup yet. Shall we table this part of the conversation until dessert?"

"Fine," said Jason his expression sullen. He'd been in such a good mood since seeing her on the platform. All ruined in a few short minutes. And the critics said his plays moved too quickly.

"Let's go back to my earlier question. What were you doing in

Phoenix?" he asked, assuming it was a safe conversational topic.

"Actually in Flagstaff. I have family there that I haven't seen in years, cousins on my mother's side. We grew up together and I wanted to see them on my way back to New York.

"And how were they?"

"Older, a mixture of happy and disappointed with life, as perhaps we all are."

"Where's home for you?" asked Jason.

"I live in Virginia."

"Where's your family from?" He was trying to stay with neutral topics, wanting to keep as far away from politics as possible.

"Excuse me," the waiter appeared. "What would you like for dinner this evening?"

"How's the fish?" questioned Betty.

"In Phoenix?" interjected Jason. Then she laughed that pretty little laugh. It sounded like music.

"I'll have the Cornish hen please."

"Soup for me, with a salad please," said Jason. The waiter nodded and left.

"Are you reducing?" she asked quizzically.

"Maybe a little. It's hard when you travel and are outside your daily routines. It's easy to find yourself eating any old thing."

"I know a bit about that. My job takes me all over the country. I always seem to be on the move."

"Where do you like best?"

"I'd say the west." She looked out the window at the landscape that was now all but hidden by the inky blue of twilight. "The west holds mysteries that you don't see back east. And the landscape is so foreign, I find it compelling."

"Do you hike?"

"As much as I can. And you Mr. Rothman, how do you get your exercise?"

"I walk, mostly in Central Park, but frequently the length of Manhattan. I like to experience the different neighborhoods that exist across the island."

"I'm not that familiar with New York. That's not to say I don't go there regularly, but not enough to understand its people." She picked up a breadstick and pointed it at him. "So what type of writer are you?"

"A good one," Jason mocked. "I write plays."

"Like Mr. Odets?"

That brought a smile to Jason's face. "I think you would find my recent plays a little less radical than Mr. Odets and probably not as worthy. I do sitting room comedies. Non-political in nature."

"Where do you stand on the war Mr. Rothman?"

"Am I on the record Miss Stern?"

"Does it matter?"

"In a word. Yes."

"Off the record then."

Jason became serious. "I'm not sure you know the difference between on or off record, but I'll tell you anyway, that I'm worried. I'm concerned that the British are the only ones doing anything to help the Jewish refugees. Does your boss care at all about these things or is his only concern the belief that we in the arts are somehow dedicated to bringing down the American way of life?"

It was a little pointed, Jason's ire had risen to the surface. His relatives were dying and being put in concentration camps. He didn't know what to do. He made a conscious decision in the last few years to keep politics out of his art. His mission to take his audiences minds away from reality for a short time and give them entertainment. And now to be accused of something he hadn't done. He couldn't wait to get started on a new play.

Betty stared at him for a prolonged moment seeing that he had worked himself up over the question. She responded evenly, "I don't know what my boss thinks about the Jewish situation in Europe. I do know he's dedicated to keeping the U.S. out of the war. However, he's also a realist and knows the war will come. When it does, he intends to round up all the Reds in this country in order to eliminate any spies living within our own borders."

"And does and your boss believe artists are the conveyors of secret messages?"

"No, however, they do have great influence over the masses. The messages they send embedded in their work are more powerful than all the stumping senators in the world."

"And you? Where do you stand Miss Stern?"

"I want us to stay out of the war. But I don't have an answer to your question about the Jews. Those that are still in Europe should have left long ago. I don't know what will happen to those that have remained."

"But it's their home, where their families have lived for generations. Where should they have gone?" Jason asked almost pleading for a real answer.

"I didn't say it was right. I'll even go on the record to say that it's wrong. Look what we have done to the American Indian, yet they still live on and we have put them in concentration camps of a sort. Perhaps that's what the future holds for the Jews in Europe."

"Perhaps." Jason said slumping back in his chair and playing with his fork.

"I really didn't come here to entrap you Mr. Rothman. Honestly, I didn't even know you were on this train. Ironically, you are on my list of people to contact in New York."

A sharp wave of fear gripped Jason – so he was being watched, his paranoia justified. Wait until he told Miriam. Betty continued, "Please don't let my profession inhibit us from having a perfectly fine conversation. I know your sympathies are with your people and whatever it'll take to free them is what you'll do. It has nothing to do with political affiliation."

"Miss Stern, forgive me, I'm not feeling well. I'm going to return to my compartment."

This startled her and she knew she wouldn't see him for the rest of the trip.

"Alright then, before you go, I'll get to the point. What do you know of Karl Klyne?"

Out of the Dark
by Alan Stipple

Now that the war is at our doorstep will anyone talk of anything else? Will art focus on patriotic themes? Will we see a return of the pro-war musicals like *Yankee Doodle Dandy*? This theatergoer hopes not. Now is a time to stiffen our resolve to leave the conflict 'over there'.

Artists who only last month had shows in the Village exploring inner truth, are now producing posters promoting the war and its machinery. You don't have to be Red to see that the war is an excuse to prop up the economy. So there you have it. Come after me, Mr. J. Edgar Hoover!

THEATER:
Morning's at Seven
Written by Paul Osborn, is a light romp into middle age and beyond. The play consid-ers, as Robert Frost suggests, the road less travelled.

MOVIES:
★★★★★ *The Women*
Hollywood's best actresses get together to rag on men and each other. Our favorite, Anita Loos, wrote the screen-play with a little unaccredited help from F. Scott Fitzgerald and directed by George Cukor. *The Women* first delighted audiences on Broadway as a Clare Boothe Luce play. A must see for all you felines out there. Meow.

★★★★☆ *Golden Boy*
Odets' Pulitzer Prize master-piece. Acted brilliantly by newcomer William Holden who plays an aspiring violin-ist turned bad by Barbara Stanwyck. And Ms. Stanwyck is just the girl to make a good man go bad.

September

Jason couldn't believe he actually thought this woman attractive. "I know the name. I believe we were introduced at an art opening this past winter. That's all I can tell you." With that he stood up and dropped his napkin on the plate.

"Safe journey to you Miss Stern."

"And to you as well Mr. Rothman."

The waiter bringing the meals watched Jason leave.

Miriam, Alex, and Bill

Miriam missed Jason so much that while he was away, she wouldn't allow herself to dream of his return. After his call giving her the date and time of his arrival home, she let herself imagine him back in her arms. In less than three days he would be with her.

To celebrate she decided to go out for dinner, something she hadn't done in the six weeks he had been away. She put on her favorite dress intricately braided her blonde hair into a work of art and headed for their favorite steak house on Sixth Avenue. Miriam decided, if there was a good movie playing at Radio City Music Hall she would go to that.

The little blue hat and the powder blue gloves she wore accented her navy dress, which highlighted her violet eyes.

"Good evening, Mrs. Rothman," George the doorman called out as she crossed the lobby.

"Good evening, George. How are you this evening?" She could barely contain herself. Even her feet were happy wanting to dance, run, or at least skip.

"I can't complain Ma'am. It's been cooling down steady since around four o'clock. A breeze is coming up off the East River."

"That's great George."

He looked at her curiously. It wasn't that great.

"What's up Mrs. R?"

"Mr. Rothman is coming home. He'll be here in a couple of days."

"Gave up on all that California sunshine huh?"

The mention of California took some of the wind out of her sails, still she refused to be deflated by the mere name of a place that existed three thousand miles away. A place that no longer held her husband.

"I'm going to dinner George. I'll see you later."

The pleasant early fall evening had drawn many of her neighbors outside. Miriam relished the warm days of September, even as the sweat ran between her breasts.

The little steak house in the modest four story building adjacent to Rockefeller Center was just south of Radio City Music Hall. As she approached from Fifty-Fourth Street, she could see the Theater's lights. The huge neon sign stood out in relief against the darkening blue sky. As she came closer she saw that the marquee boasted Wuthering Heights. She knew it starred Laurence Olivier and Merle Oberon. Miriam had met Olivier when she and Jason were in England attending theater in the West End. He was charming and handsome, a superior actor with an equally strong appeal for both men and women.

She looked at the times posted at the ticket counter and saw there was a show at seven. She decided to buy a ticket to avoid the inevitable line later. Tickets prices at Radio City were always more than a regular movie theater, because there was a floorshow and a terrific organist who played during intermission.

After purchasing the ticket, she walked down the street and up the stairs to the restaurant. The maître d' remembered her, despite the fact that she and Jason hadn't been there in over a year.

"Right this way Mrs. Rothman, I have a nice table for you." She was pleased to see it was off by itself, away from the thick clouds of cigar smoke. Here Miriam could enjoy her five-dollar dinner. The price of a pair of shoes she thought. But this was a celebration and she knew the meal would be sublime and one she'd remember.

Just after her desert and coffee arrived, a tall stranger appeared at her table and sat down. It took a moment before she recognized him as the rude man from the store last spring. "Sir, I'm leaving. It's not appropriate for you to join me."

"Now, now, we're old friends. What in the world could be wrong with you and I catching up over coffee?" said Bill smugly.

"Sir, I do not know you and I'll be forced to call the waiter and have you removed if you do not leave at once."

"Oh no, you won't do that. After all, where's your husband? Somewhere studying? He looked like a bookworm. Does he write encyclopedias?" He leaned back, puffing on a large cigar, the smoke blowing in Miriam's face.

"For your information he's a great playwright." She bit her tongue. No reason to give this cad any real information.

The maitre 'd approached the table, "Mr. Curran, how nice to see you. You know Mrs. Rothman? You artist types stick together ehh?"

"You're an artist?" asked Miriam incredulously.

"Pretty unlikely, huh? Yeah, I'm a dancer. I headline at the Rainbow Room. I guess your husband doesn't take you out much." He looked around. "Hey where is he? You're not here alone are you?" He spoke as if she were Little Red Riding Hood.

"No, I'm..., well..., I'm alone for dinner, but meeting him next door for the movies in a few minutes."

"That's perfect. I was about to leave. I'll wait for him with you. That way you'll have protection from the big bad wolves of the city." He smiled, stuck his cigar in his mouth and stood to help Miriam out of her seat. She couldn't tell if he meant it or was using the opportunity as a scam. She also didn't know how she was going to get rid of him once on the street.

They walked the block and a half to Radio City Music Hall, and stood before the large brass doors, bathed in the blue neon light. Three doormen were attending the lobby. Miriam felt safer. Bill tossed his cigar into the street and pulled out a cigarette case. He offered one to Miriam. She refused.

"Why are you bothering me, sir? I just wish to be left alone. I don't know you, please go away." Miriam was feeling braver. She could see a policeman across the street.

"Why Madame, I'm crushed. You have dinner with me and then throw me away like so much rubbish. How cruel." Bill was ready to make a scene if Miriam wanted one. No dame was going to get the upper hand on Bill and what's more, he had some unfinished business with her. He doubted she was meeting anyone, in which case, he had plans for her during the next couple of hours until his floor-show began.

174

"It's Miriam right? Now come on little lady, be nice and I'll be real nice." He leered at her and for the first time Miriam was frightened.

"I beg your pardon. You may not use my name. Please go away or I'll call a policeman." He reached over and grabbed her roughly. He placed his arm around her and she suddenly realized that she couldn't defend herself against this man. He whispered into her ear.

"If you cause a ruckus I'll tell the cop that it's a domestic squabble and you know he'll believe me. Then things will go much harder for you." He paused, "In fact why don't we go now. You're not meeting anyone." He began to move her away from the door, when Alex greeted them.

"Miriam Rothman? Why, Mrs. Rothman, what a pleasure to see you again. Alex Bridges. We met at the theater. Your husband introduced us." Actually it was one of Miriam's friends, but Alex had registered that something was amiss and decided to invoke Jason's name. The menacing stranger was holding Miriam a little too tightly.

"And you sir? I'm Alex Bridges."

Bill ignored Alex's outstretched hand, "Yeah, yeah. Write me a letter. Miriam and I were just leaving to discuss a plot."

Miriam looked up at Alex, tears forming in her beautiful eyes. He could smell her fear.

"Is that right Miriam? I thought you and I were going to the movies this evening. I was looking forward to seeing this picture." He spoke to Miriam, but looked at Bill. "Besides I already have the tickets." He began to fumble in his pockets.

Bill's ire was up. He was ready to fight for Miriam like a dog over a bone.

"No way, bud. She's coming with me."

"No, I'm not." Miriam kicked Bill in the shins and launched herself at Alex, who immediately placed a protective arm around her.

Bill pulled himself up to his full height. Alex would have done the same, but knew the gesture would appear comical.

"You seem like another one of those sissy college boys to me" He turned to Miriam, "Is that what you like, bookworms and sissies? I bet you've never had a real man. Why I'm just the...." He paused and stared at Alex. In a low, feral voice he said, "Hey, I know you."

Alex hoped against hope that Bill didn't know him. That he couldn't place him with a different woman every month. Alex didn't want his life spelled out so vividly in front of Miriam.

Alex began to guide Miriam toward the door and they had almost reached it when Bill grabbed his shoulder and spun him around. Miriam fell towards the building but Alex stumbled towards the street. People were beginning to notice the scuffle.

"You bring married women to the club," said Bill, "I see you all the time. You're a high priced call girl." Bill looked at Miriam with loathing, as he assumed she was on a 'date' with Alex. "Are you telling me you didn't go with me in order to get it off with this low life?" Bill spit on the ground. "You disgust me, bitch."

Just then a policeman joined them, billy club in hand.

In a thick Irish brogue he asked, "What seems to be the trouble here?"

"No trouble officer," said Miriam. She didn't want any publicity, certainly not this sort, with Jason on his way home. "These two gentleman were just arguing over the war. You know how lively these political arguments can get."

"Well keep it down. This is a public street. Take it home if you be wantin' to fight." He looked up at the marquee. "Or go to the movie, why don't you? They say it's a pip." He motioned his stick to the posters. "That Olivier, he's some actor, even if he is a bloody Englishman."

The four stood staring at each other. The policeman spoke next.

"So what's it goin' to be? Who's movin' on first?"

Bill spoke up, "Mr. Bridges, how about you and I go somewhere and we settle our differences."

"I would, except I promised to take this charming lady to the movies. We'll have to settle our differences later."

"Good call," said the officer.

"I won't forget this, college boy. Next time you show up at the Rainbow Room, I'll be waiting." He looked at Miriam. "This isn't over. I'll be seeing you around."

Damn, now Alex recognized him. Bill Curran, the dancer at the

Rainbow Room.

"Let's go inside Miriam." He turned back, "Thank you officer."

"Just doin' my duty." The four moved away from each other. Inside the doors of the theater Miriam tried to compose herself.

"Thank you Mr. Bridges. I'm afraid I was in a bit of mess out there."

"How do you know that man? He's very dangerous."

"I know, and no, I don't know him. I work at Bergdorf's and he came in one night at closing and started harassing me. Luckily Jason showed up," she paused as the emotion of the moment descended upon her. Alex guided her to the couch in the lobby.

"It's over, you're safe." He rubbed her back lightly as she leaned forward gulping the air.

"I had gone out to dinner to celebrate. My Jason's coming back from California and I wanted to celebrate." She began to cry and Alex held her.

She looked up, with tears streaming down her face. "But what about you? Won't that man cause you trouble?"

Alex thought a moment. "Perhaps he will, but it was trouble I had to face sooner or later." He decided to tell her. No one knew and saying it out loud would make it real. "You see I'm an architect and I couldn't get any work and one thing led to another..."

Miriam put her hand on his. She already knew, "These past few years have made us all do things we never thought possible." Miriam was not one to take the high ground where people were concerned. She left morality to the soapbox orators in the park.

"Alex, why don't you join me for the movie? I have one ticket but I'd be happy..." she was going to offer to buy him one, but then realized the awkwardness of the situation.

"No, Mrs. Rothman. You really shouldn't be seen with me." He studied his manicured fingers. "That monster was right. Being with me could be bad for your reputation."

"I'm not worried about that. Please come to the movies with me."

"But your husband?"

"My husband will want to shake your hand for interceding this evening." She lifted his chin.

"Have you anywhere else to go? Any previous engagement?" She hated that she had phrased it like that. There were landmines everywhere.

"Why no."

"Then it's settled. You get a ticket and I'll get the popcorn."

He hesitated, unable to ignore the feeling that this woman was a friend who wanted nothing from him, other than his company. Alex felt a genuine relief that he had not experienced for a long time. He decided to go with her.

"Good," Miriam said, "And afterward you can put me in a cab and my doorman will make sure I get inside safe and sound."

Just like a woman, Alex mused, always thinking ahead.

He realized that tomorrow he would have to make some hard decisions. Bill Curran having his number would make it impossible to go to one of the best clubs in the city. His current 'profession' would have to be altered by content or geography. He decided to worry about that tomorrow.

Karl and Jason

Karl went down to Penn Station to meet an old friend coming in from Chicago. A musician friend he hadn't seen for years and who was going to try his luck at the clubs in New York. Karl had agreed to let him sleep on the floor of his humble abode while he looked for a gig.

As the first class passengers disembarked, Karl saw Jason Rothman among them. They had met briefly at the Labor League art exhibit in Harlem.

"Mr. Rothman."

Jason tried to place the face and then recalled Karl, from the art show. He remembered that he had liked Karl, even if he was with a sloshed Hemingway.

"Hello there. I'm sorry, I'm bad with names. It's Karl isn't it?"

"You're not so bad with names. Karl Klyne at your service. Were you out in Chicago?"

"No, California. I've been away for almost six weeks." In a flash

Jason recalled the dinner with Betty two days ago. It was Karl that she wanted know about. How odd that he should be here now, meeting the train.

"Where's the tan? I thought everyone who went to California came back with a tan." He laughed good-naturedly.

"No tan I'm afraid. I spent my time indoors working on a script." Jason looked over his shoulder, back at the train. "I haven't stopped yet, I've been holed up in my compartment for the past three days.

"You know, don't you?" Karl's expression became gravely serious. "You know about the war?"

All Jason could do was nod.

Karl continued, "I know many of the German people are against it. There have been demonstrations. The elected German officials seem deaf to the protests of their constituents." He paused and studied Jason who seemed to be taking the news hard.

"Would you like a cigarette?" Karl asked as he pulled Jason off to the side, out of the passenger traffic.

"Yes, but I have my own." Jason took out a pack and offered a Camel to Karl, who accepted it as an act of solidarity.

Karl continued, "I still have family in Germany. I keep begging them to leave. They hate Hitler and everything he stands for, yet they think they'll be able to serve the German people if they remain, perhaps inhibit some of the insanity." He gave a wry chuckle. "Imagine, there are members of my family that are more idealistic than me."

"Have the bombs fallen yet?" Jason instinctively looked up towards the sky, but could only see the beautiful arched roof of Penn Station.

"Warsaw has been pummeled and the rest of Poland captured. Warsaw is the only city still holding out. Unfortunately, it's only a matter of days. The Brits have not begun any type of retaliation bombing yet."

Jason didn't want to believe it. He had hoped that Hitler would stop after annexing Czech-Slovakia. Perhaps the murder of the Romanian Prime Minster by a Nazi youth would cause Hitler to cease his aggression and be content. But Jason knew, deep down, that an insane glutton like Hitler would never be satisfied.

Jason continued his thought aloud, "Italy is set to take over Albania and the Soviet Union will take Finland. After that, I believe we're in for a long bloody battle. I had hoped the U.S. would mediate the madness. If only Theodore Roosevelt were still alive."

"Yes, Theodore Rex. He would have been a good match for Hitler. But as it is, the American people don't want us in this war. And whether they do or don't, the industrialists have figured out they can make more money staying on the sidelines and supplying both sides rather than getting involved and cutting their profits in half," said Karl.

"War, in the end, is nothing more than a lesson in economics isn't it?" Jason took a long deep pull on his cigarette, then threw it to the ground and stamped it out under his foot.

"I'm afraid you're right." Karl paused, "but I'm working to keep us out of this war. Other friends of mine are active in getting friends and family out of Europe. Do you have family in Europe, Mr. Rothman?"

This conversation made Jason almost desperate to get home and hold Miriam. Abruptly he pulled his hand from his coat pocket and thrust it out to Karl. "It was good seeing you. Keep up the good work. I need to get home to my wife."

"I understand. Take this with you. Read it if you wish. It's the English translation of Hitler's Mien Kampf. The particularly relevant sections are highlighted. Let me warn you, it's disturbing reading." With that Karl held out his hand to shake Jason's, "I hope to see you again soon. And perhaps by next year the war will be behind us."

Jason nodded, but neither man believed the war would be anything but a long and protracted ordeal.

OCTOBER

The Starlight Club

Ernestine loathed even being near Bill. She had come to expect his blows when they were out of the public eye. The good news was that the violence usually occurred at the studio and Bill had mostly stopped coming to rehearsals. Ernestine was leaving town. She planned with caution, fully aware that to make a move too quickly would be folly, because Bill would kill her.

After plying a few waiters with ten-dollar bills, Ernestine discovered that Bill worked for Meyer Lansky and that it was Lansky's connections that were propelling Bill and Ernestine's career. Meyer was using Bill to access New York's elite, for his own purposes.

Ernestine's dream of creating a new dance form was over. Meyer Lansky ran Murder Incorporated and he didn't let his partners leave on their own volition. Ernestine would need to start over, somewhere far away and with a new name. She had decided to go to Australia and she was ready to leave tonight.

Wanting to avoid Bill in the dressing room, she sat in the ladies lounge, before the first set. The Starlight Club had a large and comfortable lounge area complete with couches and makeup tables. Each vanity contained French cosmetic samples to entice women to purchase the products in the future. As Ernestine played with a tube of lipstick she wondered what would become of the manufacturer now that the war had come?

She awoke from her daydream and began touching up her stage makeup. A woman in her early thirties entered and sat down at a vanity beside Ernestine. The lounge was empty save for the two of them and the old woman who catered to the patrons by providing safety pins, combs, perfume and smelling salts.

The young woman wore a beautiful gown by Elsa Schiaparelli; a black crepe number slung low in the front and back, decorated with glass beads and sequins. Her skirt flared out just below her derrière all the way to the floor like a peacock's train of feathers. Her shoes were black heels that continued the sequin theme. Her dark hair fell about her beautiful face in ringlets.

Ernestine's trained eye recognized the woman's make-up and hair had taken over an hour to prepare and yet she could also see this was not a pampered society woman. Those women were desperate for attention and required that other women notice them. This woman barely glanced at Ernestine. She just sat down, reviewed the damage and after deciding it was acceptable went into a stall.

Ernestine was curious. It had been a long time since she had spoken to another woman about anything beyond the weather. As a ballerina, Ernestine had always felt she had to stay aloof. Now that she was about to begin a new life, one that didn't include the competition of her past, she found she wanted to speak with this woman.

Kim McIntyre emerged from the toilets, washed her hands and turned to take one more glance at herself in the mirror when Ernestine spoke.

"Hello, I'm Ernestine Robertson. I'm the performer tonight." Ernestine held out her hand.

"How do you do?" Kim was taken by surprise. Why was this woman speaking to her? Kim had so much on her mind that it was only with an effort that she could bring her attention into the moment.

"I'm sorry to bother you, do you have a minute?" Ernestine asked.

Kim was uncomfortable. Her boss was waiting at the table. Not that she particularly wanted to be with him, but that it seemed rude to leave him out there unaccompanied.

"Is there something I can do for you?" Kim asked with hesitation.

"What do you do? I mean, I can tell you're a career woman, which is unusual for the patronesses of this establishment. I'm curious, what's your career?"

"I'm the curator at the main art museum at the World's Fair," she said with pride.

"Very impressive. That's what I thought, that you managed something important. Tell me have you ever thought of doing anything else? Trying another profession I mean?"

"Excuse me?" asked Kim confused by the question.

"I'm asking because I've been a dancer since I was ten years old. I'm twenty-seven now and thinking about changing careers. Of course I don't know anything else, but it seems like this might be a good time to be born a woman. The depression seems to have given us a level playing field. Women are entering non-traditional professions and considered equals to men." She looked at Kim, who didn't understand.

"Even in my own family," Ernestine continued, "there are women doctors and lawyers, musicians and politicians. It seems anything is possible, especially in the arts. Don't you agree?"

Kim sensed something amiss, that this woman was in trouble. At the museum she had seen strangers reach out from their malaise, needing to share a simple kindness. Kim decided to sit and listen. She would return to her boss with a story to share, once Ernestine began her dance.

"I'm not sure I'd use art curation as your measuring stick," Kim said. "Truth is, my curator position is relatively new. I've been an artist for ten years with little success. My current position has a lot to do with being in the right place at the right time."

"Ah, but don't you believe experience is cumulative? That you wouldn't have been in the right place if not for all the years that had gone before?" Ernestine looked at Kim with unnaturally large eyes. Her face was made up for her performance, so all of her features seemed bigger than life.

"Perhaps." Kim read Ernestine's desperation. "You want out, don't you? I can feel it." Before Ernestine could respond Kim raised her hand to stop her. "Go to Hollywood. If your theory is right, someone with your experience should move to Hollywood. There's no other place on earth where women have as much clout. There are great women actors, designers, directors, writers, cameramen, you name it, the world would be your oyster and you could leverage all of your expertise and talents."

Ernestine began to argue, yet something told her to keep quiet and listen. And in that moment, her path became clear. She knew what to do next and how to do it. She began to shake her head slightly from side to side. "I knew there was a reason I stopped you. I have never done anything like that before. Thank you," Ernestine stood and held out her hand, "I'll be in Hollywood. Thank you again."

Ernestine left the room and Kim felt like a great queen had dismissed her. Yet Kim was certain she had performed a mitzvah, a good deed, for this troubled stranger.

Kim returned to her table to find her boss holding a smoldering fat cigar in one hand, while he drank a Rob Roy from his other. Three empty glasses sat before him on the table.

"Where have you been?" His tone was curious not angry, which relieved Kim. "I've been wanting you to see this band and I have all sorts of ideas for the museum."

Kim realized it was going to be a long night.

A Tour of Rockefeller Center

One of his regulars had given Alex a ticket to the World Series as a tip. Rather than go to the game alone, he decided to ask Kim to join him at his favorite spot – Rockefeller Center. As Alex waited for her he marveled that almost all of the buildings were now finished. Only number Fourteen stood with its bare bones reaching towards the sky, waiting to be draped in flesh. Alex marveled over the straight lines of the complex, the angular deco look of the buildings, each with its own decorative motif. Sitting with his back to the main plaza looking towards Sixth Avenue, he could see the boastful image of the wind on the Associated Press building, blowing the hats off of unsuspecting passersby. The silver trio that emerged from the building actually represented the varied forms of communication. The ability to interpret the art and make it one's own made Rockefeller Center unique.

At times, as he stood looking up at a piece of art, an employee from within the building would stop to gaze with him. Then inevitably he or she would exclaim, "Has that always been there?" The designs were exquisitely incorporated into the structures and streetscape, each building with its own bold and modern icons. Alex shook his head, impressed by the imaginative work. He studied the symmetry of the buildings and considered their functional purpose; retail, office space, and storage. Fourteen buildings erected amidst the frigid grasp of the depression.

When no one would invest with Rockefeller, he decided to go it alone. He worried and managed every detail. When something didn't work, he didn't hesitate to fix it. The center of the complex was originally a sunken outdoor retail bazaar, but after six months, minimal foot traffic pointed to its demise. Rockefeller took a bold step and employed a new invention in refrigeration replacing the bazaar with an outdoor ice skating rink. This stroke of genius brought thousands of visitors to the complex. From the first day the rink opened the surrounding retail stores experienced an instant and sustained rise in business.

Alex found inspiration here in the art and originality.

Kim found him standing on Sixth Avenue in front of the main building. They kissed each other on the cheek in greeting.

"So what did you want to show me?" asked Kim.

"I want you to see John D's vision for the West Side. When he began, everyone believed that anything west of here would remain a

WAR CORRESPONDENT

Nancy Ames - Paris

I sit here in Paris and wonder is anyone listening? Our country appears to be asleep as evil extends across borders and into the homes of average citizens.

In case there were any lingering doubts as to the authenticity of the persecution of the Jews, Britain has recently disseminated to the world several reports regarding the atrocities being committed against Jews throughout Europe, including the concentration camp system.

The Nazi party has institutionalized a program of euthanasia for the sick and disabled, Jews and Poles. Eichmann is heading the effort to move all Jews from occupied lands to Poland. More than 50,000 journalists, university professors and Polish citizens have been executed in the last four weeks.

Turkey has agreed to support Britain and France, should fighting occur in the Mediterranean. This is the first country to break neutrality in what is being called the Second World War.

The Scandinavian countries stand ready for invasion by Stalin despite Sweden's ties to Hitler. And nervous they should be. Last week Stalin's troops marched into half of Poland and overwhelmed Estonia, Latvia and Lithuania. The Soviet troops are now positioned to enter Finland.

How is it Germany could rally behind a man who has never been beyond the borders of his own country? How could he possibly have perspective to rule the rest of the world?

Who knows? The next Dalai Lama of Tibet has been discovered, reincarnated as a four-year old boy. Maybe he will be our salvation for world peace. Hitler's rise has made anything possible.

slum. John D. knew, what few others knew, that the elevated train was being torn down. Look at it today, a thriving area of commerce." He waved his hand towards the broad street with the pride of a father.

"In less than a week, Rockefeller will personally drive the final rivet into the last building of this complex." He looked to see if she grasped the enormity of the accomplishment. She didn't, which was all right, he had brought her here to look at the art.

"I wanted to get your opinion on the art Rockefeller's son chose to decorate his edifices. I'd like to see if you can explain it to me." She looked at him, puzzled. "Kim, I attended your art exhibit back in the winter. I loved your architectural paintings. I think you have the heart and eye of an architect."

Kim blushed, "Thank you for such high praise."

"Not at all, all accolades for your work are well deserved. To reciprocate I wanted to share with you some of my favorite buildings in New York along with their unusual motifs.

Let's start here," he said, as they stepped into a covered entrance of Thirty Rockefeller Center just off Sixth Avenue. Kim looked up at a gigantic mosaic by Barry Faulkner, originally designed in 1933. The tiles were one inch square, each dyed a rich color, glazed to a high polish and sprinkled with gold so that they shimmered. The entire mosaic stood approximately 15 feet tall and 50 feet long. The center-piece was a goddess in white robes. Beneath her feet, in large letters, was the word 'THOUGHT'. Flanking her to the right were two winged assistants, speeding away with their own messages: 'written word' and 'spoken word.' Beyond each of the assistants, also depict-ed in rich colors, were fairies bearing the words -philosophy, hygiene, publicity, physics, biology and sports. These words they delivered to mere mortals, who appeared to be healthy farmers, the man in his undershirt and the woman, full figured and in a house-dress. To the far right were a naked man and woman, burning in a fiery pit of hell crowned with the words poverty and fear."

Alex turned to Kim. "So Miss Curator, what do you make of it?"

Kim was baffled. She had seen rarely seen this type of interpretive work on buildings. "Didn't the artist leave an explanation?"

"None that I'm aware of. But it gets better. Let's start from the Thought Goddess again and move to our left." He guided her by the elbow back to their starting point and turned left.

"Here the fairies deliver the words - news, politics, poetry, religion, drama, and music to another couple, who appear tormented. The man holds his palms up to the sky in supplication, as though asking, 'Why?' The woman is blindfolded, her fist clenched to her chest.

And again, beyond them, another naked couple burning in hell with the words cruelty and ignorance." Alex turned to her, "I just don't get it. What are your thoughts?"

Kim shook her head. "The only possible message I get from the mosaic is that poverty is a form of an individual's moral failure. Yet that is impossible since the piece was finished during the worst of the depression. I'd like to meet this artist."

Alex smiled, "Let's take a look inside and see if you have any better luck there." They stepped through the revolving doors and walked down a somber hall on floors made of black marble with brass concentric squares.

The murals were subdued and blended with the rich cream-colored walls. The artwork began above their heads and extended across the ceiling. They looked like charcoal drawings. The images were of half-naked slaves and workers toiling for a demanding overseer.

"You're right, this is even stranger," said Kim. "Is the artist trying to say capitalism is built on the backs of the people and that slavery is justified in the name of progress? Or is this Rockefeller's penance for destroying Diego Rivera's mural? Wait a minute. Isn't this where Diego's mural had been?" They had walked the length of the hall and were now in the lobby of the building, which faced the center or the plaza not the main street.

"That's right. Somehow a diatribe against managers and owners is better than a portrait of Lenin. But I can do you one better," grinned Alex. He placed his hands on her shoulders and moved her just to the left of the massive black marble reception desk. "Now look up."

Kim reflexively put her gloved hand to her mouth, trying to stifle the sound of surprise she emitted. It was not every day that she found herself looking into the underwear of a naked giant.

"Why? What does it all mean?" asked Kim.

"You've got me. That's why I brought you here, to explain it to me."

As they laughed and talked about the rest of the murals, Alex felt certain that he would one day design buildings rivaling these colossal structures. He would go to Europe, where the bombs were falling and architects were fleeing. There he would make his mark.

He didn't mention to Kim that he had in his pocket a ticket for passage on a cargo ship, The City of Flint, which sailed out of New York in two weeks.

Jason and Miriam

"Miriam, I've had it as a playwright."

Miriam didn't stir or speak. They were lying peacefully in each other's arms and she was certain that Jason was just going through one of his moods after a hard day.

"I'm serious. If I were Cole Porter or Irving Berlin or touched by the angel that sat on Gershwin's shoulder, I might feel otherwise. But there are so few people in the audience these days and those that do show up want musicals. I can't write musicals. Hell, I don't even like them."

Miriam took his hand and brought his fingers to her lips. "Darling, you're working yourself up over nothing. *An Evening of Mirth* will make it to the end of the year. That's an amazing run for a new play. And your next play has Carole Lombard. Hollywood on Broadway always fills the house."

"It's more than that." He turned to face her. "I really think I'm done. I don't think I have anything left in me. I need to move on, to do something else." He played with the nubbin pattern on the bed-spread.

Miriam became nervous. She had heard him complain before, but never threaten to quit. Not with the tone of finality his voice now possessed.

189

October

"Jason what are you saying?"

"Perhaps I should look for another profession, teaching or something." He avoided her eyes.

"Jason what is it?"

"I don't think I'm ready to tell you."

She felt a solid mass, tightening in her chest, a cold block of ice that threatened to freeze her from the inside out.

"You'll tell me when you're ready, Jason. Meanwhile, what can I do to help you?"

He touched her face and then began to kiss her. He murmured into her neck. "I'm sorry, I'm sorry. You're the dearest wife." He hugged her tightly, as if his life depended on it. "I'll try to be in better spirits."

"You can be in whatever spirits you need to be." Miriam knew instinctively that this was not a passing fear, but a ghost that had come to haunt them. She would fight for him with the physical weapons of a woman.

Sarah and Buddy

It was a perfect fall evening, a warm day followed by just enough nip in the air to justify the beautiful silk wrap Sarah had bought at Saks. She had been seeing Buddy for two months. Each date was a romantic adventure, filled with music and flowers. Tonight he had given her a gardenia wrist corsage. She repeatedly brought the flower up to her nose, mesmerized by the sensual aroma.

Buddy hadn't traveled for the last few weeks and every night (or day on the nights she worked) he would find something fun to do. One afternoon they flew to South Carolina to play golf. When she had three consecutive days off, he drove her in a white Cadillac convertible to Mt. Cadillac, in Maine, just as the fall leaves began to change.

There were dinners in his penthouse overlooking the city. One night he even rented the observatory atop the Empire State Building. He had taken her to see La Boheme, Tosca and a peculiar opera called Nabucco by Verdi, all viewed from the best seats in the house. The Metropolitan Opera orchestra was superb this year. Sarah winced to think she had turned down their offer to be first chair harp. Of course, if she'd accepted, she would not have been able to spend time with Buddy, since the orchestra lived by a very rigid schedule.

No, she was pleased with her choices. These last few weeks had been the happiest of her life.

Buddy never hid anything from her. Every question she asked he would answer without hesitation. He made it clear that he had given her the key to his heart – loving her without reserve – she was careful to make few demands. She feared that one day she would learn something she didn't want to know. For now, she didn't want to break the spell of their romance.

Sarah knew she would soon have to decide how she felt about him. He was like no one she had ever known. So giving and generous, yet for all the gifts and experiences he showered upon her, he never pressed himself. He never tried to take advantage of her and seemed satisfied simply to hold her hand or touch her coppery hair. Sarah knew that one day this wouldn't be enough, but since the abortion, she could give nothing more.

The contrast between Buddy and Alex was clear in her mind. Alex was energetic. Their relationship had been physical. She wanted him from the moment she saw him at the art exhibit. She had fantasized about him for months. Touching his skin seemed only an extension of what had gone before in her thoughts.

Alex's handsome face and smooth body were the stuff of Greek legends. And yet, there was something dark about him. Where Buddy was open and light, Alex kept things hidden from Sarah. Sarah was certain there was disappointment at Alex's core. One so great he couldn't express it. Something from his childhood... a father he couldn't face and a sister he loved and would do anything for.

Oddly, Alex couldn't bear to look at his own image. He had told Sarah that the mirrors in his apartment were hung low so that he wouldn't see the reflection of his own face. She often watched other women admire his good looks and yet Sarah saw his deep insecurity. He wanted to love, but he was too wounded to let it happen.

The pregnancy had been a mistake. By the time it happened, she knew she would always care about Alex, as a sister would for her brother. They couldn't see each other without embracing, kissing, and wanting one another and yet the emotion, was no longer that of passionate lovers, but of friends.

Alex had broken it off. After the procedure he couldn't bear to face her, to be confronted with what he had done and how he hurt her. She still missed Alex intensely. Buddy couldn't replace him and she knew she would always feel this way.

She came back from her thoughts and found herself sitting with Buddy at a table in the Starlight Club, atop the Waldorf. A talented group of musicians were playing a tango. She frequently sat in with this orchestra since she lived just downstairs. When the tedium of the radio got to her, she would jam with her friends.

Tonight she wouldn't leave Buddy. He looked over at her, aware she had been far way, lost in her thoughts.

"Happy anniversary."

"Excuse me?" asked Sarah.

"This is our thirtieth date. Let's dance to celebrate."

Ernestine and Bill's Last Dance

Ernestine had put on Bill's favorite dress, a coral and black silk number consisting of four large swatches that came together at her waist. She vacillated between thinking she looked like a giant checkerboard or a jockey. She wore coral shell earrings and black shoes with heels just slightly higher than were comfortable. Bill complained endlessly that she was too short, so tonight, although she couldn't stop the insults and complaints, she could eliminate the elevation problem.

After five months dancing with Bill, Ernestine had begun to lose much of her self-confidence. She now questioned everything she thought and did, a dramatic shift from the self-assured dancer and star of the New York Ballet. She placed a hibiscus flower in her hair that she plucked from the plant she kept in her dressing room. The color of the flower was a perfect match with the coral in her dress.

She never expected Bill to knock, nevertheless, when he barged into the room that night she tensed.

"The bums. You would think someone could beat that team," Bill grumbled as he entered.

"You mean the Yankees?"

"Yeah. If they win again it'll be four World Series in a row. It ain't natural. Who's ever going to want to go to a ball game again if the Yankees just keep winning?" He threw his coat on one of the armchairs and pulled at his tie.

Ernestine knew better than to argue with him or to challenge his logic. She simply asked, "Did you go to the game or hear it on the radio?"

"Don't you ever listen?" He shook his head in disgust. "I went to the game." Glancing around the room, he snarled, "Where's my scotch?"

He had taken to drinking before, during and after dancing which did nothing for his temper or his footwork.

She looked around, "I don't see it. Would you like me to get a waiter to bring you a glass?"

"Were you born stupid or are your brains in your fat ass?" he sneered. "You should have a drink ready for me before every performance. Make sure you get that straight or I'll have to knock some sense into you."

Ernestine rose slowly. She didn't want to give him cause to lunge at her by making any fast moves. Once outside the door she sighed with relief. As she headed for the bar, she noticed a cute redheaded couple at a table beside the dance floor. Neither of them were strikingly good looking, yet it was clear, that they were destined for happily-ever-after.

Ernestine just wanted to live through this evening. She would work on the happily-ever-after later.

"Hi Mike, how about a drink for my stud dancer?" she smiled. Mike the bartender and she had an ongoing joke about Bill. Neither of them liked him. Curran believed himself to be a lady-killer. And who knew, maybe he had killed a lady or two in his day, but as for turning heads it wasn't true. Most women picked up on his vibe and kept their distance. Unfortunately, Ernestine's 'vibe' mechanism failed her on the day she met Bill.

"Ah, the big man needs a little lubricant in order to get his feet working?"

"He's in need of something," said Ernestine. They laughed a slightly uncomfortable laugh. Then Ernestine decided to bring Mike into her plan.

She drew closer to the bar, "Hey Mike, I need a favor. Are you game?"

"What is it, Ernie?"

"I need to" she looked up at the mural above the bar, "get Bill, shall we say, very drunk by the end of the evening. I'm taking off tonight, Mike and I don't want him following me." She locked eyes with the bartender, "Do you get it?"

He spoke slowly and thoughtfully, "Yeah, I get it. You want me to slip him a mickey. Are you sure you know what you're doing kid?" He hesitated and looked both ways down the length of the bar. "You leave now and you'll never work in New York again. But maybe more important, I mean, Bill has some friends it isn't healthy to make mad."

"I know, thanks Mike, but I'm going to get lost someplace. No one will find me."

"That's good, because I wouldn't want to know you if they did."

"Mike if you …." She didn't finish the sentence before he held up his hand to stop her.

"Hey, I can take care of myself. You just give me the sign."

"Thanks Mike. You're a gent."

"Don't mention it. You take care of yourself, kid." He smiled and reached over to pinch her chin. Ernestine was anticipating that her nightmare was almost over. She need only face Bill one more time.

The Closing of the World's Fair

Jason was pleased that Miriam had convinced him to experience the World's Fair. He could see instantly why it would not be the same the following year. In order to make the working class man more comfortable, the glamour would be stripped away. Simplicity would

Out of the Dark

by Alan Stipple

Life magazine ran a spread on Hitler's paintings, suggesting that had he been a successful painter he may not have become Fuhrer. The weakness of the work suggests that it was not likely that painting, besides houses, was in Hitler's future. However, his fanatical dislike of modern painters has delivered to our shores a great many artists of repute.

Unfortunately, those German artists who didn't escape have been hunted down and killed and/or publicly humiliated. Many are still trapped behind enemy lines. To honor these great artists, this week the Metropolitan Museum of Art will display their work, now banned in their home country.

THEATER:
The Man Who Came to Dinner – another Kaufman and Hart success. Based on our very own naughty boy Alexander Woollcott (who,

by the way, whole-heartedly approved of the play). He's portrayed by none other than Monty Woolley whose mannerisms are so similar to the great man's that it causes one to do a double take. What's more, the madman Harpo Marx and the gallant Noel Coward both have small parts that add even more spice to the concoction.

MOVIES:
★★★★☆ Wuthering Heights - Boy has girl, boy loses girl over the love of money. Girl realizes her folly and dies broken hearted. Oh brother. Still, Olivier makes it seem simple. Despite wanting to hate the movie (which most men do), you find yourself clutching the edge of your seat waiting for some big emotional explosion which will take out all the characters at once. Instead, we sit through a stewing venomous broth that slowly eats away at the characters from the inside.

replace splendor. What's more, the countries that sponsored pavilions along the Lagoon of Nations might either be gone or annexed by aggressors.

Jason tried not to be melancholy, but he couldn't hide his feelings from Miriam. They had been together for too long. While he managed to ignore the coming war while working on the play with Lombard, he could not ignore it now.

As they entered the Soviet Union pavilion, an oppression so great overcame him that he asked Miriam if they could step back outside into the sunshine.

"What is it Jason?" asked Miriam as she placed her arm around him.

"It's just me. I can't explain it. It has something to do with the war." He looked at her and tried to smile. But it came off as a grimace.

"I'm taking you home."

"No Miriam," he said forcefully. "I need to see this. I want to see this. Perhaps this might be the last time to view the exhibits of Poland, Finland, France and even Great Britain."

Miriam pulled him over to a bench in the sunlight, "We can stay, but you have to tell me what's going on. You've acted so strangely since you've been back." She hesitated slightly, "Jason, is it the letters? Have you learned something about my family?"

He removed his glasses and looked at her. "Alright, Miriam, I'll try to explain what's happening to me. I guess it has to do with the Germans and their attack on Jews or rather the extermination." Miriam started to respond, but Jason shook his head.

"Miriam hear me out. One mad man has the power to wipe out every Jew on the face of the planet. That includes us. "He let his words sink in. "I feel that I must try to do something about it."

Miriam suddenly realized that he wanted to leave, to go to Europe and save the Jews. To face real danger and unfairness in the world without her.

"Jason, you're a playwright. Write a play to expose what's happening. That's what you do. That's what you're good at." She tried to keep the hysteria out of her voice. This was much worse than losing her husband to another woman. She could wage war against another woman, but she didn't stand a chance against Hitler.

"Jason, how many times have you told me that you're too sensitive to be involved on the front lines? That's why your plays carry a message of hope." He began to fade before her eyes. She shook his arm to refocus him, "Why can't you write a play? Let people know how bad it is. You'd reach more people every night with a play than you will going off with a gun." Still he didn't stir. "That's what you're saying isn't it, that you want to go and fight? Is it my parents? Are you trying to save them? I should go with you."

He hadn't really thought it through. He didn't know what he wanted to do. As soon as Miriam put it into words, he knew the answer.

"Yes, Miriam, I want to go abroad and help. Varian Fry is putting together a group. You know Varian, the reporter with Foreign Affairs. He's looking to save the artists and intellectuals. I don't care who I save. I'll join any resistance that might get one Jew away from Hitler. I want to establish an Underground Railroad like Harriet Tubman did for the slaves. I know it can be done and I want to be part of it. But, I don't want you with me. I must do this alone."

Miriam's face turned to stone. "Jason, let's go home."

"But." He said nothing more. Together they rose with mutual hesitation. She had unmasked him. The one woman Jason had ever loved, he was set to destroy. She would let him go, and he had broken her heart in the bargain. Yet Jason felt it was totally out of his control. His need to serve, to help, to save people was not going to fade. He had to act.

He took her hand as they moved toward the Perisphere and Trylon. "I'll come back," he whispered and squeezed her limp and unresponsive hand.

That night they made passionate love, exploring each other's bodies as if they were blind, trying to remember every inch and nuance. It was important. They both knew it. Somehow they would get through this, but they would never be the same.

October

Kim and Betty

Kim loved her job. She even preferred curating to her own artistic endeavors. Here her aesthetic sensibility and deep understanding of painting were put to good use. She analyzed the color, brush strokes and mood. She envisioned where it was painted, for whom, how the artist felt as he or she brought it to life.

Now that she was in charge of the classics as well as the modern collection, she prided herself on having a hand in adding several important women painters from the Renaissance and beyond. These were women who, due to their gender, were not able to paint for the church. They were limited to painting family portraits of the nobility and the wealthy merchant class. Yet a woman like Elisabeth Louise Vigée Le Brun became one of the most famous painters of her day, in demand throughout Europe during the late 1700's.

Kim chose to ignore the subtle pressure from her boss to focus on male artists and highlighted the splendid work of women such as Lavinia Fontana, Anne Peale and Angelica Kaufman. Perhaps, she thought, one-day women would have a museum of their own.

Today, Kim was not thinking about artist gender. She was concerned about the sheer volume of artwork that was showing up at the museum's back door. Works of the masters were discretely finding their way to her from the Polish, Czech-Slovakian, Romanian and French pavilions. At first, their curators complained of failed air conditioning units, which endangered the paintings. As days turned into weeks she realized that she now housed priceless works of art, smuggled away from the pervasive grasp of the Nazis. She took the paintings in like orphaned waifs, acutely aware that left to the Germans, they would be destroyed or confiscated at a great loss to humanity. She took pains to find each piece a safe temporary home.

One afternoon, as Kim gazed upon a Flemish painting of a vase of flowers, a woman approached her. The thirty-year old, honey colored blonde, had the build of an athlete. Her eyes were an icy blue. For a moment Kim felt mousy in comparison, with her tortoise shell glasses and hair pulled back into a bun. Looking every bit the spinster librarian versus the Aryan beauty that stood before her.

Then Kim remembered who she was, the curator of one of the greatest art collections in the world. The finest artists known to mankind stood behind her like an army-in-waiting. This woman was no threat to her, yet still Kim felt intimidated.

The woman held out a strong, freshly manicured hand. "How do you do? I'm Betty Stern."

"How do you do, Kim McIntyre."

"I know. I was wondering if you had a few minutes? I've something I need to discuss with you in private."

Kim suspected it wasn't safe to be alone with this woman. Miss Stern wanted something. Kim knew the walls in her office had ears.

"Let's go outside," said Kim.

"Wonderful, let's take a stroll shall we?"

The overcast sky gave off a weak light and a persistent wind caused Kim's scarf to try to escape. She knotted it at her throat, thankful for her cardigan, as the first hints of winter were in the air.

"Where's your favorite spot to sit in the fairgrounds?" asked Betty. Kim looked at her puzzled. Betty added, "to sit and think?"

"Near the Italian pavilion. I'm partial to the fountain."

"Then by all means, let's go there."

They strolled along the lagoon. Kim felt a pang of regret that the Fair would be closing in three weeks. Presumably she would sit in her little apartment, pretending to paint.

"So what are you planning on doing once the Fair closes?" asked Betty. Kim looked at her suspiciously. Betty pointed, "Ah, there's a coffee vendor. Let's see what he has." At the stand Betty motioned for Kim to order.

"A hot chocolate please," said Kim.

"And a coffee for me, with two biscotti." She turned to Kim. "So, what are your plans?"

"I don't know. I haven't made any definite plans. I'm hoping they'll hire me back when the Fair re-opens next April."

"You mean if the Fair re-opens, don't you? I'm sure you know that the investors have taken a bath, that the expected sponsorships didn't come in and unless the Fair changes dramatically, it'll be scrapped."

"I've heard that. I don't believe it. The Fair is too...." She wanted to say perfect, but held back.

"I'm sure the powers that be have a plan. I wouldn't worry. In the meantime, I have a proposition for you." Betty handed Kim her hot chocolate. They both sat on a bench facing the fountain of the four horsemen.

"Kim, I represent the museum and the U.S. government at the same time. You probably have never thought of the two as tied together, aligned, as it were, yet they are. Much of the Fair has had the blessing and/or the direct involvement of the federal government. I'm here to ask for your help in ensuring a victory for the United States."

"A victory over what?"

"The enemy," said Betty. "We may not be at war with bombs and men in uniform, but don't be fooled we are at war. We're shoring up defenses and balustrades. You, Kim, are one of our lines of defense."

Kim turned to her with surprise. "I beg your pardon, I'm an art curator. You must have the wrong person."

"No, you are exactly the right person. Let me get to it." Betty took a sip of her coffee. "We're aware that you have been storing artworks for a variety of countries currently under attack by aggressors. We would like you to keep doing that. We want you to coordinate a road show of your favorite paintings, to travel across the United States while the Fair is closed. This will give you the opportunity to accept additional pieces being smuggled out of Europe."

Kim said nothing, frozen with fear and uncertainty. Her heart beat wildly.

Finally she spoke. "There's more isn't there?"

Betty's thin lips formed into a smile of appreciation. "I told your boss you were more perceptive than he realized. Men always under estimate women."

She leaned back on the bench stretching her arm out behind Kim. Kim leaned forward.

"Yes, Kim, there's more. We would like you to accept the works of art in order to keep custody of them. Until things sort themselves out in Europe." Betty didn't say it, but Kim knew the U.S. had no intention of returning these pieces. She would be an accomplice to an art heist of unimaginable proportions, under the guise of curator and patriot.

"We also want you to gather information. The OSS, which focuses on terrorist activities by foreign nationals in this country and the Un-American activities group who watches U.S. citizens, needs information from you, based on your contacts." Her eyes pierced Kim. "Please don't misunderstand, I'm not making a request. I'm telling you the way it will be."

"I'm sorry you have been ill-informed. I'm a second rate painter who landed this wonderful job which," Kim hesitated for a moment, "appears to be over."

"I know nothing of your artistic accomplishments, however, I can assure you your work here's not over. If you were to refuse us, we'll arrest you for smuggling the paintings you have already accepted."

"What?"

"The best way to think of this is to consider the great service you'll be doing for your country. The U.S. will be at war soon and any information you provide our intelligence agencies now, will help ensure a speedy victory."

"I'll get back to you," said Kim flatly.

"There really isn't much of a choice here - jail or doing your patriotic duty. What's more, we haven't much time. We need you in place before the Fair closes."

"Whom do you work for, exactly?"

"Let's just say, the President."

"Of what?"

"The United States."

Kim needed time to think, so she said the most expedient thing, "Sure, I'll do it."

"That's my girl." Betty's demeanor towards Kim changed as though they belonged to the same sorority. "This is what we have in mind and we're always open to suggestions."

October

Bill and the World Series

Bill had a box seat ticket at the World Series courtesy of Meyer Lansky. He couldn't believe the Yankees were going to win their fourth World Series. It wasn't right. So there in the Bronx, he found himself cheering for the Cincinnati Reds, who didn't have a chance.

In the fifth inning, one of Meyer's henchmen sat down next to Bill. He didn't remember the guy's name, something like Lefty, Louie or Lucky.

"Enjoying the game?" The thug sounded greasy, the words slipped from his tongue. He wanted something.

"What is it?" Bill said with irritation.

"Your girlfriend left town." The man watched the game instead of looking at Bill. Charlie Keller hit a home run and the entire stadium was on its feet. Everyone except Bill and the man in the camel colored felt hat.

"What girlfriend? Are you crazy? I don't have a girlfriend," said Bill.

"Your dancing partner then."

"Ernestine? Nah, you're nuts. She's probably over there at that studio of hers on Fifty-fourth Street rehearsing her little heart out. She wouldn't go anywhere without me. She's afraid of me. I've got her right here." He placed his thumb into the palm of his other hand.

"Afraid not buddy. And Meyer ain't happy about it. He feels that it's time for you and he to meet again. Renegotiate your contract that is." Lucky Louie continued to lean forward and watch the game. The score was seven-to-three, Yankees.

Bill stood abruptly, "Let's go."

The crowd behind him began to shout, "Get down in front."

Lucky Louie didn't move, "He's not ready to see you yet. Go ahead and enjoy the game. He wants you to meet him on Friday at this address." He handed Bill a matchbook. Looking at the cover, Bill recognized the name of the club and knew it to be over on Fiftieth Street.

"Be there at nine." Lucky Louie started to leave and turned to add, "Don't be late."

He was gone and Bill was left at a ball game he had no more interest in. He needed to see if it was true and decided to go back to the city. It seemed impossible. When did she leave? He had to find out. He stood and the fans behind him shouted.

Bill spun around and growled, "Fuck you."

Karl and Kim at the Fair

It was around sunset when Karl found Kim deep in thought, sitting on a bench outside the Italian exhibit. He went over and sat silently beside her.

It took her a moment to notice him and then it was like being startled from a dream. "Karl!"

"Kim, what's wrong?"

She had always liked that about Karl, no pretense, no small talk.

"Nothing," she lied. "I was thinking about what this will be like come next year when the Fair re-opens."

He nodded, "I came by for the same reason. I wanted to look around at the pavilions one last time. Next year, who knows." They sat in a comfortable silence and then he asked, "Are they going to keep the Soviet Union pavilion? I've heard rumors…"

Kim broke in, "No, they're bulldozing it as soon as the Fair closes."

"Will the artwork be returned to the Hermitage?"

"I don't know," she shrugged. This was the first lie she had told in her new role, she suspected the first of hundreds. She knew the United States would confiscate the goods, claiming them as 'spoils' taken from an aggressor nation.

Karl would know she was lying, aware that her position as curator left her responsible for the museum's contents. She doubted he'd guess why she lied, although he certainly could sense her state of mind. They knew each other completely.

"Kim, is there anything I can do for you?" His gentle voice soothed her. Helping people was all this man ever wanted to do. How could he be suspected of wrongdoing?

With a harsh laugh she said, "Yeah you could pay back the twenty five dollars you borrowed." She didn't look at him. Lashing out was the only way she could keep from crying.

"I'm sorry, I don't have it on me. I have at least twenty back in my room." He reached out to her.

"Why don't we go back into the city and go out for dinner? We haven't seen each other in a long time. I'm sure there's lots to catch up on." She continued to stare at the ever-moving fountain. "What do you say?" He nudged her gently.

Kim wanted to turn and scream at him. Why had he become involved with the people he had? Why didn't he know when he was in danger? Why did he always want the best for everyone, when others wanted only the worst for him? Now she was trouble for Karl and he didn't even know it.

"I don't think I'd better," she said. Yet with all her heart she wanted to be with him. Sleep with him. Feel safe and innocent again.

They sat in silence for a long time.

"It's almost closing time. Let me at least accompany you back to the city." He could feel the pain emanating from her. He needed to protect her from something. He sensed it lurking near her, an imposing threat that consumed the light of her spirit. Karl wanted to grab hold of her. But he couldn't say or do any of those things. If he were to touch her, she would recoil, as though burned by a flame. He needed to be patient. Let things unfold at their own pace.

Night had fallen and the lights in the park glowed. Finally Kim turned to him and said. "Sure, you can take me home. I need to go over and lock up the museum. Why don't you come with me?"

They stood up together. He held out his arm and she placed her hand in the crook of his elbow. Kim decided to spend the night with him. Her new employers would think they had influenced her, causing her to spy on a notorious communist. The truth was she would seek only solace. Kim had compromised her values today - having chosen 'patriotic duty' over prison. While nothing would change that, she could, for a little while, remember with a good friend what it was like to be loved.

Bill at Ernestine's Flat

When Bill reached Ernestine's apartment he discovered that Lucky Louie was right. She had left town. Her furniture and bric-a-brac were there, but her clothes and personal items were gone.

He went next door to the studio where she had always insisted that they practice. He never liked the place. It felt too much like a schoolroom, with her the teacher. Bill couldn't stand anyone lording over him.

"Shit," he muttered, under his breath. Now he was at the mercy of Meyer Lansky. There was nothing he could do to get himself out of this one. Bill always thought it was a sweet deal. The money, booze, dames all supplied by his boss. All he had to do was whisper some information, a demand, or veiled threat into the ear of one of the wealthy patrons that frequented the fancy nightclubs where he danced. No job could have been easier.

Now this bitch had wrecked everything and he didn't see it coming. Betrayed by a skirt. There wasn't any point in his skipping town and he sure as hell wasn't going to look for her.

NOVEMBER

Buddy and Sarah to Marry

Sarah decided she loved Buddy enough to marry him. Although their love lacked passionate lust, it proved to be something more grounded and real. True comfort came from Buddy's calmness and the respect he showed her. He never treated her as a second-class citizen. They were equals although she would never be able to understand or move in his business circles, Sarah knew they had much more to share.

She anticipated that he would ask her to marry him tonight and she was ready to say yes.

The day was stunningly clear with the mercury pushing into the seventies – it was an Indian Summer. Luckily she had opted to wear a lightweight flouncy rayon dress of cream that flowed with her stride up Fifth Avenue as she searched for an engagement present for Buddy. She passed by Rockefeller Center and saw the skaters already circling on their small pond. It wasn't even Thanksgiving, the skating seemed too soon. She felt a slight chill as she walked in the

WAR CORRESPONDENT
Nancy Ames - Odessa

Masters of propaganda, the Germans have been quick to photograph their successes and send them around the world. There isn't a newspaper or magazine in this country that isn't using German photos of the war. Many excellent pictures show Germans blowing up British warships.

Meanwhile Hitler has embarked on one of the oddest resettlement plans in history. The Fuhrer has demanded that any German family that moved to Latvia, Estonia or Lithuania, during the last 700 years now return to the Fatherland. 120,000 so-called German refugees were given just days to liquidate their belongings. They have been promised equivalent properties and housing in Poland, which was taken from the Jews. These German/Russians have been given twelve months to divorce their Jewish spouses.

Mohandas K. Gandhi has used the British announcement of war to his advantage in India. He has argued Britain for self-rule.

As if Britain doesn't have enough trouble – the Irish Republican Army (IRA) exploded three bombs in Piccadilly Circus and the Germans have parachuted mines into the Thames River in London.

In a move of solidarity Canada has stepped forward as a powerful British ally and will be the training ground for British pilots.

In Washington, the White House and Capitol buildings are now off limits to tourists.

shadow of the tall buildings.

She decided to skip Tiffany's and go directly to Cartier. She always felt they displayed more substantial items and she enjoyed the staff. They were knowledgeable as well as solicitous.

From the street, the building looked like a fortress. Upon entering a pleasant older woman greeted her.

"How may I assist you?"

"I'm looking for a gift for a man."

"This way Miss," and without another word the greeter took her to the far side of the store and introduced her to a salesman in his mid-forties. "This is George Krendal. He'll be happy to assist you."

"Thank you," said Sarah.

Sarah sensed that George took great pride in his work.

"Mr. Krendal," she said as she looked down into the cases. All she could see was glitter. "I believe the gentleman I have been seeing is about to propose and I would like to purchase an engagement present for him." Sarah was surprised at her own boldness and confidence. She felt neither embarrassed nor presumptuous.

George reflected for a moment. She suspected he was sizing her up – young woman, well dressed and of means. If George was good at his job, he would realize that she would be turned off by gaudy jewelry.

"What if you presented him with a ring?" said George.

Sarah responded with a puzzled look.

"Not an engagement ring, per se, but a pinky ring. Does the young man have one already?" Sarah watched as George mentally kicked himself for using the word young. They both knew her beau was not young.

"Actually, I think I saw him wear a ruby ring on his little finger once. He doesn't wear it regularly."

"Well, there's a new style in women's engagement rings and that's diamonds. It'll soon be the stone of engagement." True, Sarah had been seeing more and more diamond engagement rings lately. When she was a girl, other precious stones were more popular.

George continued, "May I suggest a pinky ring with a diamond as a reciprocal gift?"

As he spoke he began laying out five gold rings. Each ring embedded with diamonds of different sizes and shapes. One contained four diamonds creating an ornate half moon, which she immediately dismissed. Whatever Buddy wore, it would have to be discrete.

"Not this one," Sarah said, and with the skill of Houdini, George made the ring disappear. Of the four remaining rings, lying on the deep blue velvet pad, there were three she liked. She pointed to the fourth and shook her head no. It too disappeared.

She chose the simplest of the three. "Ah, a fine choice Miss. This is a three-quarter carat diamond. A baguette cut, set high enough to allow light underneath to give it sparkle. Its rectangular shape offers a masculine feel."

"How much?" Sarah asked. She didn't really care about the cost but knew that by asking, George would shave a few dollars off the total. Mostly, people who came to Cartier never asked the price.

George was taken aback for a moment, then, like a trained soldier, he quickly recomposed himself. "This ring is three hundred dollars, Miss." It seemed a good price.

"And how much are these other two?" George now appeared flustered. He hadn't sized her up as one concerned with price.

"The half carat trilliant cut is two hundred and twenty-five dollars and the one carat oval is three seventy-five." He paused trying to find the upper ground in this unfamiliar territory. "My apologies. I should have asked earlier if these rings were within your budget."

"I hadn't originally thought about diamonds and I'm surprised at the price they command, compared to other fine stones like sapphires."

"We have a great many loose stones, many beautiful Ceylon sapphires, that could replace the diamond. I would be happy to show you."

"Perhaps," was all Sarah said, waiting for George to improve on the prices.

"The resizing of the ring, if it should be required, will be free. I believe if I confer with my manager, we might be able to offer you an additional ten percent off," he said in a whisper.

"Alright Mr. Krendal, you have a deal." She slipped the ring over her gloved finger and admired it. It spoke to her. "At two-hundred-seventy dollars you have yourself a deal."

"Yes, Miss."

"Would you please wrap this for me?"

"Immediately, Miss."

While not a blue Tiffany box, the distinctive red Cartier box and ribbon would do. Sarah was pleased with herself. Now she need only wait for Buddy's proposal.

Ernestine in Hollywood

Ernestine stepped from the train in Los Angeles feeling hopeful and exhilarated. Having escaped her nemesis, the three-day train ride had given her time to reflect on the future. Ernestine, as always, could imagine only one kind of future for herself and that was one of fame. She believed this to be her destiny, so much so that she was slightly crestfallen when there were no fans, press or city officials to meet her train. Ernestine conveniently forgot that she was more likely to meet up with a bullet from one of Lansky's crew. Instead, her fantasy of becoming famous in Hollywood was so complete, that the only thing left was disappointment.

She took a room at the Beverly Hills Bel Air and began calling old friends who had moved west. She was astonished to discover they had either disappeared, (having gone home to the Midwest) or they had chosen to forget her. The new Californians wanted nothing to do with New York. Naturally, they mildly protested the lack of good deli food, pastrami sandwiches, bagels and lox, but no one wanted to return. And they didn't want to hear about what was going on back there.

In less than a week, Ernestine realized she would have to move to more modest accommodations and took up residence in a Santa Monica bungalow. She loved getting up every morning to the sea breeze. At night, if she felt lonely, she would walk down to the pier and watch the tourists play at the arcade games.

During more somber moments, in those first few weeks, she

Out of the Dark
by Alan Stipple

This month we New Yorkers received a gift from Miss Bernice Abbot. Miss Abbot has made it possible for us to stop snapping our fingers trying to remember, "What building used to be there?" In her new book, *Changing New York*, funded by the Federal Arts Project, Abbot has collected the changing scenes of New York over a five-year period (1935-1939).

Edna Ferber has written a new book about her career as a movie scriptwriter and playwright. She goes into to great detail regarding *Dinner at Eight, Stage Door, The Royal Family* and *Showboat*. It's a pleasure and leaves the reader wishing that *Showboat* would return to the Great White Way.

THEATER:
Life With Father - A look at New York in the last century. Keeping with the current political climate, father says, "Why did God make so many damned fools and Democrats." The goal of the piece is to show a world where fathers still dominate the home or believe they do and how women actually run the show.

MOVIES:
★★★★☆ ***Ninotchka***
Worth it just to see Garbo laugh. Garbo in a comedy is something this critic never thought possible. A little old for the part, she still presents a wonderful spoof on communism. And just for the record, Garbo is not Russian, she's Swedish. Melvyn Douglas plays a believable gigolo. My favorite line, "They can't censor our memories."

★★★★☆ ***Drums Along the Mohawk*** - John Ford is not yet finished settling the Wild West except this time it's upstate New York in the 1700's. Same difference, there are bad Indians and British officers out to get 'em and strong women ready to take them all on. A nice teaming of Henry Fonda and Claudette Colbert. As always, John Ford delivers first rate entertainment.

concluded that breaking into the Hollywood scene would be grueling work. Although still young, she wasn't certain her body had the stamina. The endless circle of logic would collapse upon itself and she would alleviate her sadness with long walks along the palm-lined esplanade.

On one of her dark days, during a walk along the ocean, a jaunty couple from New York stopped her.

The husband spoke first, "Excuse me, but aren't you Ernestine Robertson, the dancer?"

"I am."

Remembering his manners the man removed his hat and reached out a hand, "How do you do, Miss Robertson. I'm Oscar Jurzakowski and this is my wife Edith."

"How do you do?" Ernestine replied tentatively. In New York she would have brushed this type of recognition aside, here in L.A. it felt like rain in a desert of anonymity.

"Do you live here now? Or are you doing a picture? Perhaps just on holiday?" Mr. Jurzakowski rushed questions at Ernestine faster than she could register them.

Ernestine smiled and held up her hand to block the glare of the sun, "I'm living here temporarily, on an extended holiday."

"So you aren't dancing anywhere? Not at any clubs here in L.A.?"

"Oscar, she told you she was here on holiday. She's not going to be dancing if she's on vacation," said Edith.

Mr. Jurzakowski looked disappointed, and then he perked up again. "We saw you at the Starlight Club two months ago. You were extraordinary." He paused, "Oh yeah, and your partner was good too. But you were terrific."

"Thank you." Ernestine was ready to move off the topic of her partner. "And what brings you to town?"

"A little business and a little pleasure." Oscar turned to Edith and smiled. "We're going to see Fanchon and Marco tonight at the Brown Derby. Have you seen them yet? I hear they're the cat's whiskers."

"No, I haven't," said Ernestine "I'll make sure to catch their routine."

"Why don't you come with us?" Oscar replied quickly. Edith gave him a quick jab in the ribs. No woman wants to go on a romantic dinner date with another woman in tow.

"No, I think not tonight. But I'll make sure to see them," said Ernestine politely.

Oscar continued, "I'm sure no matter how good they are they won't hold a candle to you." Edith began tugging at his arm. "You have a good visit here in LA. We'll see you back in the Big Apple."

In that moment Ernestine remembered her dream. Now that she was out from under the constant threat of Bill, she recalled her desire to start a school, a place to teach and to explore new styles of dance. She would start it right here in Hollywood. She would hire one of the best publicists in town to promote Ernestine Robertson (under a new name) as the next Martha Graham. She had learned something from watching Lansky's public relations machine make Ernestine and Bill overnight headliners.

Filled with purpose, Ernestine turned and headed back to her apartment, suffused with a plan that she felt couldn't fail.

The Wedding

Buddy and Sarah originally planned to have a small, lavish wedding, executed with impeccable finesse and charm.

However, the Waldorf begged Sarah to hold the reception at the hotel and offered to make it the social event of the season. They understood that the guest list would include the best of high society and would be good for future business.

Sarah and Buddy invited friends and family. Creating the invitation list proved as difficult as choosing the right combination of harp strings. Sarah found that her guest list was based on sympathetic chords and notes that would produce a beautiful melody together.

Painters, poets, playwrights, and dancers made up Sarah's list. Alex was not on the list, their relationship still too fresh in her memory. She did invite Karl Klyne, for they were kindred spirits. While they had been high school sweethearts years ago, they still remained good friends, despite seeing little of each other.

Sarah regretted that her father would not be able to give her away. Although his passing was several years ago she still missed him. She did invite her mother, from Illinois, but Sarah knew the trip would be too much. Mrs. Karofsky never ventured more than twenty miles from the farm.

Even now, Sarah's thoughts occasionally drifted back into those slow, calm days, measured by the rhythm of the seasons and the plow. Yet it was not the life for her. She remained ever thankful to her father for letting her study music, allowing her to leave home and go to the big city. He knew that becoming a farmer's wife would dampen Sarah's spirit. And her father believed spirit was God's greatest gift.

Buddy's list was much more complicated. It included the anticipated family members, cousins and aunts, as well as a preponderance of business associates. His list contained senators, assemblymen, judges, ambassadors and even a few members of royalty. Buddy would introduce Sarah to the world and she was thrilled.

In the end, 350 invitations went out. Sarah had played at enough weddings and large parties to know what to expect. Her smile would last for hours, so much so, that her face would hurt the next morning. She and Buddy would be ever so slightly aware of all the little dramas going on behind the scenes. Each guest would be touched with a few words, even if just for a moment, and ultimately the couple would be spirited off amidst the fanfare of well wishers.

She and Buddy would remember the highlights for the rest of their lives: the "I do's", the pronouncement of "man and wife", the first dance, the best man's toast, their change into travel clothes and the rice thrown at them as they dashed to the car painted with good wishes. All this Sarah knew and she faced it with neither trepidation nor great excitement. She reserved her excitement for being married.

It was funny. Sarah had spent months determining her feelings towards Buddy and in the end realized she trusted him. And upon that she could build a life. And a life with Buddy, who loved her unconditionally, would always be a surprise and delight.

As for the honeymoon, they were to sail first to Bermuda and then on to St. John in the Caribbean. Sarah had never taken a vacation since leaving home except for the occasional long weekend. The extended respite might give her a chance to reflect on what her music meant to her. Although Buddy never asked her if she intended to continue playing harp professionally after the wedding, she knew he would support whatever decision she made. A new world was about to open up to her, a world full of options.

Jason and Miriam at the Wedding

The wedding transcended all of Buddy's previous parties - a fountain of champagne, members of the NY Philharmonic playing for the wedding procession, with Fats Waller, Louie Armstrong and Billy Holliday scheduled to play at the reception.

Everything was swathed in imported silks. Male guests received gold key chains from Tiffany's while the women enjoyed gold bracelets from Saks Fifth Avenue. No expense was spared.

Sarah had invited Jason and Miriam, whom she knew as casual friends, having attended the same events for years. They were among the few people Sarah invited who also knew Buddy. Jason and Miriam were happy to get out of the house and away from their thoughts.

"Jason Rothman, you old so-and-so." It was Lillian Hellman. Jason felt a bond with Lillian, unfortunately Miriam found her too bold, and so Jason never invited Lillian to dinner. He often thought of Hellman and used her as the critic in his head, because he felt she wrote first-rate plays. She might not be much to look at, but she knew her way around fast-paced dialogue. "Lillian," he gave her a quick hug as she held her champagne glass out of the way.

"Lillian it's so nice to see you," said Jason kissing her on both cheeks.

"I hear you have Carole Lombard all wrapped up for your new play. You dog, how did you do that? I always thought she was scared to death of the theater and what's more, how did you convince Clark to give her up for a four month run?"

Feigning shock, Jason said, "I beg your pardon. Five months at least."

She laughed her throaty laugh and said, " A five month run. How did you do it?"

"I went out there and sat with them every day for six weeks until they felt perfectly comfortable."

"You didn't? You did? Aren't you dedicated to your work." She took a long drag off of her cigarette. "Jack Warner has been hounding me to go out there to work on *The Little Foxes*. Since it's been so successful here on Broadway he figures that the average movie Joe will like it too. He's threatening to put Bette Davis into the lead role." She leaned towards Jason and lowered her voice. "But I've got to tell you Jason, I don't think he's read the script. I mean it's Red through and through. I can't believe he's willing to take on the Un-American Committee over this movie. Shit, I don't know if I'm ready to take those guys on. I mean it's fine until you step into their headlights and then, Pow."

"Yeah, out in Hollywood the Committee was on everyone's mind. You should have heard Dorothy Parker. She never gave them an inch. Called them all kinds of expletives. Every chance she got."

"Dorothy's out there?"

"Yep, they have her fixing broken scripts. They'd love her if she'd let them, but you know Dorothy."

Lillian let out another one of her famous laughs, "I know Dorothy. I guess I'm going to have to go on to California. I haven't had a good tongue lashing by Mrs. Parker in months and I need my prescription filled." She looked around for another drink and raising her glass added, "Speaking of prescriptions, I'll see you later."

Jason nodded sympathetically. He turned to speak with Miriam and saw she had slipped away. Clifford Odets was holding court, waving a pate'-covered cracker in the air. "I think the Committee just doesn't like the cold weather," said Odets, "I believe that, like fleas, they'll be back in the spring to torment us all."

"So are we talking about our favorite topic, the censorship of ideas in America?" asked Christopher Isherwood, holding a long cigarette, giving him a feminine look.

"Yes, my pet," responded Odets. "It seems to be the topic du jour." Odets turned to Jason, "Rothman, you should be alright, at least you never signed up behind Stalinist communism. Now that the schmuck went and invaded Finland and Poland, we're all screwed." He plucked a canapé from a passing tray.

Hellman reappeared and continued, "You're right. I turned Trotskyite, but I'll still be damned. Shit Rothman, you maybe the only one of us to come out smelling like a rose."

"Ah, but you forget, dear friends, I'm a Jew. And being a Jew, I am responsible for the war. At least that's the belief held in some quarters."

Both Odets and Hellman lifted their heads on the word Jew. It was a flashpoint in most conversations.

"Poppycock," responded Hellman, "Hell, I'm half Jewish and it's the important half. I don't think they'll go after us for that." She paused considering.

"Hard to say, when we have that shining example of Europe before us," said Jason. "Have you friends or relatives still trapped there?" he asked.

Odets responded first, "I'm working to bring them over. Everyone I know. You might have something Rothman. Your paranoia may be rooted in some reality. I'm finding it harder to get my Jewish friends out than my Christian friends. I hadn't really thought about it, but it's true."

"This bloody thing is going to get pretty ugly, both there and here," added Isherwood.

Odets stared at Jason for a long time and then asked in a quiet voice, "You *are* going, aren't you?"

"What!" screeched Hellman, "You wouldn't. Are you nuts? What do you think a rich Jew could do in Europe these days to help?"

"For one thing Lillian," Jason responded, "my plays don't run for as long as yours or Clifford's, so I'm not rich." Jason and Hellman gave each other a mock bow and smile. "However, Clifford, you're very observant. I have indeed decided to go. I don't know what I can do or how I'll contribute, but I feel a need to be there. A need to participate, even if I can only save one life," he trailed off.

"Good God, Rothman, you're more of a bleeding heart than I suspected," said Hellman.

"Listen old man," said Odets. "Why don't you stay here and

write a play. Expose what's going on from the pulpit of the stage. Dump the Lombard thing or get it going and then work on what matters. I'm sure you could do more good here." Odets was worried for Jason. He had heard reports from his friends. He knew that Jason, idealistic and naive as he was, would be in harm's way.

"You sound like my wife. That's what she wants me to do," said Jason.

"Although I know Miriam has never liked me, which makes me question her judgment, I must say she's right on this one," said Hellman. "Listen to the girl. She's possesses true wisdom." She winked at Jason.

"No, I'm afraid my mind's made up. I sail on the Rex, January first."

"What a sweet New Year's present for Miriam, Jason. Thank you for reminding me that there are bigger shits in this world than Hammett."

Odets held out his hand to shake Jason's, "I think it's a mistake, but I wish you all the luck. If you run into trouble over there, remember you have friends here in New York."

Jason shook his hand. Hellman stood on tiptoes and kissed his cheek. "That goes double for me. There's always room on the funny farm if you ever need a place to come back to." They hugged and he was grateful to have shared his decision with them. He knew everyone in town would know by tomorrow. It might even help attendance for his current play. Wasn't his producer always telling him he needed to do more publicity?

Meeting with Meyer Lansky

Bill walked the few blocks to the nightclub where he was to meet Meyer. The high rollers and swells frequented the Manhattan Club. He'd been there a few times. You got in via a slide that dropped you at the main floor.

Bill ordered a scotch, to fortify himself for his audience with Lansky. He knew he could handle anything Lansky dished out.

A voice at his elbow said; "Meyer is ready to see you now." The midget wearing a big fedora squinted at Bill. "Hey, are you sober?"

"Sober enough, little man."

The short gangster pulled back his right fist and punched Bill hard, right above the kneecap. Bill's leg buckled and it brought him face to face with his assailant.

"I'd watch who you're calling little, Mister" He waved a stiletto knife in front of Bill's face. "I'd be happy to cut you down to size anytime."

Bill knew he shouldn't pick a fight with this guy. There was nothing to gain and his position was already precarious. He might need him later.

"Sorry buddy. I didn't mean anything by it." Bill tipped his hat.

The man in the fedora snorted, "Yeah and neither did I." He moved toward a side door and called over his shoulder, "This way."

Bill followed, straightening his tie and hat. His knee smarted. There'd be a hell of a lump, but that was the least of his worries.

Meyer was in a private room off of the main floor. He sat on a dais at one end of the room, chairs spread out in front of him as if he was royalty. Three of his thugs stood to the side. A big guy in a banker's suit leaned over, whispering into Lansky's ear as Bill arrived.

Meyer looked up, "Have a seat Bill, I'll be with you in a moment." Meyer listened attentively to the middle-aged man in the suit. Then he nodded and said, "Do it," and the man was gone.

"Sorry to keep you Bill. That was my lawyer and it always pays to listen to your lawyer. Or I guess you have to pay, even if you don't listen." He laughed and his lackeys laughed with him. Bill didn't laugh.

"So, it looks like your dancing career is in the crapper. What should I do with you now?" asked Meyer. "You haven't come close to paying off the debt you owe me, what with all that publicity and high living."

Bill said nothing, still Meyer held up his hand as if to fend off any objections.

"Now, I admit you did me some favors over these last few months, which is why I think it's worthwhile to keep you alive."

Bill thought the conversation a bit dramatic. Meyer Lansky had nothing to gain by killing him.

"One of my industrialist friends has asked me to do a little job," continued Lansky. "It's some pest control. A guy's gumming up the works at one of his factories. The bird is a union instigator, a damn Red. Joey here is going to take you around the corner and give you the low down on this guy and what we need done. Can you live with that Bill?"

Bill knew there was only one answer. "Of course."

Meyer sat back in his chair, noticeably relieved. "Good, you do this little job for me and we'll see what we can do about getting you another dance partner. I don't think bringing that old broad back would do you any good, especially considering the condition we'd have to bring her back in. What do you say?"

"Forget her. I never liked the bitch. I think we can do better."

Meyer smiled an eerie smile and for the first time Bill felt a tingle of fear.

"Good. Very good. Until we meet again." And with that Bill was dismissed. One of Meyer's thugs directed Bill out the back door, where little Mr. Fedora sat at a single table in the middle of boxes of booze. There was one chair across from him. Bill sat in it.

"Here's the drill. The Joe's name is Karl Klyne. He lives down in the Bowery. He seems like a nothing guy, I guess he has stirred up enough trouble for the big wigs that they want him out." Mr. Fedora stopped and looked at Bill to make sure it registered. "We want this done by the day after tomorrow. You got it?"

"I got it. You want the guy ended."

"Yeah." Mr. Fedora stood up and patted Bill's back as he left. The last time someone had patted Bill's back they had placed a 'kick me' sign on him. At least this time, Bill knew it was there.

Kim Prepares to Tour

Kim's new bosses were subtle. They were never visible and yet she could feel them all the time. She knew she was being watched and yet no one ever stepped out of the bushes to introduce themselves.

November

She suspected they were waiting until she was in a strange city and off-kilter before starting to needle her for information.

No one had spoken to her about the night she spent with Karl, even though Betty had mentioned him by name as a labor instigator and a confirmed Red. Clearly, they would have liked to know more, but Kim wasn't about to give up anything. She respected and trusted Karl. To hell with the goons she worked for, even if they did drape themselves in the American flag.

As for collecting valuable pieces of art, Kim supported the effort. She didn't feel good about extracting them from other countries, but realized if they were going to be destroyed by the Nazis, she would rather keep them protected under her appreciative and watchful eye.

The espionage group she worked for had indicated a number of safe houses along her transcontinental route, places where she could drop off the precious cargo. Kim was to provide for proper humidity, temperature control and security. The best spots were old abandoned fur storage vaults. They were plentiful in metropolitan areas. What's more, trucks backing up to them would never be given a second thought. She wanted Alex to design a container with several hidden compartments, one that could easily be loaded onto the trains and trucks. But he had disappeared without a word.

She sat for a moment, overtaken by memories of Alex. He was someone she really liked. She never thought about marriage, yet she was certain there was something real between them. Kim wished him well, wherever he might be.

As she stood, ready to face the job of determining which art to take on the tour, she considered several parameters. Nothing too celebrated, but good enough to attract the crowds. Nothing too valuable in case it were damaged in transport or stolen. Engrossed in thought she didn't notice George Whalen standing beside her.

"Deciding on the show?" George Whalen asked good-naturedly.

"Yes, Mr. Whalen. Figuring out what to take and what to leave behind."

"If it were up to me, I would take the Picassos and the Van Goghs for sure. No one will understand them and yet the viewer can identify the subjects. You take too many Braques or Gunthers, you'll lose them for sure." He looked around with a serious expression for a moment. "Actually, I'd go light on some of the classical stuff too, especially the old religious art."

"You mean like the DaVincis and Raphaels?" He couldn't tell if she was being sarcastic.

"No, no the crowds would like those, but you can't be taking them on the road. They're much too precious." She laughed at his naiveté.

"Don't worry, Mr. Whalen, I have it under control. The great masters will not be joining me, instead I'm opting for the Whistlers, Burne-Jones, and Rockwell Kents." She paused and turned to him in seriousness.

"I'm intentionally not bringing the Germans. I'm leaving behind the Kandinsky, Klimt, and others because I'm afraid...." she trailed off.

He patted her shoulder, the way a dog owner absent-mindedly pats a dog's head. "This is wise my dear. I suggest no Germans or Russians. I'd keep it to Americans, Brits, French and Dutch. Anything else might stir up feelings of nationalism that you don't want associated with this exhibit." He seemed satisfied that she had the project in hand. He started to leave the hall then turned back and asked, "Have you thought about next year? What will you exhibit?"

This was the first time anyone with authority had mentioned a future for the Fair. Something in his demeanor made her realize that he worked for the same people she did now.

"I think I'll get a better sense after the tour. After all, the entire theme next year is, 'Art for the Common Man.' Who better to tell me what they like and don't like than the citizens of middle-of-the-road U.S.A.?"

Whalen mocked, "Ah, how I wish I was going with you." He thrust his hands into his pockets and wandered off, jingling his change and whistling a happy tune.

Kim decided she would take more Manet's and Monet's and leave Pissarro behind, since there was still so much unrest around Spain.

She pulled a pencil from behind her ear and added, 'Matisse, everyone loves Matisse.' She felt her knees buckle and leaned against the wall feeling faint, as if the wind had been knocked out her. She collapsed onto one of the nearby marble benches. For the first time she realized that Matisse, Chagall and so many others were in harm's way in Europe. She would have to do something about protecting their work and protecting them. She didn't know what to do or how to do it, but was certain something would come to her.

Unsummoned, thoughts of Alex re-emerged.

Alex Sails

For Alex, the thrill of setting sail was even better than he had imagined. He was beside himself, giddy as a child, unable to hold still, shifting his weight from foot to foot in anticipation.

He had never been to Europe, never done the grand tour and now he was setting off to a land of gas masks, bombs and shrapnel. Alex knew he could make a difference overseas. After all, the war wouldn't go on for long. The British were bound to finish off the Germans in short order and then Alex could get down to the business of designing new buildings.

In his trunk were his best clothes, all of his drawing tools, samples of his work, several blank journals, a tin of hard tack and chocolate bars. He wasn't quite sure about the chocolate bars, it seemed like they were something people used to trade when traveling.

He paid up his rent, happy to be leaving his 'love den' behind, a form of prison cell of his own making. During these last few months, he found that more and more of his patronesses chose to come to his apartment. He had planned to move into a fine hotel, thinking his society ladies would be more comfortable there, then it became clear that they didn't want to risk running into someone they knew. What's more, the fact that his apartment was outside of mainstream society and had no doorman, ensured a level of privacy even a second tier hotel could not offer.

So instead he had turned his apartment into a boudoir, full of elements that were exciting to the touch and eye. Luxurious fabrics in subtle colors covered the pillows, bedspread and sheets. Unique and innovative recessed lighting accentuated every contour of even the fullest figure. He had made a science of his work and had saved enough money to live frugally for a couple of years abroad.

He considered at length who he should say goodbye to. There was the dark haired beauty, Kim. He had begun to like her, to become emotionally attached – but this was why he ended the budding relationship. And then there was the fiery Sarah – he couldn't gather the emotional strength to see her. After he offered her the thirty dollars for the abortion, she ripped it up in his face. The memory was still painful. He knew in his heart that Sarah and he were too much alike. They would each need to find fortitude with another mate, someone who would help drive them toward their goals.

The only other face that swam to the surface of his mind was Miriam Rothman. He had always felt he could be honest with her. Alex could imagine a long-term friendship with her and her husband. Ever since that day, when he had protected her from that cad, thoughts of Miriam came unbidden.

For now he decided, he wouldn't let anyone know who he was or what he had done for a living. He would treat this episode of his life like a war story that would never be shared.

Alex knew he was no Albert Speer, the giant who rebuilt Berlin after the war. No, he would not play at that level of genius. But after this war there would be cities and towns that would need new churches and office buildings. In these simple dreams, Alex knew he was headed in the right direction.

A handful of people stood beside Alex on the deck of the City of Flint, a passenger/cargo ship, waving to friends on the dock. Alex would return one day and while no one would know his name in America, a building or two in a foreign land would bear his stamp.

DECEMBER

Karl's Memorial

A haunting melody filled the church. Kim wanted the pianist to stop. The chords pierced her heart. A comely young woman with red hair played accompaniment on the harp. Kim vaguely recognized her.

By the end of the song the mourners were wiping tears from their eyes. Even the harpist pulled a handkerchief out of her sleeve. Kim could barely hold herself together. She came for Karl. She told herself she would of come even if, Chicago hadn't been the first stop for her traveling exhibit.

The minister took the pulpit.

"Karl Klyne left this community many years ago and settled in New York. We all assumed he went there to become a famous pianist. Karl composed the piece you just heard for his mother at the age of sixteen.

I had the great pleasure of watching Karl grow up. A leader of children and later, of men, he guided others with integrity and great compassion." The minister paused and looked down at the black casket covered with a blanket of white roses. Kim held a single red carnation to place there. She hadn't anticipated anything this emotional.

"We of Elgin knew we couldn't hold him. Even the metropolis of Chicago was not large enough. Karl found himself in New York where the greatest number of people needed him. His desire to help the poor and to support their most basic needs for food and shelter put him at cross-purposes with those in power. Unable to accept the inevitable, Karl fought injustice with determination and a sense of purpose, never asking for help or money from his family." The minister turned towards Karl's affluent parents and both shook their heads no. "Karl built shelters, worked to institute new standards in housing and secured food to support the lives of countless individuals in need."

The minister looked out at the congregation and pleaded, "Is this a reason to end a person's life? To stop him from doing the good work? A reason to prevent him from living up to his potential? To take this life, Karl Klyne's life, is to commit more than the sin of murder. It is a sin against humanity." The minister gripped the podium before him.

"The fact that a stranger, William Curran, could take Karl's life, leaves us to wonder about Mr. Curran's fate. Will he ever be able to repay his debt to society? Unquestionably guilty, found at the scene of the crime with the gun in his hand, should we take judgment into our own hands and say, 'Mr. Curran' you are guilty and must pay with your own life? I know what Karl would say. He'd say, 'Let's leave Mr. Curran's fate to God.'

Karl would, of course, be right again. Neither we, nor the state of New York, are capable of determining if William Curran should pay for this sin with his life. No, we must leave this decision up to God. What we are left with is the responsibility of keeping Karl's memory alive in our hearts and our deeds." He paused and wiped his eyes. "Let us honor Karl and the principles he represented. In the back of the chapel you'll find envelopes for donations to the causes that Karl lived to support. Please donate generously in Karl's name. After the service there'll be a reception at the home of George and Carol Klyne.

"Now let us pray."

Kim knew for a fact that her actions hadn't killed Karl. She had never told Betty about their evening together.

When she had heard about the shooting, she remembered Bill Curran. She had seen him perform at the club where her boss had taken her. She had even met Bill's dance partner who, thinking back, was surely afraid of him. She wished the woman peace.

Kim felt certain the harp player was from New York. After the ceremony she would speak with her.

Sarah hears of Karl

When Sarah heard of Karl's murder her heart went out to his parents. She and Karl had grown up together outside of Chicago.

Sarah flew out for the funeral with Buddy. She agreed to play at the service and tried to explain Karl's motivations to his parents. She knew Karl didn't have many friends in New York. He had hidden the great wealth of his family from his acquaintances and associates.

She shared with his parents the pride he took in implementing some of the first housing code reforms in the country. She recounted his close relationship with Eleanor Roosevelt, who despite not being able to attend the service sent a beautiful bouquet of flowers and a generous donation to one of the orphanages Karl supported.

Sarah wished she had spent more time with Karl, but their schedules never seemed to mesh. He had even missed her wedding, a fact that now brought her real sorrow.

After the last of the mourners had paid their respects, Karl's parents remained in the little chapel, immobilized, on their knees, praying. Sarah went to them, placing her arms around their waists and lifting them gently to their feet.

"Mr. and Mrs. Klyne, you must remember that Karl died believing he was making a difference in this world. He would not have had it any other way. Your son was a angel. He'll not be forgotten."

Mrs. Klyne broke into tears and clung to her husband for support. They stood there and cried together, thankful for Sarah's comforting words.

December

Miriam's News

Miriam knew the moment she had conceived. It had been that awful night when she and Jason had fought. She had always wanted a baby, just not now, not like this. She was losing Jason. Each day he drifted farther from her. Emotionally he was already on the front lines of a war four thousand miles away. A war so terrible, with such atrocities, that she couldn't speak of them.

She wanted someone to blame: Lillian Hellman, Clifford Odets, anyone on whom she could focus her anger. For someone must have snatched away the man she loved, leaving this phantom of sadness. Yet Miriam knew in her heart that what was destroying Jason was the very thing she loved about him, his tenderness and intense empathy towards others.

She tried to explain to Jason that when he saw a person, brutalized or in pain, his sensitive nature would be overwhelmed, that his journey to Europe would be filled with impossibly difficult situations. Situations he could not resolve. Then she would ask him what of the danger? In response he would turn away from her and stare blankly into space. The pain of the war was something they both lived with like a third person in the apartment. How could it hold a fourth?

Miriam didn't have many close friends. Those she did have from her college days were superficial and offered no insight into human nature. She loved spending time with Auden and Isherwood, but they always viewed the world (especially a relationship between a man and a woman), from a skewed perspective. Their attitude suggested that if only men knew better, they would *never* be with women. This wasn't the companionship or counsel she needed. No, among all the people she knew there was only one woman who would give it to her straight. Miriam reached for the phone.

"Operator, Pleasantville, New York. The Hardscrabble Farm. Lillian Hellman, please."

In a few moments there was a response on the line.

"Mrs. Hellman, I have a person-to-person call for you from a

WAR CORRESPONDENT
Nancy Ames - Helsinki

I thought it would be best to end this year with the courage and stamina of the Finnish. Here's a country out-gunned, out-manned, attempting to defend a border larger than most European countries, against an enemy ten times stronger and yet they are succeeding. If ever there was a *David and Goliath* story this one is it. Finland, who is recognized by the League of Nations, has come under attack and asked for help simply to have their request ignored. Yet do they give up? Do they accept the impossible odds stacked against them? No. Not only this, but they are winning! Take that to heart America and all you other countries now under the cruel tyranny of a maniacal despot. The good and righteous can prevail.

Let us hope our people and our Congress come to their senses before it's too late, before all of Europe has been laid to waste. Remember that Hitler has made no secret of putting America next on his list of acquisitions. Let us help our friends before being consumed by the enemy ourselves.

From the trenches, your war correspondent, wishing you a New Year of peace and courage.

December

Miriam Rothman. Will you accept the call?"

"Gladly, operator." Lillian had always wanted to be friends with Miriam. She felt that Miriam had to be more than the simple housewife she portrayed or Jason wouldn't love her so. Lillian was flattered by the call.

The 'gladly' in Lillian's response pleased Miriam.

"Lillian, its Miriam. Lillian, I need to speak to you. May I come out there?"

The directness with which Miriam spoke surprised both women and revealed in no uncertain terms that the topic at hand was important.

"You may come right away dear. But if you prefer, I'll be in town tomorrow. We could meet wherever and whenever you like."

Miriam was silent for a moment.

"Miriam, if you would rather see me today, please don't hesitate."

"Thank you Lillian, I can't tell you how much I appreciate it. I'm sure this can wait until tomorrow," she paused. "It is important. It is all I can do not to jump out of my skin."

"If it's so important then you must come. Come now. What time is it? My watch says 3:30 there's a 4:00 that will get you to the farm by 6:00." There was no response. Lillian ventured a little further. "Will Jason be with you?"

It was as if a pin had pricked a balloon and the air went out of Miriam with a pop.

"No, no this is about Jason and no, I need to be home when he gets back."

"Is Jason alright dear?'

"It's nothing I wish to discuss over the phone. No, I guess tomorrow will be fine. What train will you be on? I'll meet you at the station."

Now Lillian was ready to race into the city. This was more serious than she imagined.

"Miriam do you want me to come in tonight? I could stay at my room at the Savoy."

Miriam paused for a long time then finally responded, "No Lillian, it's all right. Tomorrow morning will be fine. It'll give me a chance to get my thoughts together. Reaching out to you like this is so impetuous. I can only imagine what you are thinking. Tomorrow will be fine. What train did you say you would take?"

"The nine o'clock. It's an express and should get me in at ten-ten."

"I'll meet you at the track entrance in Grand Central." The women were silent for a long moment.

"Thank you Lillian, I can't tell you how much I appreciate this."

"Darling, whatever you need. You let me know. I'll see you tomorrow. Stiff upper lip."

"Good-bye," said Miriam hanging up and bursting into tears.

Buddy and Sarah

"Good morning sweetheart," Buddy said softly to Sarah. "Happy New Year's Eve."

Sarah awoke to the sight of her husband holding a present about the size of a loaf of bread. "Get up, get up," he urged, gently, as he sat beside her on the bed.

Sarah squinted, looking around the room for the clock. She noticed a hint of sunrise in the pink and blue clouds peeking between the buildings along Central Park.

"What time is it?" she said, yawning.

"Time to open your present." He smiled and handed her a glass of orange juice. "Here you go. I have many surprises for you today and this is just the first."

"Crazy man. I don't suppose one of them is to let me sleep for another hour or two." She attempted to turn over.

"No my dear. There's much to do this morning and in order to get everything done before 1940 you must get up now." He stood and swatted her rump affectionately.

"Come on darling, the early bird, you know." He walked out into the living room. Sarah knew there was no point arguing with him when he was in one of these chipper moods. She might as well get up.

She slipped on her mules and a purple velvet robe. "Alright you,

I'm up. What is it you want me to do? Would you like some break-
fast?"

"No, no I haven't woken Margaret. Just you. I wanted to share the
sunrise with you and begin a game of fun."

She felt confused. "How about a cup of coffee first and then, perhaps, I'll be able to make some sense out of what you're saying?"

He hustled into the kitchen, while she sat enjoying the view of the
park. They were like eagles soaring high above the treetops thirty-
eight stories above the earth.

Buddy emerged from behind the counter with a tray of sliced
banana, cantaloupe and a carafe of coffee. Once she had doctored her
coffee with milk and sugar she looked up.

"Now I'm fortified and ready for you, husband." She smiled a
devilish smile that she had discovered after marrying Buddy. Every
day with this man she felt older and wiser and he seemed to grow
younger and more spontaneous. The seventeen-year age difference
between them was vanishing.

"Here you go, my pet." He again handed her the package. Upon
accepting it she discovered it was heavy. The wrapping was a luxuri-
ant handmade paper bearing an Asian motif. The ribbons were red
and black silk with glass beads at the end.

"The packaging is remarkable Bud. Do I have to open it?"

"You do." He said with a mischievous grin.

She managed to pull the ribbons off, planning to unknot them
later. The paper fell away and exposed a beautiful enameled wooden
box. The wood was exotic, of a reddish color highlighted by intense
figuring. Embedded in the wood were thin colorful strips of resin
and brass, which continued the Asian theme of bow ties, segmenting
the top and sides.

"Buddy, it's beautiful." She looked up at him, as always surprised
at the gifts he lavished upon her.

"Open it," he said. She did and the sweetest sound emerged from
the music box. When she recognized the tune, she laughed.

"I knew it had been some time since you played the Blue Danube
and I thought you might have forgotten." Again he grinned. "But
there's more. Look in the drawer."

She couldn't imagine what the little drawer could possibly hold. It was a quarter of an inch high. Within it there was a folded piece of wrapping paper. Sarah picked it up and saw the elaborate calligraphy. At first she thought it was a love poem.

Sarah read out loud, "The reader of this note holds the first of many clues that begin a treasure hunt to usher in the new decade. Today will be a day of discovery as we say goodbye to the past and bring in the New Year."

"I'm prepared to go on your hunt, sweet husband. Where do I start? And will you be joining me?"

He beamed at her. "I'll be with you the whole day." Then he added, almost apologetically, "I promise you, it'll be fun."

"I have no doubt my love, I have no doubt." She leaned over and kissed him. She did love this man. She wondered once again what angel watched over her, making her so lucky.

December 31st 1939

The Rex was scheduled to raise anchor at midnight on December thirty-first 1939. It seemed auspicious in every way. The ship was filled with individuals who were venturing out into dangerous waters, feeling compelled to do so for reasons beyond reason.

German U-boats had been seen off the shores of every major U.S. city although the populace was not always informed, to avoid mass hysteria. Despite a lack of support by congress, Roosevelt funded the building of bunkers along the eastern seaboard.

He had also planted spies on board the Rex. Roosevelt had taken to enlisting the affluent of New York, with Vincent Astor heading the spy ring. Astor personally reported to Roosevelt regarding the movements of most of the armaments and the political intentions of the warmongers currently living in the U.S.

Roosevelt always said, "Follow the money and we'll know why, when, and where this war will heat up." This wisdom held true from the very beginning of hostilities in Europe. In the U.S., Roosevelt made a point of spreading money around, so that none of the big dogs would turn on him.

December

Buddy arrived at the dock riding in the back of his big black Rolls Royce. Sarah sat beside him, attempting to appear cheerful. He took her hand. "It's alright darling, neither Hitler, nor Stalin are man enough to keep me away from you. And if you're not convinced of that, remember, I'm the one who makes their war possible. They won't let me be harmed."

Sarah knew he said these things just to reassure her, but for the first time she considered that he could be kidnapped and held for ransom or worse. Buddy continued, "Besides, I'm going to the Middle East, where the royalty is quite civilized. The princes and emirs simply want to have weapons in case a greedy aggressor tries to take what's rightfully theirs."

"Darling, I know this is your job and I knew this day would come, but why the Rex? It has such a checkered past, having been turned around by the British just last month. Couldn't you find a more neutral boat to sail on?"

"Dearest it's an Italian ship. The Italians are, at the moment, allies with everyone. They have flip-flopped so much that no one knows for sure what side they're on. Besides, it's common knowledge that the Italians are so low on weapons that there's no point in shooting at their ships. In addition, we're leaving out of New York, the safest port in the world. None of the aggressors want to bring the U.S. into this war."

He hugged and kissed her, knowing she wasn't convinced.

"I'll be home before the first tulips are pushing their heads up in Central Park. And by then you'll have seen all the best theater and opera and saved me hours of sitting through mediocre renditions." He squeezed her hand tightly.

"Actually I have plans for a little remodeling while you're away," she said.

He pulled away and studied her face. She couldn't tell if this worried or pleased him. He simply said, "Splendid. I promise you, I'll be home as soon as I can."

"You wouldn't reconsider letting me go with you?" She attempted some dark humor. "Remember the passengers of the Titanic were thankful for having musicians aboard."

He feigned amusement. "Very funny. After this crossing, I'll decide if it's safe to have you join me on the next trip, but for now, think of me always." Buddy produced a jewelry case from inside his coat.

He handed the box to Sarah, who opened it like a child at Christmas. It was an exquisite brooch encrusted with gemstones.

He watched as she lit up over the bauble. He wasn't sure he could reach such an independent woman with such a trifle. Her pleasure in the object satisfied him immensely.

"Happy New Year darling," he said and kissed her.

"Happy New Year husband." She kissed him back with enthusiasm. She knew in her heart he would return.

Buddy stepped out of the car, never taking his eyes off of her. He was leaving a piece of himself behind and he grasped the significance of immortality. That he and Sarah would have a child was now a forgone conclusion. He couldn't wait to get home.

"Good bye, my darling." He blew a kiss to her and she caught it and placed it on her lips.

Nearby, another tearful separation was taking place, but it was not so full of hope as Buddy and Sarah's. Miriam and Jason were parting, although Jason had already left emotionally weeks earlier he was just now taking the physical voyage.

"I'm so sorry to be doing this to you Miriam," said Jason. He looked down and kicked at the confetti and packing materials that had accumulated around the dock. "I wouldn't go if I didn't have to – you know that."

"I'm trying to understand," said Miriam tenderly. "It's just, well there's one more thing. A reason for you to return with great haste."

"I know darling, I love you too."

"I'm one of the reasons, however, there's now a second." She took his hand and placed it on her stomach.

Jason looked up in surprise. "Are you saying?" She nodded. "When?"

"When did it happen or when is it due?" she smiled mischievously.

"When is it due, you silly?" For the first time in weeks Jason

Out of the Dark

by Alan Stipple

How fitting the opening dialogue of the most anticipated film in Hollywood history should begin with,

"War, war, war. Is that all anyone can talk about?" Miss Scarlett O'Hara may have been talking about the foreshadowing of the Civil War in *Gone with the Wind*, but she might as well have been talking about our next great World War. This art critic has found that fewer and fewer column inches are available for the discussion of art as they are now dedicated to the maneuverings of the world powers.

It saddens me to think that remarkable art is never produced during the years of war, but rather during peace. I see a dark time coming for art in this country and in all countries. It might be years before we again see the light of day.

Until then, your faithful watcher of the creative will immerse himself, with the rest of the planet, *Into the Dark.*

THEATER:
Time of Your Life - Mr.
Saroyan's first full-length play is fresh and full of bite. This critic would not be surprised to see it make the Pulitzer short list this year. With the world in chaos and the future unknown, we can take heed from Mr. Saroyan's opening:

In the time of your life, live – so that in that good time there shall be no ugliness or death for yourself or for any life your life touches. Seek goodness everywhere, and when it is found, bring it out of its hiding place and let it be free and unashamed.

MOVIES:
★★★★★ *Gone With the Wind* - Finally, on a
windy cold day in Atlanta, the movie we have all waited for was premiered. *Gone with the Wind* has not only lived up to the hype associated with the multimillion dollar production, but has also remained true to the book. Congratulations to all the screenwriters and directors affiliated with the picture.

regained the look of his old self, the haunted Jason was gone and she saw the optimistic genius she had married.

"Probably June. That'll give you a good six months to go over there, end the war and save the world. Does that seem about right?" She smiled broadly at him now.

"Oh you. Maybe I shouldn't go. I mean who's going to take care of you? What are you doing standing even now? Let's find a place for you to sit." His fawning was amusing and for the first time she recognized the benefit of not having him underfoot while she suffered miserably from morning, afternoon and evening sickness.

"No, you need to go. Just remember, I expect you back." She hesitated and bit her lip. Then with her hand on her pregnant belly she said, "We both insist on your return."

"As quickly as I am able. I promise." And for the very first time, Miriam believed him. Until now she was certain he was leaving to face his death and that he was resigned to leave her forever. Now she had a beacon within her that would guide him home.

She could have made him stay. Instead she was following Lillian's excellent advice. If he didn't go now, he would never be completely with her. He would always wonder if he had done the right thing. Now, even if he only sailed across the sea and turned right around, he would have gotten it out of his system. Miriam would be forever grateful to Lillian.

As they hugged, Miriam saw over Jason's shoulder Bud Rawley striding towards them. "Look dear, it's Buddy. He must be sailing with you."

"Jason Rothman. Are you on this ship?"

"Indeed I am."

"I'll let you say your good-byes and look forward to seeing you on board." Buddy bowed graciously to Miriam.

Jason turned back to her.

Miriam offered, "I actually feel better, knowing that you're going to be sailing with Buddy. No one will want to shoot him out of the water. He's too valuable to all sides of the war."

Jason was filled with emotion and drew Miriam close. "Don't worry darling," she said, "we'll be here keeping the home fires burn-

December

ing. We love you, come back soon."

He kissed her once more, then reached down and picked up his small attaché and walked up the gangplank. Although Jason did not turn around, Miriam saw him remove his glasses to wipe away the tears.

On Deck

After all the farewells and the Happy New Years, Buddy and Jason were standing at the rail watching the brightly lit buildings of New York drift by.

"May I join you?" asked Alex Bridges.

"Please," said Jason. "Alex Bridges this is Bud Rawley."

"How do you do?" said Alex.

"Superb, and yourself?"

"Ready to get back out to sea," said Alex. "Last month I sailed on the City of Flint. Unfortunately, we were captured by the Germans and sent to Norway and then back – it's a long story. I'm happy to be off to Europe at last."

Alex gazed at the bejeweled city. In some neighborhoods bonfires burned in celebration of 1940. "Sure is a thing of beauty."

Now that Jason's veil of melancholy had lifted, he could see New York as Alex did, sparkling and adorned in her finest. He heard Rhapsody in Blue coming from somewhere inside the ship and thought it to be the perfect background accompaniment.

The three men stood silently by the rail. The destroyer, the builder and the storyteller. A triumvirate destined to sustain each other during the terrible days ahead.

ABOUT THE AUTHOR

Paula Phelan is the CEO and founder Nadel Phelan, Inc.,
a Public Relations firm focused on technology since 1993.

Ms. Phelan divides her time between the company headquarters
in California and its offices in New York
where she is an avid theater-goer.

1939 - Into the Dark is Ms. Phelan's second book and follows her
award winning novel *1919 - Misfortune's End,* also a work of historical
fiction. She is currently working on her third book entitled,
1969 - The Dream of Aquarius.

Ms. Phelan's nonfiction writing appears internationally in
management publications and technology journals.
Ms. Phelan holds a Ph.D. in psychology.